KU-517-193

Enhancing Student-centred Learning in Business and Management, Hospitality, Leisure, Sport, Tourism

ALSO PUBLISHED WITH THE HOSPITALITY, LEISURE, SPORT AND TOURISM AND
BUSINESS MANAGEMENT ACCOUNTANCY AND FINANCE SUBJECT CENTRES:

*Enhancing Graduate Employability in Business
and Management, Hospitality, Leisure, Sport, Tourism*
edited by Nina Becket & Patsy Kemp (2006)

*Enhancing the International Learning Experience in Business
and Management, Hospitality, Leisure, Sport, Tourism*
edited by Richard Atfield & Patsy Kemp (2008)

Edited by John Buswell and Nina Becket

Enhancing
Student-centred Learning
in Business and Management
Hospitality
Leisure
Sport
Tourism

Threshold Press

Introduction, editorial matter
and chapter contents © Oxford Brookes University 2009
All rights reserved.

This publication may not be reproduced in whole or in part, translated, stored
in a retrieval system or transmitted or distributed in any form or by any means
(electronic, mechanical, photocopy, recording or otherwise) without the prior
written consent of the publishers or under a valid license for limited copying
issued by the Copyright Licensing Agency Ltd.

First published 2009 by
Threshold Press Ltd
152 Craven Road
Newbury Berks RG14 5NR
Phone 01635-230272 and fax 01635-44804
email: publish@threshold-press.co.uk
www.threshold-press.co.uk

British Library Cataloguing in Publication Data
A catalogue record for this book is available from the British Library

ISBN 978–1–903152–24–9

Printed in Great Britain by the MPG Books Group, Bodmin and King's Lynn

Every effort has been made to trace the copyright holders and we apologise in
advance for any unintentional omissions. The editors and the publisher would be
pleased to insert the appropriate acknowledgement in any subsequent edition.

The editors

John Buswell is principal lecturer in the Department of Leisure, Tourism and
Hospitality Management at the University of Gloucestershire and chair of the
ISPAL Professional Development Board. He is also Liaison Officer for Leisure for
the HE Academy Subject Centre for Hospitality, Leisure, Sport and Tourism, based
at Oxford Brookes University. He is a member of the Open University Validation
and Awards Committees. His research interests and publications are in pedagogy
and in the area of service quality in leisure, tourism and sport.

Nina Becket is currently lecturing in hospitality and tourism management in the
Business School at Oxford Brookes University and is the former assistant director
of the Hospitality, Leisure, Sport and Tourism Subject Network.

Contents

Introduction
John Buswell

This book is the third in a series jointly published by the Hospitality, Leisure, Sport and Tourism (HLST) and Business Management Accountancy and Finance (BMAF) Subject Centres. The series sets out to inform the sector about practice in particular aspects of teaching and learning. The first book was concerned with enhancing employability and contained an eclectic mix of topics and case studies focusing on the development of students' employability skills, and the second addressed enhancing the international learning experience across the subjects.

The purposes of this book are to:

❑ explore the conceptual and practical aspects of personal development planning and student-centred learning addressed by initiatives in a range of institutions
❑ highlight examples of practice which have worked (or perhaps have not)
❑ consider the lessons learnt from these interventions.

This book is closely related to the first and addresses the cognate subject of Personal Development Planning (PDP) as a sector-wide scheme and as student-centred learning. It clearly embraces employability but also highlights the importance of lifelong learning and the encouragement of independent, autonomous and self-empowered learners. It is published at a time when the QAA *Guidelines on Progress Files and PDP* (Quality Assurance Agency for Higher Education, 2001) are being revised and the recommendations of the Burgess Report (2007) are encouraging institutions to place more emphasis on student profiles and to move away from the preoccupation with the degree classification system.

The emphasis on PDP in the UK, with its statutory requirements, has also begun to pose questions for pedagogy in UK higher education. As we observe later in this introduction and throughout the book, questions about the way in which we engage with students are raised by the rapidly changing nature of life in the 21st century and the subsequent dynamics of globalisation, technology, diversity and increasing numbers of students entering higher education (HE). Indeed recent research by Quinton and Smallbone (2008) suggests that there are many challenges in implementing PDP; their evidence to date reveals a considerable variation in the way it is implemented and, indeed, perceived by both staff and students across English universities. They suggest that the implementation of personal development planning is still at a fairly preliminary stage, and that universities in England need to reflect on and learn from the experience of change. This book is designed therefore to inform the enhancement of this process. The case studies highlight some very thoughtful and innovative approaches to engaging students in PDP and student-centred learning and the lessons learnt to date.

The context of PDP in student-centred learning

Such a context lends weight to the growing significance of PDP and its key role in enhancing student-centred learning. PDP's primary objective is to help students understand their own learning through reflection and gradually take more responsibility for their learning through action-planning and further review. The QAA (2001) suggested that PDP is:

> a structured and supported process undertaken by an individual to reflect upon their own learning, performance and/or achievement and to plan for their personal, educational and career development (QAA, 2001: 9).

This definition encapsulates the need for balance between mediation and structure in developing student-centred learning, and also the opportunities for reflective learning and the development of self identity and self-regulation. As Bourner points out, 'reflective learning is not what happens to a student: it is what the student does with what has happened' (2003: 259).

The emphasis on reflective learning and metacognition also addresses an important element of employability, and at the same time an increasingly significant challenge to higher education (Barnett, 2000; Edwards, 2001; Jackson and Ward, 2004), which is to prepare students for the unknown. Such a philosophy recognises that the requirements of employers and the needs of society are not fulfilled by what graduates know but, increasingly, by their ability to acquire new knowledge and skills and to understand how they can best achieve this. It demands that the student be capable of reflecting on their experience and learning from it. Jackson and Ward (2004) refer to this as 'transdisciplinary learning', which recognises the changing demands of the world of work, and the requirements for graduates who can think across the traditional boundaries of knowledge in order to deal with increasingly complex and multi-faceted problems and challenges. It places emphasis on the development of skills and capabilities and suggests that students' educational achievement is defined more by what they can do than simply what they know or even understand.

What is student-centred learning?

Personal autonomy is seen as important in the 21st century because the complexities and rapidly changing demands of modern society require the capacity to change and to regulate learning and behaviour (Clifford, 1999; Jaros & Deakin-Crick, 2007). Most higher education programmes in the UK purport to develop independent and collaborative learners, although sometimes the processes for achieving this are less than transparent. We encourage our students to become critical thinkers and to be active learners, and set out to create deep learners (Case and Gunstone, 2002). These goals are often represented in a range of educational aims and learning outcomes.

PDP may not be the most attractive of terms, and perceptions of it can be of a mechanistic and instrumental process, but its potential to contribute to a more student-centred approach, founded on the principles of active and self-regulated learning, has gathered momentum in recent years (Burgess, 2007). Indeed, Broadfoot (2006) suggests that PDP provides the opportunity to transform the HE experience by developing curricula which focus on the student rather than simply subject-based content. It also moves us closer to the notion of a lifelong-learning curriculum in higher education and one which places less emphasis on academic disciplines. Annette suggests:

> The development of a 'lifelong learning curriculum' in higher education might possibly lead to a reconfiguration of the map of academic knowledge and a change to the dominance of the academic discipline (2007: 18).

The process of the student thinking critically, not only about the subject, but also about how they engage with the subject – and develop as a learner – represents a paradigm shift in how we approach teaching and learning in higher education. It is a shift in emphasis from content-based, subject-led approaches and models to context-based, student-led approaches. PDP is viewed by some observers as atheoretical and superficial and a strand of work to be located outside the formal curriculum. Yet, if we consider that it is based on reflective thinking and learning, the highest order cognitive skill, and the even more complex skill of metacognition, then such scepticism may be unfounded.

Indeed nurturing critical thinking skills and a deep approach to learning involve the student in constructing their own meaning for the subject matter and its impact on their learning as well as their personal and academic development. If we extend this constructivist approach to experiential learning in which important events and incidents in work experience, students' own work and other activities like volunteering are reviewed, then we are guiding students to the highest level of critical thinking, that of contextual knowledge (Baxter Magolda, 1996). She sees the active learning in events such as work experience as a major contribution to the development of epistemological beliefs. This can be either in a disciplinary or a transdisciplinary context, although in situations outside the formal curriculum, like work experience and volunteering, we will also want to encourage students to apply subject theory to the context and to examine its impact on their epistemological beliefs and their capacity for adapting the knowledge and skills acquired. This comfortably aligns with the reflective and strategic aspects of PDP in which the student is reviewing development and achievements in the context in which they occur, and in which they are a participant. It makes important connections between their personal development and their knowledge and understanding of the subject.

A significant aspect of the active engagement of the student in learning environments is included in the first contribution to the book, Colin Beard's philosophical piece on the features of student-centred learning. This learning requires not only reflection, reflexivity and self-awareness but also emotional engagement by the student. 'Student-centred' implies that the student is more than a passive recipient of knowledge and actively participates in all the mediated learning experiences to develop the capacity of self-regulation.

Self-regulation

Self-regulation is the ability to understand and manage our use of cognitive skills and strategies; because of this perspective, the concept of metacognition is often applied here. Self-regulation involves identifying and setting personal goals and monitoring progress in achieving them in a systematic way. It is therefore intentional learning (Jackson, 2004) and leads to the individual taking control of their learning (Biggs, 1985). This is meta-learning – one of the main goals of PDP and student-centred learning – although we must accept that students will not find it easy or comfortable and, for some, it may not be achieved until the end of their programme. It therefore requires mediation and method on our part as tutors and a set of 'other' regulations, especially in the early stages of the programme – as we shall see later. Indeed, Rosie (2000) suggests that deep learning is not an attribute but can be a strategy that people can adopt and, if they are supported in examining alternatives and making informed decisions, then their learning achieves a higher level.

Mediation and method: Can PDP be taught?

It is often less clear how we should support students to become more strategic and create the learning environments that enable such goals and outcomes to be realised or indeed what constitutes such environments. How they work and how we know that they work are also important questions facing us as we design our teaching, learning and assessment strategies. The dangers of ignoring substance and educational theory in the pursuit of personalised learning have been highlighted recently (Ecclestone, 2007; Hartley, 2007). Indeed, Ecclestone reminds us that, within the rhetoric of empowerment, there is often emotional vulnerability and fragility in approaches to learning that we have to address as well.

In other words, in order to support individual development towards self-regulated learning, we need to invest in other forms of regulation along the way (Jackson & Ward, 2004). Such scaffolding poses the challenge of achieving balance and progression, so that the student is not over-supported or directed and can gradually develop the confidence and the skills with which to take control, but alternatively is not left to 'drift' too early. Many of the case studies feature examples of direct support and 'other-regulation' of learners as they gradually develop greater self-awareness and the capacity to manage and regulate their own learning. We have identified several key aspects of work, although some case studies relate to more than one aspect:

❑ Self-management through addressing the constraints to learning
❑ Feedback, including self-assessment, on learning
❑ Recording and reflecting through eportfolios
❑ The role of staff in inspiring and supporting students
❑ Embedding PDP and student-centred learning in the curriculum
❑ The diversity of learning spaces.

Self-management

We need to treat different students in different ways and acknowledge the fragility and lack of resourcefulness of an increasing proportion of our students, particularly in the first year of their programme. There are factors which inhibit learning, or, in some cases, lead to withdrawal. Helping students to learn more about themselves and their approach to learning is a common theme in many of the case studies and can enhance the skills and capabilities of self-management. Sue Lea and Derry Corey's case study addresses the challenge that many students find in writing correctly and critically particularly across our subjects. This is the means to tackling most assessments in our subjects, and increasing numbers of students seem to require initial support and guidance to help them develop both the skills of academic writing and the required academic confidence and self-reliance. The case studies by Peter Cox, Will Bowen-Jones and Karen Bill, and John Buswell and Angela Tomkins explain how students are helped to understand their strengths and weaknesses through the use of skills profiles or learning inventories and, crucially, demonstrate how they can actively do something to improve their approach to learning.

Pru Marriot's case study is of a slightly different order, but still tackles a very real constraint to learning and progression that increasing numbers of students face. There is much evidence that many students drop out because of financial difficulties, or the demands of long hours of part-time work. Marriot's chapter offers insights into the pressures facing students and how the provision of support to help them manage their finance is another form of regulation which can develop self-reliance and more empowered learning.

Feedback and self-assessment

A second form of mediation, which has a central role in encouraging self-regulated learning, involves feedback on student engagement in learning, including assessed work and other experiences like volunteering and part-time work. The challenge of how we encourage students to collect and read feedback is well-documented, but we know that the more strategic students do act on their feedback as Jackie Lynch's case study demonstrates. PDP requires students to act on reflections around their achievements and performance, and feedback on academic work provides the opportunity for some rich, if painful, experiential learning. She reminds us of how difficult it is to get students to separate the mark from the grade and to act on feedback and she provides some useful thoughts and observations about how we can do this. Another form of feedback is provided by self-assessment in various guises. Cox's case study examines an approach to engagement through self-analysis and skills audits. In a similar way, the Student Qualities Profile in Bowen-Jones and Bill's chapter provides feedback and opportunities for reflection on some key skills.

The case study by Angela Tomkins and John Buswell takes a different perspective and considers reflective processes and the use of learning inventories to provide some personal and meaningful feedback about approaches to learning. Susan Lea and Derry Corey's case study focuses more specifically on writing skills and helping students to reflect on and improve their approaches to writing critically, while the use of a personal response system by Wendy Beekes enables students to not only participate in sessions, but also to receive immediate feedback on their judgements and understanding in a simple but effective way. It is a relatively expensive system, although if costs are shared across programmes and modules then it may be a sound investment, particularly if it achieves the positive reactions from students that we see in the case study. The key message from these examples is the significance of how we encourage self-assessment, or provide feedback, on learning and approaches to learning; the responses to the feedback are also important and enhance self-regulation.

Eportfolios

Another piece of the scaffolding which offers support is the way that students are encouraged to record and reflect on their achievements, and to plan for the future, through the use of eportfolios. Portfolios are an integral element of PDP and student-centred learning, but the emergence and rapid growth of eportfolios has offered another dimension of considerable importance. We know that not all students are comfortable with using them, but their value to reflective learning is considerable so we need to know how to make them appealing and useful to as many students as possible.

The use of eportfolios provides the opportunity to move on from fairly sterile paper-based portfolios (although if done well they can have their place), to a medium which can encourage a sense of ownership and control when integrated into students' learning with thought and sensitivity. Peter Robinson, Debra Wade and Crispin Dale's case study illustrates their use of PebblePad, and compares the experience with a paper-based system used in another module. PebblePad is one of the most common dedicated eportfolios in the UK system and it was developed at Wolverhampton University, so they are in a very good position to assess its effectiveness and impact. Their balanced evaluation highlights the benefits of an eportfolio system, but they also remind us that a more traditional approach with higher levels of face-to-face contact also has its merits. The chapter contributed by Mark Moss, alternatively, examines the journey staff in the School of Psychology and Sport Sciences at Northumbria University have undergone in moving from a paper-based system, comprising a collection of forms and activities, to a much tighter electronic system and eportfolio using Blackboard. He highlights the struggle to engage students but suggests that the appropriate use of an eportfolio offers a pragmatic solution to the pressures on staff and student time.

Staff and student engagement

A further element in student-centred learning involves the role and impact of staff and student engagement. Staff are key to how students are encouraged to understand and manage their own learning and, even more importantly, how they are inspired and motivated to engage in student-centred learning. The HLST Subject Network PDP survey of 26 institutions suggests that staff attitudes and perceptions of PDP are even more of a barrier than those of students (Buswell & Gush, 2008), and this was reinforced by Quinton and Smallbone's research (2008). It would seem that one of the most important factors in developing students' capacity for self-regulation is the understanding of what is required by staff and their commitment to the cause. Clearly the engagement of both staff and students is critical to the success of PDP and there are a number of case studies which address this requirement from different perspectives.

Sarah Nixon and Caitlin Walker's case study examines how we can inspire students to engage in student-centred learning through the process of actually understanding the diversity and individual needs of students. Through the use of non-leading 'clean' questions to avoid influencing responses, they obtained some very valuable feedback from students about what they feel encourages their engagement: students said that they value the opportunities to reflect on experiential learning including their own and the examples of role models in their industry.

Dominic Micklewright's case study sets out to examine the socio-psychological factors shaping PDP behaviour and through the use of a PDP questionnaire, develops a conceptual model of learner beliefs about PDP. He found that it was students' attitudes and their sense of control over the PDP process which inspired them to engage, rather than the presence of subject norms such as employability requirements. The case studies by Keenan, and by Baker and French also reaffirm the benefits of encouraging a sense of ownership and control for students. Indeed, Christine Keenan began with a pre-induction programme called Stepping Stones2HE which included some negotiated content and collaboration with the students' union. The case by Graham Baker and Robert French describes a new student-focused module with several themes aimed at getting the best out of students and developing independent, self-reliant learners. They point to discernable improvements in student performance and in staff engagement although they also highlight the tensions between the centralised elements of a PDP approach and the academic freedom necessary for intrinsic motivation. It was apparent that some students and staff found these tensions a little uncomfortable, but the challenge to all of us is how we manage these and achieve the right balance.

Bowen-Jones and Bill's case study focuses on the role of the personal tutor and how this can be pivotal in providing and then gradually removing the scaffolding helping students to develop key skills, particularly entrepreneurial and networking skills. Louise Grisoni, Carol Jarvis and Margaret Page's case study highlights the use of enquiry-based learning. This develops self-awareness and confidence but also takes students out of their 'comfort zone' and requires the 'safe uncertainty' of a structured tutorial system to allow students to share deeply personal insights with their peers and tutors. This case study also suggests that the process is very

xiv   Enhancing Student-centred Learning

challenging but potentially rewarding for both student and tutor with considerable 'emotional labour' for both parties, echoing the suggestion in Beard's first chapter.

The curriculum

The overall aim is the development of self-awareness, which is the key to meaningful PDP and student-centred learning, but the impact of staff is most effective when supported by the curriculum. This aspect concerns curriculum development and, particularly, the attempt to embed PDP and student-centred learning in the curriculum. Many of the case studies involve elements of curriculum design: induction (Nixon and Walker); pre-induction (Keenan); a new student-centred module (Baker and French). However, the QAA *Progress Files Guidelines* (2001) suggest that we fully embed PDP in our curricula and we have already seen how Buswell and Tomkins' use of learning inventories can help students to make sense of all their learning experiences including work experience. Jacqui Gush's case study also involves the pivotal impact of work experience and describes how she has attempted to integrate learning from other units in a second-year module which prepares students for their industrial placement. It draws on the USEM model of employability (Knight and Yorke, 2004b) to enhance reflection and self-awareness, and complements subject-based learning by linking theory with practice and achieving the necessary balance between direction and self-empowerment.

Mark Atlay, Petia Petrova and Dorota Ujma, referring to the work of the Bridges CETL at the University of Bedfordshire, show how their approach has evolved in recent years to the point where PDP is integrated and fully embedded across the curriculum. Students are encouraged to reflect on their learning experiences across all modules and also on their experiences outside the curriculum, such as part-time work and volunteering. These authors demonstrate the benefits of such an approach and confirm the need for balance between independent thought and action, and the support and structure provided by the institution.

Learning spaces

The final element of mediation which merits scrutiny is the increasing diversity of contexts for students' learning and how we can harness the many informal, social settings for rich, experiential learning. Some HEIs are beginning to invest in these settings for collaborative and independent learning. Colin Beard, in his second contribution, explains the importance of learning spaces and highlights the growing provision and relevance of informal, social environments for learning, including for example, refectories and the spaces in teaching blocks for independent and group learning around computers and sofas.

Beard's thoughts in the last chapter help to bring together the messages from the range of case studies featured, by encouraging us to link learning spaces with active and reflective learning as it is increasingly understood and managed by the student. It connects with the thoughts in his earlier chapter in which he focuses on the individual learner.

Conclusions

The case studies examine the interrelationships between learner, tutor and learning environment. They show how the role of the student and the nature of the learning environment have subtly become more significant in their impact on student learning. They have also demonstrated that, although we may now be seen more as facilitators than teachers, our ability to understand how students learn and how we can construct and shape learning environments is central to student-centred learning. The case studies collectively demonstrate how we mediate and structure students' learning environments and learning experiences so that they will be empowered and encouraged to manage and control their own learning more actively.

A feature of all the case studies is the attempt to engage students in active and experiential learning, in which they are not passive recipients of knowledge but are active in the development of skills and capabilities gained through making sense of the contexts in which their learning takes place. We have seen that important outcomes for students are self-empowerment, self-identity and the capacity for meta-learning. They help students to cope with the progressive challenges of their programme, but also help prepare them for the increasing complexity and demands of the twenty-first century.

References

Annette, J. (2007) Lifelong learning, research based academic disciplines and the undergraduate curriculum. *Academy Exchange* 6 Summer 2007 pp 18–19

Baxter Magolda, M. (1996) Epistemological developments in graduate and professional education. *Review of Higher Education* **19** (3) pp 283–304

Barnett, R. (2000) Supercomplexity and the Curriculum. *Studies in Higher Education* **25** (3) pp 255–67

Biggs, J. (1985) The role of metalearning in study processes. *British Journal of Educational Psychology* **55** pp 185–212

Bourner, T. (2003) Assessing reflective thinking. *Education and Training* 45 (5) pp 256–72

Broadfoot, P. (2006) 'Empowering the learner: theories, tools and techniques'. Keynote address to *Researching and evaluating PDP and e-Portfolios*. International Seminar, Oxford, October 2006

Burgess, R. (2007) *Burgess Group Final Report: Beyond the honours degree classification*. London: Universities UK/GuildHE

Buswell, J. and Gush, J. (2008) *HLST Network Benchmarking Survey: Implementing Personal Development Planning (PDP)*. Oxford: HE Academy Subject Centre for Hospitality, Leisure, Sport and Tourism

Case, J. and Gunstone, R. (2002) Metacognitive development as a shift in approach to learning. *Studies in Higher Education* 27 (4) pp 459–70

Clifford, V. A. (1999) The Development of Autonomous Learners in a University Setting. *Higher Education Research and Development*. **18** (1) pp 115–27

xvi   Enhancing Student-centred Learning

Deakin-Crick, R., Broadfoot, P. and Claxton, G. (2004) Developing an effective lifelong learning inventory: the ELLI project. *Assessment in Education* **11** (3) pp 247–72

Edwards, G. (2001) *Connecting PDP to Employer Needs and the World of Work*. LTSN Generic Centre

Ecclestone, K. (2007) Resisting images of the 'diminished self': the implications of emotional well-being and emotional engagement in education policy. *Journal of Educational Policy* **22** (4) pp 455–70

Hartley, D. (2007) Personalisation: the emerging 'revised' code of education. *Oxford Review of Education* **33** (5) 629–42

Knight, P. & Yorke, M. (2004a) *Learning, Curriculum and Employability in Higher Education*. London: RoutledgeFalmer

Knight, P. & Yorke, M. (2004b) *Employability; judging and communicating achievement in Higher Education*. York: LTSN

Jackson, N. (2004) Developing the concept of metalearning. *Innovations in Education and Teaching International* **41** (4) pp 391–403

Jackson, N & Ward, R. (2004) A fresh perspective on progress files – a way of representing complex learning and achievement in higher education. *Assessment and Evaluation in Higher Education* **29** (4)

Jaros, M. & Deakin-Crick, R. (2007) Personalized learning for the post-mechanical age. *Journal of Curriculum Studies* **39** (4) pp 423–40

NCIHE (1997) *Higher Education in the Learning Society. Report of the National Committee of Inquiry into Higher Education*. (the Dearing Report)

QAA (2001) *Guidelines for HE Progress Files*. QAA: Gloucester

Quinton, S. and Smallbone, T. (2008) PDP implementation at English universities: what are the issues? *Journal of Further and Higher Education* **32** (2) pp 99–109

Rosie, A. (2000) Deep learning: a dialectical approach drawing on tutor-led Web resources. *Active Learning in Higher Education* **1** (1) July pp 45–59

Transforming the student learning experience
A pedagogic model for everyday practice

Colin Beard
Sheffield Hallam University

This chapter sets the scene for the argument of the book with a discussion of the nature of learning, emphasising that it is a process of experience and the importance of engaging the whole person.

The role of the educator

Although some consensus exists as to the roles that educators perform, Tennant (1997: 140) considers that there is 'ironically, an unnecessary dichotomous conceptualisation of teacher and taught in much adult education literature'. Other writers such as Moon argue that we should consider 'learning and teaching as separate operations' (Moon, 2004: 12), while Knowles (1980) suggests that educators should be sound procedural technicians and resource providers, but advocates that the learners themselves also need to be active explorers in the design and management process.

The terms educator, designer, architect, choreographer, animateur, trainer, and facilitator all indicate a range of roles and identities and there is a tension at the boundaries of these meanings pertaining to the extent to which they are *aiding* or *providing*, *for* and *of* learning. All these roles involve, to some degree, an *intentionality* of design (Andreson et al, 2000), an 'approach or procedure, an acknowledged practice by a trainer or educator as a way of teaching or promoting learning' (Beard, 2005b: 342), yet these titles and role descriptions (Miller and Boud, 1996, 1997; Beard and Wilson, 2006) posit a crisis of identity. Within constructivist approaches the learner is seen as the *central* actor, fundamentally separate from his or her environment in the meaning making process, intimating perhaps a curbing of the educators' impact in the ability to influence this internal and external experience of the learner. Underpinning my thinking in this chapter is the recognition that learning and teaching are inextricably interlinked processes, and there is a need for a co-constructive approach to student learning.

The pedagogic limitations of existing models

Many educators are unable to articulate a coherent view of what it is that informs and shapes their design of teaching, though typically this involves the application of certain models. Objective setting often starts the process and though problematic (Hussey and Smith, 2002; Watson, 2002) it is nevertheless a valuable approach to a question-based learning-needs analysis, beyond, as Fenwick notes (2003: 5), 'the usual "what" and "how" questions. Indeed the *where, when, what, why,* and *how* of learning form some of the fundamentally reflexive questions required of us in pedagogic fieldwork. Significant contributors to the field such as Boud and Walker note that

> while there has been extensive discussion of models in theory-building and research, less emphasis has been given to the development of models to aid teaching and learning. (1993: 19)

Mortiboys (2002) regards three dimensions of teaching as key: technical knowledge, subject knowledge and emotional competence.

Brooks and Brooks (1993:3) in presenting a case for constructivist classrooms, note that many promising educational propositions fail to address the core 'processes of teaching and learning that occur daily, relentlessly, inexorably'. In 2001 Heron voiced concern that 'the old model of education, going back to classical times, dealt only with the education of the intellect, theoretical and applied' (2001: 208); his new model integrates emotional, interpersonal and political competence. He also noted that 'nowadays we have people who are learning by *thinking, feeling* and *doing* – bringing all these to bear on the acquisition of new knowledge and skills' (Heron, 2001: 208 – italics added). These categories are expanded still further in the new model offered in this chapter. At variance with Heron, Illeris posits cognition, emotion and the social as critical dimensions, noting that 'there do not appear to be any earlier learning theories that fully recognise and deal with this complexity in its entirety' (Illeris, 2002: 9). Thus, within constructivism the central pedagogic concern and key philosophical debate appears to be the extent to which knowledge is socially, psychologically, emotionally, bodily, politically, environmentally or otherwise constructed.

Snyder notes the institutional difficulties of generating effective approaches to student learning:

> The cultural environment of higher education does little to foster active learning to strengthen critical thinking and creativity skills in its students... Faculty are given little time, budget, encouragement or support to develop 'active learning' tools that assist in developing these skills. Incorporating 'active learning' pedagogic techniques, for example, developing and running exercises, group projects, or simulations, is risky for a faculty and there is no guarantee that these techniques will work or that students see the benefits of this form of pedagogic method. Fortunately, but slowly, the cultural environment that places barriers to moving toward more innovative

pedagogical tools is eroding away. (2003: 159)

In offering a pedagogic tool (Beard, 2007) I expand the three dimensions offered by both Illeris (2002) and Heron (2001) (see figure 1). I also deal with the issue of *connectivity* (Nicol, 2003) between the primary, outer, public world experiences and the secondary, inner, private world experiences; learners 'explore inner space as well as the physical world, entering deeply into the inner being of the mind and seeking to be fully connected with the outer world' (Fenwick, 2003: 52). The framework presented here attempts to provide a logical framing of the milieu of themes arising from case material within a set of six categories of *being, doing, sensing, feeling, thinking* and *changing* that have a synergy with the six fieldwork questions about the *where, what, how, hearts* (affect) and *minds* (cognition) of learning to create learning and change (see Figure 1).

Figure 1 A new framework that extends the practical efficacy of experiential teaching and learning

EASTERN PHILOSOPHY
Confucian aphorism (AD 551–179)
I hear – I forget

I see – I remember

I do – I understand

SIMPLE WESTERN MODELLING
Dales Cone – 'Instructional' techniques triangle – 1969

Tell

Show

Do

Kolb – Experiential learning cycle – 1984
1 Concrete experience – doing

2 Reflective observation – reflecting

3 Abstract conceptualisation – forming new concepts

4 Active experimentation – application

Experiential approaches to student learning

I am proposing that experiential learning is not just learning by doing, despite having a history dating back to Eastern, Confucian philosophy, with the aphorism 'I hear I forget, I see I remember, I do I understand' laying the very early foundations for subsequent Western interpretations. Many writers have contributed to the debate about the notion of learning from experience or learning from doing (Dewey, 1938; Rogers, 1969; Kolb, 1984; Revans, 1980; Boud and Walker, 1993). In this chapter I seek to establish that *experiencing by doing* is central to effective learning but that the learning experience is enriched when it involves learning from *being*, *doing*, *sensing*, *feeling*, *thinking* and *changing*.

Because of this long lineage, experiential learning has evolved within many disciplines and fields of study and while this offers a strong interdisciplinary diversity, a further consequence is that experiential learning exhibits escalating ideologies, meanings and problematic defining parameters. My proposal here is that there is a need to respond to calls within a range of disciplines for learning approaches to provide greater synergy between the interaction of the inner-world and the outer-world experiences of learners, and so my starting definition of experiential learning (EL) is:

> A sense-making process of learning that actively and reflectively engages the inner world of the learner as a whole person (physical-bodily, intellectually, emotionally and spiritually) with the intricate 'outer world' of the learning environment (nature, place, social and political).

This definition forms the basis of a new model that I wish to propose for pedagogic purposes: for learning design and delivery in higher education.

A new model: a visual metaphor

The model I am proposing is shown in Figure 2, as an abstract, visual metaphor representing a *combination lock* with several categories or cogs that can all be independently rotated. Its simplicity lies in the fact that it involves six basic learning-design categories yet it has the potential to produce several million possible permutations. The left side of the framework represents the outer, public world of learning. The central, lighter-shaded cog represents the sensory modes, as conduits between the outer world and the inner, private world of the individual learner (shown on the right-hand side).

The framework is however much more than a set of categories; it has been built upon a distinctive grounded synthesis of theory and fieldwork, and uses a substantive body of data from ongoing research that has been developed over a period of twenty years, emerging from my personal interactions, from discussions with significant stakeholders and informants, and from seeing and being in the learner's immediate experience and environment. This in turn has lead to the creation of a milieu of *themes* within the six categories that present limitless possible combinations for the design and management of learning.

Figure 2 The learning combination lock

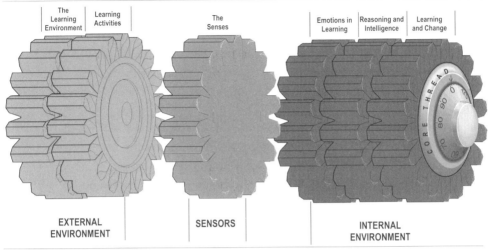

Working with the learning environment

The first tumbler in the model represents the learner environment: the space, place, social, emotional and political context that provides opportunities and stimuli for student learning. New spaces increasingly provide very real opportunities for the individual to learn in a deep way about themselves and their interactions with their outer world. The design and use of the student learning environment is beginning to metamorphose. In the past it was strongly associated with the lecture theatre and textbooks; nowadays, even in higher education it includes distance education sites, common areas such as halls, social group work space with café culture sofas and coffee, outdoor green spaces, amphitheatres, video clips, and virtual discussion groups. An illustration of the transition in thinking can be found in the following Indiana University definition of a learning environment:

> A physical, intellectual, psychological environment which facilitates learning through connectivity and community. (www-lib.iupui.edu/itt/planlearn/pert1.html)

While traditionally students spent many hundreds of hours learning in lecture theatres and seminar rooms, learning is spilling out into informal learning spaces that are increasingly being used for more formal learning as is illustrated by the case study in Figure 3. In Finland there are lecture theatres with seat hammocks, specifically designed to enhance the creation of certain mental states, such as relaxed alertness, and in Lancaster University students learn about countryside recreation within Mongolian style tents with wood-burning stoves, located in the grounds of their countryside campus (see Chapter 18, figures 1 and 2). There is a considerable, and growing body of literature highlighting the rapid evolution of new learning spaces, not least an intense interest in future 'classroom' design. The lecture theatres and seminar rooms that we inhabit as lecturers never encourage ephemeral relationships, as we arrive and occupy the space for one or two hours at a time and then move on to another 'given' space. Replacing or upgrading old learning spaces such as classrooms with new learning spaces is expensive.

Floor space and wall space can be used far more creatively to actively engage learners. Tiles or squares of carpet or masking tape can provide perfect grids to use in developing learning models, to create patterns or for generating active discussion or reviewing techniques. History can be mapped out on the floor with colour coded cards (see Figure 3 Walk the Talk for a fuller description below), and students can kinaesthetically 'walk-the-talk', for example, demonstrating their understanding much more effectively. Technological tools are also influencing learning space, with items such as interactive whiteboards and large plasma screens, which can enable the instant capturing of fresh, 'live' and indigenous intellectual property. As pedagogy interacts with the operational facilities and the media technology, the learning environment will undergo rapid change. This will change the future layout of walls and learning space and enable active movement of people and information. This is important, for I believe that good learning environments will increasingly provide areas that maximise the flexibility and mobility of information, people, and space.

Designing learning activities

The second tumbler in the model explores some principles involved in the design of learning activities. Snyder (2003) notes that a number of studies comparing active learning with passive learning, show that active learning methods generally result in greater retention of material at the end of a class, superior problem solving skills, more positive attitudes, and higher motivation for future learning. Creating a real sense of engagement in an active learning journey over periods of time such as a semester or a year or the duration of a degree, can be a transformative experience for students. Journeying, with its sense of setting off, building, constructing, changing and arriving are all important conceptual ingredients in generating powerful experiential learning. Experiencing learning as separate modules will need to change so that the whole experience is more connected to the journeying through stages of dependence, counter dependence, independence and interdependence.

By 'active' learning methods I mean more intellectually, physically, socially and emotionally active. Active learning can offer a greater depth of information processing, greater comprehension and better retention, in contrast with the passive learning techniques that characterise the typical classroom, in which lecturer wisdom is offered for students to dutifully record in notes. Active learning involves students doing something and taking a participatory role in thinking and learning. The mélange of activities can include elements such as: kinaesthetic activity; mental challenges; experiencing a learning journey; overcoming obstacles; following or changing rules; and altering reality. Although much more research is needed into learning activities used in higher education a basic typology of activity might include:

1 Creating a sense of a learning journey for students, with a clear vision of the bigger picture, with a destination and route maps to guide.
2 Creating and sequencing an array of intellectually, physically and emotionally stimulating activities.
3 Adjusting or suspending elements of simulation or reality to create learning steps.
4 Creating activities to stimulate and regularly alter moods … acknowledge the student experience, create relaxed alertness, understand peak or flow learning.
5 Using the notion of constructing or deconstructing activities, such as physical objects, or non-physical items e.g. the gradual construction of a model, a concept, historical maps, key ingredients, typologies, a phrase or poem.
6 Creating and managing the learning community through a mixture of collaborative, competitive or co-optative strategies.
7 Creating and acknowledging feelings, values, targets, ground-rules, restrictions, obstacles and allowing students to address change, success and failure.
8 Consider multi-sensory teaching – experiment with building in a holistic 'sense' of the material covered … consider the sensory enhancement of material e.g. touch, smell, colour …
9 Providing elements of real or perceived challenge or risk … and allowing students to address risk and the stretching of personal boundaries.
10 Introducing complex design, sorting and/or organisational skills.
11 Developing generic functional student skills alongside specific course content work – such as literature searching, writing introductions, conclusions, researching skills, etc.
12 Designing quiet time for reflection – using the notion of physical and mental 'space'.
13 Allowing the story of the learning experience (including emotions) to be told by the learners (student progress files, learning logs, reflective exercises, group reflective dialogue).

Working with the senses

> The natural attitude of common sense leads us to overlook the phenomenon of the perceived world ... as we get on with life we do not notice the role of the senses in organising experience and constituting the physical world; it is precisely their business to make this role invisible to us... Hence to rediscover and articulate it we have somehow to get a detached sideways look at ordinary experience. (Introduction by Thomas Baldwin in Merleau-Ponty, 2004: 1)

The third tumbler considers how the senses – sight, touch, taste, hearing and smell – have the role of transmitting information which may then be interpreted and subsequently acted upon. Just using sensory-laden language appears to support more effective learning. Neuro-linguistic programming, for example, tells us that good educators use communication that conveys visual, auditory and feeling messages to engage a broader range of learners in a more effective way, and learners also generate clues as to their preferred ways of receiving and handling sensory data in order to construct their own 'map' of reality (O'Connor and Seymour, 1995). 'I hear what you are saying' (auditory), 'I see what you mean' (visual), 'I get the hang of it' (kinaesthetic): these indicate sensory preferences for learning. Lecturers too often use their preferred representational systems when communicating. Auditory dominant students might like audio tapes, talks, rhythms and sounds. Kinaesthetically dominant students like physical activity, which might include physical challenge or active drama and role play. With large groups of students, sample products can be passed around the lecture theatre to enable students to feel, see, move, explore, and try out.

Environmental awareness in product-design students is heightened when I wind up a clockwork radio and show students my mobile phone charging off my solar rucksack while we discuss the basic principles of sustainable product design: the experience becomes more sensory, more engaging and memorable. Enhancing and awakening the senses and linking them to learning activities can create more powerful learning. The more senses we stimulate in an activity, the more memorable the learning experience will become, because it increases and reinforces the neural connections in our brains. We also know that moods can be influenced by background music, by smells and by room colours. Music can be used to generate energy or for relaxation and contemplation that can enhance learning (Miles, 1997; Rose, 1996). Sensory reduction is also often used – blindfolds, for example, are the stock-in-trade of many outdoor education programmes.

Figure 3 An experiential learning case study

Walk the Talk
Mapping the history of the environmental movement

What it achieves
It develops a kinaesthetic learning imprint in the mind and body generating spatial awareness: learning by mapping and then walking the history of environmentalism.
It develops a deep understanding of complex information.
Active kinaesthetic reinforcement of learning increases active energy levels.

Underlying principles
The technique actively encourages group **research** and **collaboration** into specific allocated areas such as the voluntary sector, the laws, or government departments.
The technique uses spatial arrangement of **colour-coded cards** (visual-spatial), with collaborative discussion (oral) and walking (kinaesthetic) the historical map of **events**.
The activity uses **space** (the room) as a time zone/line. A form of testing can be added using a **viva** principle if needed.
This activity develops a **'kit'** presented in a video box to give to students (see resources).

Details

Students form groups to research specific aspects of environmental movement history using a prepared record of events spanning the last 300 years. This database is now available free on the Higher Education Academy HLST Network website at: (http://www.heacademy.ac.uk/hlst/events/detail/Learning_for_sustainable_futures).

In week six, the students map out on the floor their environmental history using coloured cards offering additional information in both written and oral form. Blue cards represent environmental laws such as the National Parks Act, yellow cards are used for the NGOs, grey for Quangos such as the Countryside Agency or English Nature, orange for key events in history such as the War or the Mass Trespass. The front of the room is the present day, the back of the room is the early 1800s.

The picture-map layout on the floor or large table demonstrates student knowledge and interpretations of the subject. Students thus walk the talk presenting their historical map as they journey through time and floor space. This kinaesthetically reinforces the learning and tests understanding in a visual-oral way.

The same can be done in other subjects, such as:

1 Literature reviewing techniques exploring key texts (The texts are spread out in a large space and debated and discussed as people move around them – the spatial re-organisation and debate is key. They can explore similarities and differences, spatial temporal issues (for example, the international geographical spread of literature). Newspaper stories can be introduced first to explore these skills with less experienced learners.

2 The history of philosophy/philosophers.

3 The history of computers.

Working with the emotions

Boud, Cohen and Walker note:

> emotions and feelings are the ones which are most neglected in our society: there is almost a taboo about them intruding into our education institutions, particularly at higher levels. (1993: 14)

Fineman made a similar observation and stated that:

> Learning is inextricably emotional and of emotions. The traditional cognitive approach to management learning has obscured the presence and role of emotion. (1997: 13)

During the past few years this neglect of emotional awareness has diminished as a result of writings on emotion and emotional intelligence. Goleman championed the subject in his book *Emotional Intelligence* (1996) and drew on the work of Salovey and Mayer who classified emotional intelligence into five main domains: knowing one's emotions, managing emotions, motivating oneself, recognising emotions in others, and handling relationships (1990). In spite of this societal and institutional pressure for objectivity the emotions have a powerful place in the process of learning. Boud and Miller stressed that

> The affective experience of learners is probably the most powerful determinant of learning of all kinds... (1996: 17)

Managing the emotional climate, accessing emotion, mapping or encouraging change in the basic emotional make-up of students is a difficult yet necessary skill for lecturers (Mortiboys, 2002). Being able to sense, and where appropriate steer, the emotional bases of student behaviour is a key skill. Yet this needs emotional maturity, responsibility and personal understanding by tutors. Students are also increasingly being encouraged to undertake personal and professional development portfolios and progress files that, through reflective exercises, examine emotional states in learning.

Working with the many forms of intelligence

The fifth tumbler addresses the nature of intelligence. In addition to emotional intelligence there are also other forms of intelligence which need to be considered and addressed in learning design. Before Gardner's book *Frames of Mind* (1983) much emphasis was placed on the Intelligence Quotient (IQ) which was based upon the narrow consideration of mathematical and linguistic skills. Gardner drew attention to the notion, and importance, of other forms of intelligence and proposed seven types: linguistic; logical/mathematical/scientific; visual/spatial; musical; bodily/physical/kinaesthetic; interpersonal and intra-personal. Stimulating these many forms of intelligence is key to inclusive pedagogy, and verbal/linguistic-learning activities might include: reading books, journal logs, debate, storytelling, verbal humour, poetry, or creative writing.

   Bodily/kinaesthetic learning activities might include: role play, moving laminated cards, things to touch/feel, using physical metaphors, encouraging movement, or using stick-it labels that can be rearranged. Mathematical logical activities might use mind maps, systems processing, force field analysis, or assigning numbers to things. Visual/spatial learning activities might use wall charts, spatial anchors, gestures by lecturers, guided visualisation or imagery, visual aids, sketches and diagrammatic representations. More examples can be found in Beard & Wilson (2002).

Advantages of the learning combination lock

Having investigated the six tumblers of the Learning Combination Lock (LCL) above, it is now possible to consider some of its merits and applications:

❑ The experiential learning model and LCL are meta-models which attempt to provide a broader perspective of the learning process and its various elements and theories.

❑ Some learning theories tend to operate as closed systems operating in isolation from other theories. The LCL encourages a broader perspective which has the possibility of incorporating new theories with existing ones.

❑ The LCL provides the opportunity to consider other learning models rather than being like the golfer who is only able to use a limited number of clubs from the golf bag.

❑ The LCL is sufficiently flexible to incorporate the main behavioural, cognitive,

and humanist schools of learning without placing them in opposition to each
other.

❑ The LCL provides a systematic approach to the support of learning.

❑ The checklist of elements for each tumbler provides an *aide memoire* for the
educator, trainer and developer.

❑ The metaphor of the combination lock should not limit the use of only one
ingredient from each tumbler. In practice, learning events may incorporate
several elements from a tumbler.

❑ The metal rod running through the core of the Learning Combination Lock
represents the needs of the learner. These should be central to any consideration
of the various options available in each of the tumblers.

❑ The LCL should not be used as a one-armed-bandit approach to selecting the
ingredients for experiential learning activities. The learning needs and objectives should be carefully considered before addressing each tumbler in turn and
selecting those combinations which are likely to be effective.

❑ The LCL is not an exclusive list of the tumblers and elements which might be
considered in the design of a learning event. It allows trainers, educators and
developers to add to the lock and build their own personalised set of learning
permutations which respond to learning needs, thus adding to the millions of
combinations. I encourage you, the reader, to customise the model for your
own particular requirements.

❑ The LCL should not be applied in a mechanical fashion without an understanding of the tumblers and the principles of learning. Rather it should be considered a form of reference to guide the design and delivery of programmes.

Conclusion

In this chapter I have emphasised the importance of using the concept of experiential
learning as a means of drawing together theory and practice. Drawing upon a new
innovative pedagogic model for effective practice, many of the elements involved during the interaction between the learner and the external environment, i.e. the whole
experience, can be built into the learning design process. The tumblers encourage a
systematic questioning of six fundamental ingredients of learning while simultane-
ously providing an almost infinite number of learning design permutations.

The value of the Learning Combination Lock will be in the extent to which it is
applied and further developed. Please feel free to use and adapt the model for your
own purposes. For a full description of the application of the model see Beard and
Wilson (2006).

References

Abram, D. (1997) *The Spell of the Sensuous.* New York: Vintage Books

Andreson, L. Boud, D. and Cohen, R. (2000) Experience-based learning. In *Understanding Adult Education and Training.* Sydney: Allen and Unwin pp. 225–39

Beard, C. (2005) The Design of Effective Group Based Training Methods, in J. P. Wilson (ed) *Human Resource Development,* 2nd edition. London: Kogan Page

Beard, C. (2008) Experiential Learning: The development of a pedagogic framework for effective practice. Unpublished PhD thesis, Sheffield Hallam University

Beard, C. and Wilson, J. (2006) *Experiential Learning: A Best Practice Handbook for Educators and Trainers,* 2nd edition. London: Kogan Page

Beard, C. (2007) Towards a Theory of E-learning: Experiential e-learning, *Journal of Hospitality, Leisure, Sport and Tourism Education* **6** (2) November

Boud, D. Cohen, R. and Walker, D. (1993) *Using Experience For Learning.* Buckingham: Open University Press

Boud, D. and Walker, D. (1993) Developing Models of Learning from Experience, paper presented in the Conference Proceedings, Paper presented to the Annual SCUTREA conference

Boud, D. and Miller, N. (1996) (eds) *Working with experience: animating learning.* London: Routledge

Brooks, J. G. and Brooks, M. (1993) *The Case for Constructivist Classrooms* Virginia VA: The Association for Supervision and Curriculum Development

Dewey, J. (1938) *Experience and Education.* New York: Collier

Fenwick, T. J. (2003) *Learning Through Experience: Troubling Orthodoxies and Intersecting Questions.* Florida: Krieger Publishing

Fineman, S. 'Emotion and management learning' *Management Learning* **28** (1) pp. 13–25

Gardner, H. (1983) *Frames of Mind: The Theory of Multiple Intelligences.* Basic Books: New York

Goleman, D. (1996) *Emotional Intelligence: why it can matter more than IQ.* London: Bloomsbury

Heron, J. (2001) *Helping the Client: A Creative Practical Guide.* London: Sage

Hussey, T. and Smith, P. (2002) The trouble with learning outcomes. *Active Learning in Higher Education* **3** (3) November pp. 220–33

Illeris, K. (2002) *The Three Dimensions of Learning.* Florida: Krieger Publishing

Jarvis, P. (2004) *Adult Education and Lifelong Learning: Theory and Practice,* 3rd edition. London: Routledge/Falmer

Knowles, M. S. (1980) *The Modern Practice of Adult Education: From Pedagogy to Andragogy.* Chicago: Follet

Kolb, D. A. (1984) *Experiential Learning.* Englewood Cliffs NJ: Prentice Hall

Merleau-Ponty, M. (2004) *The World of Perception.* Introduction by Thomas Baldwin. London: Routledge

Miles, E. (1997) *Tune Your Brain: Using music to manage your mind, body and mood.* Berkely CA

Miller, N. and Boud, D. (1996) Animation in learning from experience. In Boud, D. and Miller, D. (eds) *Working with experience: animating learning.* London: Routledge pp 3–13

Miller, N. and Boud, D. (1997) *From teaching to facilitation to animation: crossing the boundaries between traditions and perspectives in the promotion of learning from experience.* Paper presented to the 27th Annual SCUTREA conference.

Moon, J. (2004) *A Handbook of Reflective and Experiential Learning: Theory and Practice.* London: Routledge/Falmer

Mortiboys, A. (2002) *The Emotionally Intelligent Lecturer.* Birmingham: SEDA Publications

Nicol, R. (2003) Outdoor Education: Research Topic or Universal Value? Part Three, *Journal of Adventure Education and Outdoor Learning* **3** (1) pp. 11–28

O'Connor, J. & Seymour, J. (1995) *Introducing Neuro-linguistic Programming: Psychological skills for understanding and influencing people.* London: Thorsons

Revans, R. W. (1980) *Action Learning: New Techniques for Management.* London: Blond and Briggs

Rogers, C. R. (1969) *Freedom to Learn.* Ohio, Charles E. Merrill

Rose, C. (1996) *Accelerated Learning.* UK: Accelerated learning Systems

Salovey, P. & Mayer, J. D. (1990) Emotional Intelligence. *Imagination, Cognition and Personality* **9** pp. 185–211

Snyder, K. (2003) Ropes, Poles, and Space – Active learning in Business Education. *Active Learning in Higher Education* **2** (4) July pp 159–67

Tennant, M. (1997) *Psychology and adult learning,* 2nd edition. London: Routledge

Taylor, H. (1991) The Systematic Training Model: Corn Circles in Search of a Spaceship? *Management Education and Development* **22** (4) pp. 258–78

Watson, P. (2002) The role and integration of learning outcomes into educational processes. *Active Learning in Higher Education* **3** (3) November pp. 205–19

COLIN BEARD is a faculty teaching fellow at Sheffield Hallam University. He is also a National Teaching Fellow and Fellow of the Royal Society of Arts. Colin advises many higher education institutions on innovations in teaching and learning, and he works extensively with international companies advising on the effective experiential education and training of staff.

2

The Writing Project
'Bridging the gap' into undergraduate study

Susan Lea and Derry Corey
University College Plymouth: St Mark & St John

How can we most effectively respond to increasing
concerns about the ability of students to write for
both employment and academic purposes?

The starting point of the study was an exploration of our own ability to adequately communicate the complex set of skills involved in writing. Our research quickly demonstrated the need to move away from the skills-based deficit model of writing, and to consider the complexity of teaching and learning writing within the framework of the subject discipline.

Summary

This chapter reflects on a small-scale enquiry currently being undertaken at University College Plymouth: St Mark & St John (Marjon). It is the initial phase in a research process designed to explore the different ways in which academics approach the development of writing skills within different disciplines. The aim of the study is to explore the most effective ways of enabling students to improve their writing skills.

Objectives

Due to the different disciplinary background of each of the researchers, and the different programmes of study of the students, this case study should be understood as an examination of only *one* of the approaches taken in the overall research. The objectives of this case study were to enable students to learn to write more effectively by helping them to understand how to:

❑ Value their own tacit knowledge, understand their epistemological orientation and build academic assertiveness.

❑ Learn to learn, by using Honey and Mumford's learning styles (1982), and Kolb's learning cycle (1984).

❑ Learn to reflect on 'real life' issues in dialogue with peers and tutors.

❑ See themselves as co-researchers capable of understanding and constructing knowledge about their own learning and writing needs.

❑ Trust in the process of transitional thinking and knowing.

❑ Ultimately, to express knowledge and meaning making, in confident spoken and written 'voices'.

All the above objectives were embedded in the materials of one first-year module *Social Science for Community Context*, and the delivery of discursive lectures, reading packs, seminar discussions and writing-skills workshops.

Rationale

Two external forces are having a powerful impact on the role of the university and on academic and student identities. First, the globalisation of the market has led to demands for economically useful education to support business. Secondly, the impact of this on national policy drivers which now require the university to work more closely with business, widen participation in higher education, educate students and re-educate the existing workforce to meet employers' needs. Both forces identify the university in the UK as a key organisation to equip existing and potential *workers* with the type of knowledge required by business. These drivers indicate a profound change in the meaning and purpose of the university, and of learning and teaching. While these issues are beyond the scope of this study, they do provide an important context and rationale for undertaking this work.

In response to the above, increasing numbers of students are entering the university from non-traditional educational backgrounds. Sinfield, Burns and Holley claim that widening participation is leading to debates about academic discourse, class, skills and employability. They also note that various speeches by ministers, and press commentary 'barely mask a eugenicist agenda, with elite higher education for some, and an inferior, vocational HE for the masses' (2004: 142). Vilification of the non-traditional student is typified by Starkey's comment that 'there are Mickey Mouse students for whom Mickey Mouse degrees are quite appropriate' (Sinfield et al, 2004). This has led to research enquiries into working-class students' experience of HE by the ESRC (2006–08), the Joseph Rowntree Foundation (Quinn et al, 2005) and the Sutton Trust (2000). In particular the standard of students' written work is often used to disparage graduates, and the discourse is often covertly directed at the non-traditional-entry student (see Newman, 2007).

In Britain we have one of the most under-resourced education systems in Europe. We also have a higher education system which has faced continual cuts in its budget per student over the last 20 years, and at the same time we have widened participation (Canaan, 2001). In practice this has led to an increasingly complex relationship between lecturers and students, with less time to attend to learning relationships. Increasingly there is also a cultural mismatch between the offer and the expectations of students (in terms of pedagogies, values, curriculum and the relationship of experience to knowledge). These are key issues in learning and teaching and Quinn et al (2005: 69, 70) recommend that retention strategies include

> a curriculum which reflects and affirms the experience of working-class students, a pedagogy which supports integration and better integrated learning support to prevent working-class student drop-out.

Our case study responds to each of these concerns in the context of 'extended writing skills development' as a bridge from A level and access into undergraduate study.

Context

Writing is now seen as a 'problem' in higher education by both academics and employers who claim there has been a 'dumbing down' of standards. In fact students now need a greater diversity of linguistic skills to prepare them for specialised writing in both the workplace and academia, and 'our understanding of writing has not caught up with these changes ...writing is too often assumed to be a single, easily-generalisable set of skills' (Russell, 2003: vi). The idea of what constitutes 'good' as opposed to 'poor' writing is increasingly being called into question, and writing is being recognised as a complex, developmental acquisition of skills. This perspective goes beyond the surface features of poor spelling, and the study of academic writing is becoming part of a root and branch exploration of the ways in which higher education will need to reform to meet changing expectations (Russell, 2003).

In the US there is a long tradition of expecting students to undertake a general writing course in the first year of their study, yet there is little evidence of improved writing performance by students. In contrast, in Europe the integration of writing into the discipline studied in higher education is prominent. Bjork (2003) sees this process relating to both text-type consciousness and to competence which acts as a building block towards the socio-cultural criteria of the written genre. This dual approach connects writing to 'the traditions, forms of thinking, modes of communication, and research methods of the academic world itself' (Bjork 2003: 2). Effectively then, this brings writing into intimate connection with the discipline, and in practice it is connected to pedagogical issues including the epistemological and ontological orientations of the student. Brauer (2003) claims that what is required is a move beyond skills development to understanding writing as a method of knowledge building, *and* a move from text to writer and to learning by doing. If these analyses are correct, new pedagogical approaches are implied, and academics will need to reflect on their own practice and find innovative ways of clarifying their own expectations of students and of enabling them to acquire the necessary thinking, reading, and writing skills in the transitional phase into undergraduate study.

In the UK, deficit discourses around non-traditional entry students and in particular about graduate writing skills, have led to an increasing interest in understanding how best to teach academic writing (Lea, 2006). Lillis and Turner highlight the fact that whilst lecturers foregrounded notions of argument and structure as key elements to successful writing, they were unable to specify exactly what they meant by those terms. (2001: 58)

Several different approaches to improving writing skills have been used in the UK and broadly these are study-skills orientations, academic socialisation and academic literacies (Lea & Street, 1998). The academic literacies approach is rapidly gaining favour as it is student-centred, and focuses on 'how students come to make meaning in their writing in terms of any particular writing tasks' (Lea, 2006). Lillis (2006) is already exploring how this links to a critical research frame which can contribute to the development of pedagogy, and calls for dialogic interaction around written texts to facilitate student engagement, while offering different ways of making meaning.

Description

Marjon recruits a large number of students from non-traditional academic back-grounds and delivers a range of vocationally qualifying and vocationally relevant programmes. As such, we are an institution at the forefront of widening access and participation. We are also a church-foundation university college, with a social mission to enable all students to reach their full potential. Our *Learning and Teaching Strategy 2006–09* recognises that an increasingly diverse student population may require new approaches to learning and teaching.

We knew that within the organisation different approaches to writing improve-ment were being adopted at programme level. Some programmes already had dedi-cated writing modules; two of our colleagues Hazel Sales (2006) and Alison Theaker (2008) were already involved in research and publication about writing. There were also two institutional support mechanisms for students: Personal Development Planning (PDP) and Student Support Services. A small team of interested academics, with different skills and viewpoints decided to apply for a small internal research grant. We were motivated by improving our own understanding of student writing, enhancing the student experience with support for producing written work and by the hope of reducing drop-out levels. We also hope to produce a report which might provide a focus for discussion with colleagues and lead to an improvement in organi-sational support for students entering Marjon.

Within this case study, our motivation emerged from joint working the previous year when we had attempted to deliver study skills and PDP to entry-level students. Our previous efforts to improve writing through 'skills development' had been greeted with lukewarm interest by students. Our continued interest in the students' experience arise from both our own biographies as learners and teachers, and from our shared commitment to finding better ways to support student transitions into HE. Our reflections then related to our own practice. Having achieved a positive student engagement in learning, how might we better understand and facilitate an improvement in their writing skills?

Our case study started with a systematic questioning of everything we knew about the problems facing non-traditional entry students. We were, and are, working in Schon's 'swampy lowlands' of practice' (1983). Our exploration involves uncertainty, uniqueness, and value concerns – Schon's 'indeterminate zones of practice' (1987). The research approach fits broadly within Carr and Kemis's emancipatory approach to educational action research (1986); it is informed by the work of Whitehead and McNiff in relation to ontological and epistemological standards of judgement (2006), and is part of a process of systematic reflection and research into our own practice.

We started by considering the issues of difference in the student cohort. This includes difference in age, class, gender and 'race', in educational experience, confidence and self-esteem, dis/ability (in previous years the number of students on the case study module with *recognised* learning difficulties has ranged from 20–33%), and there is a difference in programme cohorts being taught together (some with work experience, some without). Given this broad range of difference, we felt it was important to move away from a deficit discourse on learning and skills development.

Our approach to our work with students was informed by the works of Dewey on reflective thinking and experience (1910, 1938), Polyani's personal knowledge (1962), Schon on education for reflection (1987), Honey and Mumford's learning styles (1982), Kolb's experiential learning theory (1984), and Moon on critical thinking and academic assertiveness (2008). We were concerned that students should learn to reflect on their own experience – in dialogue with peers and tutors (to better understand their own epistemological orientation and to enhance critical thinking), to learn how they learned and understand the process of learning itself, to trust in the educational process of transitional thinking and knowing, and to see themselves as co-researchers capable of understanding and constructing knowledge about their own learning and writing needs. Ultimately we believed this combination would enhance their academic assertiveness and help them to express their knowledge in a confident spoken and written 'voice'.

We spent four hours each week with students in a year-one Semester A module called *Social Science for Community Contexts*. We chose this module to focus on writing skills as:

❑ It was students' first experience of learning within HE.
❑ We had four hours timetabled together, and this facilitated an easy breakdown into lecture/seminar/workshop time.
❑ The subject had a good 'fit' with ontological and epistemological orientation and the subject matter lent itself to deconstruction of prior knowledge and experience, and reconstruction of 'new' understandings.
❑ We had previously attempted (the year before) to build study skills into the module, although we know that some students regarded this as a deficit model of learning and disengaged.
❑ We already knew that students had actively engaged in and enjoyed the module

content, and that seminar discussion was often lively and intelligent, and that written work did not adequately capture this learning.

For a significant number of students, the expectation of degree learning is to get to the 'truth' through collecting the 'facts'. This creates problems in transition to university which routinely demands a more complex engagement with contested concepts and discourses. It is further complicated by the complexity of the tasks which face students. They are expected to arrive at university with reading, note-taking and writing skills. They are then expected to reflect, find their own 'voice' or form of expression in critical evaluation of concepts in which they may be 'wrong', to challenge, disagree and accept challenges to their existing experience and understanding of the world, and to understand the 'different perspectives' of lecturers, texts and other students. For this reason Moon's description of academic assertiveness was important to us.

> Academic assertiveness is a set of emotional and psychological orientations and behaviours that enable a learner to manage the challenges to the self in progressing in learning and critical thinking. (2008: 79)

In order to facilitate learning and teaching then, we chose to embed two different types of skills development in the module: skills for academic assertiveness which were underpinned by writing skills development. This required us to make explicit a range of skills developments which are often tacitly assumed by teachers, and often confuse learners. These are set out in our objectives above.

In the module introduction we made explicit our own position in teaching and learning which was based on an interpretation of *The Power of Critical Theory for Adult Learning and Teaching* (Brookfield, 2005: 350). From the first session we questioned the status of knowledge, explained paradigms, and asserted the usefulness of theory – Lewin's 'there is nothing so practical as a good theory' (Lewin, 1952: 169). We explained the importance of students being open to questioning their tacit assumptions of everyday life, and how reflective examination, deconstruction and (possibly) reconstruction of their beliefs might help them to exert more 'conscious control over their everyday lives'. We also used this session to inform students that we were learners as well as teachers, and that we were hoping to learn how better to support learners in transition to HE through research into skills development, including writing skills development, and that their contribution and commentary was both welcome and vital to us.

Having reflected on our own understanding of the complexity of the task for both teachers and learners we decided that it was unreasonable to expect students to be able to source all their own study materials in a new and unfamiliar environment immediately. We therefore handed out a module outline with directed reading for each week, and a set of questions *as a guide* for reading and seminar discussion. We made clear to students that the pack was a starting point and not a boundary for their reading and discussion. We asked students to make notes on their reading, and to make notes of examples of the ways in which their everyday experience related to the reading. For example, we encouraged them to read a daily paper and make relevant cuttings for seminars, or note relevant news items or storylines in television dramas and documentaries (and of course we encouraged academic reading around the topics). We also handed out copies of Powerpoint slides from lectures at the beginning of each lecture. This required a great deal of front-loaded planning for the module and a lot of photo-copying, all of which was felt to be worthwhile to ensure that students were 'work-ready' and focused on engaging with learning (many of the students have substantial part-time work and family commitments). We explained to students that this level of supplied material was exceptional, and the norm was that they would source their own reading materials. We asked that they valued our investment in their learning by ensuring they prepared weekly to give them a quick start into learning and study.

Each session was delivered in the same way with approximately one hour's lecture input, during which students were invited to ask for clarification or make (brief) comment. This was followed by one-hour skills development time *which focused on the lecture and seminar content*. It was important to us that the skills development period was timetabled to include all students. The thinking and learning tasks were embedded into the writing we asked students to undertake during this period. We modelled reflective thinking on the lecture content, encouraged dialogue, had a short input time on various aspects of learning to learn, discussion about students' learning and writing needs and issues of concern, followed by writing activities which lasted a standard 15-minute period each week. The input and activities were often drawn from key elements in Personal Development Planning (PDP) which students had rejected in the past on an individual basis, but which they now willingly discussed and engaged with. We also started the module with a self-evaluation skills question-naire, and ended the module with the same, so that students could track their own developing levels of confidence in relation to the task. No area of discussion was out of bounds and discussions ranged from the problems of time-management, to altered perceptions of students' everyday lives and relationships. After a break, students then split into seminar groups for discussion in the remaining time.

Evaluation

We had from the outset appreciated the need to move away from deficit discourses on writing. Early approaches quickly drove our thinking towards an 'academic lit-eracies' and 'academic assertiveness' approach to learning and teaching. What had started out as a 'writing' project quickly developed into a case study in which 'learn-ing to learn' more generally became our priority. The tacit knowledge which we as practitioners held in our approach to the study required constant reflection on our part, and the emphasis which we had placed on elements of our practice changed in response to discussions with our students as we began to question our own assumptions. We debriefed each week and adapted throughout the process. One example of this was our original idea that students would share their written work with peers for formative feedback. Given the anxiety of students about this task we merely encouraged them to privately share their work with peers of their own choice. Given Scott and Coate's work on the risks and complexity of the task of giving appropriate feedback (2003), we believe this was an appropriate decision. Students were invited to submit work to us for formative feedback, but few had the confidence to do so at an early stage, and this is an area we will need to address next year.

Overall, students valued our approach. Virtually all the students grew in academic confidence during the period of the case study. This was shown in the questions and challenges to teaching staff, and in the active engagement in seminar discussion by even the normally 'quiet' students. During breaks we noticed that students continued to engage in lively debates about the subject under discussion, and at the end of seminars we had difficulty in clearing the rooms for the next sessions. Discussion on topics often carried on in the corridors after the session had ended, and there was real evidence of academic assertiveness in student dialogue. Students were also making claims about how their learning was impacting on their lives outside the classroom. A particular area of concern was how their friends, families and partners saw the personal changes in them and the effect on their out-of-college relationships. Sometimes this highlighted the need for further contact with module staff, personal tutors, study skills tutors or the counselling team – but crucially these responses to their concerns were seen by students as a positive outcome rather than a problematic one.

On a more negative note however, the one area we overlooked was the modification of assessment tasks to reflect the changes we made to the module. This had been a real oversight on our part. Having focused extensively on a process of engagement with learning and writing skills development, we then left the traditional essay and examination as the assessment! We now believe a more appropriate assessment for the future will be the embedding of different writing tasks, which require different thinking and writing skills (such as reflective writing, keeping a journal, note-making from articles) for which we can provide high-quality formative feedback and guidance before essay writing. This will, we believe, help to embed skills development more meaningfully, and also honour the learning journeys of the students.

Discussion

What started out as a 'writing project' changed profoundly. We also found that the emerging discipline of teaching writing for academic purposes offers an important challenge to all academics, as well as to students. We would argue that it is no longer possible for academics to expect students to enter university in possession of the necessary skills to enable them to take full advantage of higher education. Our case study has also highlighted the importance of the ability of us as academics to reflect on our own ontological and epistemological orientations and assumptions, and the invisible pedagogies which emerge from them. Once clear about our own approaches, we might be more capable of providing students with a much clearer understanding of what we can offer, what they can expect in curriculum terms, and what is expected of them at university. This supports Quinn et al's analysis that the cultural mismatch between the offer and the expectations of students in terms of pedagogies, values, curriculum, and the relationship of knowledge to experience needs to be challenged (2005).

At a time of widening participation, learning and teaching need to reflect and affirm the different experience of students. We also need to acknowledge the different external drivers which are impacting on the role of the lecturer in HE. This requires critical reflection by both academics as well as students and affects not only the learning relationship, but all aspects of curriculum. Knowledge, experience, and skills will all be central to this change. Our original objectives, framed within an overall understanding of, and commitment to, academic literacies and academic assertiveness are, we believe, one contribution to providing a structured approach to the improvement of student writing. We believe that this approach, conceived of as an extended period of induction and transition into university, allows for an appropriate period of social and academic integration into the university. We also believe it stands at the heart of empowering students to become both lifelong and independent learners as well as better thinkers and writers. Our research is ongoing.

References

Bjork, L. (2003) Text Types, Textual Consciousness and Academic Writing Ability. In Bjork, L. et al (eds) *Teaching Academic Writing in European Higher Education*. Dordrecht: Kluwer Academic Publishers

Brauer, G. (2003) Centres for Writing and Reading – Bridging the Gap between University and School Education. In Bjork, L. et al (eds) *Teaching Academic Writing in European Higher Education*. Dordrecht: Kluwer Academic Publishers

Brookfield, S. D. (2005) *The Power of Critical Theory for Adult Learning and Teaching*. Oxford: OUP

Canaan, J. E. (2001) Haunting Assumptions of 'Ability': How Working Class and Ethnic Minority Students Signify Academic Failure. Paper presented at the Higher Education Close Up 2 Conference, Lancaster University. Retrieved 05/09/07

Carr, W. & Kemmis, S. (1986) *Becoming Critical: Education, Knowledge and Action Research*. Lewes: Falmer Press

Dewey, J. (1938) *Experience and Education*. New York: Collier

ESRC (2008) *The socio-cultural and learning experiences of working class students in Higher Education*: Interim Summary Report. (ESRC RES-139-25-0208)

Honey, P. & Mumford, A. (1982) *The Manual of Learning Styles*. Maidenhead: Peter Honey

Kolb, D. (1984) *Experiential Learning as the Science of Learning and Development*. Englewood Cliffs NJ: Prentice Hall

Lea, M. & Street, B. (1998) *Student Writing in HE: an Academic Literacies Approach*. Oxford: OUP

Lea, M. (2006) Writing in Today's University. *Education Developments* **7** (4)

Lewin, K. (1952) *Field Theory in Social Science*. London: Tavistock

Lillis, T. M. and Turner, J. (2006) Moving Towards an 'Academic Literacies' Pedadogy: Dialogues of Participation. In Ganobcsik-Williams, L. (ed) *Teaching Academic Writing in UK Higher Education*. Basingstoke: Palgrave MacMillan

Moon, J. (2008) *Critical thinking: An exploration of theory and practice*. Oxon: Routledge

Newman, M. (2007) Appalling writing skills drive tutors to seek help. *Times Higher Education Supplement* **17** March

Polyani, M. (1962) *Personal Knowledge*. Chicago: University of Chicago Press

Quinn, J. et al (2005) *From Life Crisis to Lifelong Learning: Rethinking Working Class Drop-Out from HE* York: Joseph Rowntree Foundation. Retrieved 05/09/07

Russell, D. A. (2003) Preface in Bjork, L. et al (eds) *Teaching Academic Writing in European Higher Education*. Dordrecht: Kluwer Academic Publishers

Sales, H. E. (2006) *Professional Communication in Engineering*. Basingstoke: Palgrave Macmillan

Schon, D. A. (1983) *The Reflective Practitioner: How Professionals Think in Action.* London: Temple Smith

Schon, D. A. (1987) *Educating the Reflective Practitioner*. San Francisco: Jossey-Bass

Scott, M. & Coate, K. (2003) Rethinking Feedback: asymmetry in disguise. In Bjork, L. et al (eds) *Teaching Academic Writing in European Higher Education*. Dordrecht, Netherlands: Kluwer Academic Publishers

Sinfield, S. Burns, T. & Holley, D. (2004) Outsider looking in or insiders looking out? In Satherthwaite et al. *Widening Participation in a post-1992 university*. Sterling USA: Trentham Books

Sutton Trust (2000)

Theaker, A. (2008) Motivating students to write well. *Asia Pacific Public Relations Journal* **8** pp 77–90

Whitehead, J. & McNiff, J. (2006) *Action Research Living Theory*. London: Sage

SUE LEA Following a long career as a community education worker, Sue Lea moved to Marjon eight years ago where she now works as a programme leader for Children, Welfare and Society. She teaches on the undergraduate and post-graduate Community and Youth Studies programme and on Education Studies. Sue is currently undertaking a DEd at Exeter University and developing a research focus on educational transitions.

DERRY COREY's background is in Geography. She has represented Marjon on two Geography Discipline Network (GDN) Projects and was a member of the writing team for the series of guidebooks on key skills in geography in HE. Derry has been involved in developing and embedding Personal Development Profiling within cross-college programmes and currently co-ordinates and teaches on the HE Accredited PG Certificate programme for new teachers in HE. She is also a registered workshop presenter for the GEES HE Academy Subject Centre and presents workshops on induction and retention and implementing PDP in the curriculum.

3

Developing engagement in professional development planning in higher education

Simon Cox
Leeds Metropolitan University

Where students find employability skills development difficult or see it as unimportant and unrelated to their 'real' subject discipline, how can we engage them in analysing and developing their employability skills?

Introduction

This chapter discusses the challenges faced by academics and presents the critical factors that influenced student engagement and motivation within the Professional Development Planning (PDP) programme at Leeds Metropolitan University (LeedsMet).

The PDP programme is designed to develop employability skills in students. It is delivered at Levels 4 and 5 of the hospitality and retailing undergraduate programmes. The Level 5 module, *Personal & Professional Skills for Managers* (PPSM), was delivered to 140 students and became the project for an 18-month period of action research. Module evaluation, student focus groups and benchmarking from best practice were the main research methods used to evaluate and develop the module and improve its effectiveness in engaging students in employability skills development. A number of key changes were made to the assessment approach, indicative teaching content and learning resources.

Objectives

The aim of this project was to improve the assessment, teaching and 'sense of values' of the module in an effort to promote students' engagement and intrinsic orientation in employability skills development. Several objectives were set by the researcher to meet this aim. These were:

- ❑ To improve students' understanding of what and how they learn
- ❑ To encourage students to review, plan and take responsibility for their own learning
- ❑ For students to see the module as central to their professional progress
- ❑ To introduce a more flexible learning approach to assessments.

Rationale

Academics have a challenging task in motivating and engaging students in PDP programmes. According to Hind (2006) students do not necessarily find developing employability skills an easy process. They perhaps regard PDP and related employability subjects as unimportant, subjective and unrelated to any specific subject discipline. Furthermore, Brockbank & McGill (1998) found that often students do not find their intrinsic orientation, which alters with time, until after leaving university. They perhaps have limited life-experiences to call upon when asked to review and develop employability skills through critical self-evaluation, thinking deeply and applying reflective practice. On the other hand, mature students tend to find PDP modules relevant, fulfilling and straightforward.

Another challenge is a lack of collaboration or 'common voice' amongst academics. Tariq (2004) found that some academics find it hard to accept the 'skills agenda' and this can have a negative impact on the student experience.

Approaches to skills development in the UK have either been 'embedded' in the curriculum – where students are not actually aware they are developing skills – or are offered as 'stand-alone' modules. The latter practice of 'bolting-on' a module to the curriculum can result in these learning skills being isolated from mainstream academic subjects (Cranmer, 2006). This can have adverse affects on a student's motivation and engagement.

The vocational nature of retail, hospitality, tourism and events courses at Leeds Met reinforces the importance of integrating employability and management skills into the undergraduate programme (Hind, 2006). Hind goes on to say that to facilitate this learning, a tutor needs to consider a variety of strategies for integrating employability skills development into the curriculum.

Context

This case study features the development of the *Personal Professional Skills for Managers* (PPSM) module delivered to 140 Level 5 Hospitality and Retail Management students at Leeds Metropolitan University. The PPSM module is a stand-alone core module worth 15 UK credits, delivered over two semesters and involves seven teaching staff. The aim of the module is to:

> provide a vehicle for the enhancement of intellectual ability, personal skills, and career development and to build on the student's personal progress file.

The module evolved over a period of years to include several learning objectives including the development of students' learning and employability skills. The latter objective was introduced to help prepare students for their dissertations in their final year.

Students were also required to complete a series of six personal evaluation and reflection tasks linked to transferable skills. This formed the personal development progress file or journal to be submitted with supporting evidence at the end of the academic year.

This project involved an action research approach over an 18 month period (January 2006–June 2007). A mainly qualitative approach was adopted. The four key stages were: student evaluation 2005–06, team involvement through consultation, internal benchmarking and post-module student evaluation in May 2007.

Student evaluation

A series of three focus groups was conducted over both semesters using open questions relating to the assignments, action plans, employability agenda, module content and delivery. Students were specifically asked how the module could improve student engagement. The key findings of these focus groups were:

❑ Purpose

Provide greater clarity about the purpose and a more logical structure to the module content.

Involve the employability office to give guidance on careers.

Provide more guest lectures and speakers from industry

❑ Personal skills development

The idea of a Personal Action Plan was good but it required further development and guidance to make it self-explanatory and easier to use.

Provide a check list.

Have more personal key skills audits.

Run workshops directly related to the key skills and more sessions on reflective writing.

❑ Use the Virtual Learning Environment (VLE) as a resource to include electronic versions of action plans, skills audits, web links and lecture notes.

Consultation

The results provided an excellent opportunity to review the module. The teaching team were sent the findings and a series of discussions followed. The researcher believed that by involving the teaching team in the module review, engagement and contribution would be more dynamic and supportive.

Benchmarking

The researcher also gained access to many internal and external resources through involvement in the university-wide PDP working group. This enabled a 'cherry picking' approach to taking the 'best of the best' from several other tried and tested approaches to PDP.

Post-module student evaluation

Module evaluation through a series of focus groups was carried out in May 2007. The results are presented in the evaluation section of this chapter.

Description

There were four key changes that had the most influence over the success of the revised PPSM 2006–07 module. These were:

1   The development of three distinct themes

These three themes were:

1   Self analysis
2   Employability and leadership
3   Research skills

Teaching in weeks one to three focused on self-analysis and evaluation or 'getting to know you'. Students had to complete a minimum of three personal skills audits, such as Belbin's group dynamics questionnaire, before completing their Personal Development Action Plan (PDAP). This gave an opportunity for the student to critically analyse their personal traits in relation to key transferable skills. Vivas in the form of individual appraisals were introduced in week eight, designed to discuss and evaluate the PDAP.

Theme two (weeks four to ten) involved a series of workshops exploring several leadership and employability skills, e.g. leadership styles, group working. The topics were linked to the ten key skills outlined in the PDAP, allowing students to collate experiential and reflective evidence.

The third theme (weeks 11 to 20) was focused around supporting students in understanding and developing their research skills. This theme was primarily included to develop student awareness for their forthcoming Level 6 dissertation but was equally important in supporting related employability skills development.

2   The Personal Development Action Plan

The introduction of a PDAP booklet had the most significant impact of all initiatives in improving engagement. The PDAP booklet was designed to improve student engagement in the 'self-analysis' stage of the personal development process. The booklet was centred on ten key transferable and academic skills.

The booklet was designed to be self-administered, containing step-by-step instructions. Ten key academic/employability skills were selected and each of these was presented in a separate section. The student was asked to provide a personal statement relating to their level of competence against each of the ten key skills. Students then had to provide an action plan to improve their level of competence through a series of SMART objectives and related resource requirements. The final page allowed for a summary of key strengths and areas for improvement.

The PDAP booklet provided a structured framework that was directly linked to the key employability and academic skills. Personal skills audits could also be integrated into the document as an indicator of performance. Students could add to and edit the PDAP at any time and so, in effect, it was adapted by some as their own living, working and easy-to-use journal that could be completed progressively throughout the year. Examples of good practice could be shared. It allowed each student the flexibility to individually tailor development needs and focus on their identified key skills.

The PDAP became the framework for the main body of the Personal Progress

File which in turn made the teaching, learning and assessment process much simpler. Students who wanted to engage fully in the process were able to demonstrate this, given the flexibility provided by the document. But for the weaker students the book- let outlined a 'minimum standard' of effort required.

Clearly, with a well-structured booklet it became easier and less time-consuming to facilitate the personal development message. Marking, moderation and feedback also became simpler. Feedback was provided online, where generic feedback could be shared between groups and individuals.

3   Use of the VLE

The university's experience with a VLE goes back several years and the university now uses X-stream, a version of Blackboard Vista. X-stream means that all lectures, workshops and supporting materials, and feedback are available 24/7. X-stream has allowed for more flexible learning approaches to support a more student-cen- tred environment. This blended approach, in the sense of combining face-to-face instruction with computer-based learning (Graham, 2004), has been vital to module development.

4   Flexible choices in assessment format

In recent years we have moved into a period of mass higher education and the uni- versity is moving towards being a manager of knowledge, with a focus on industry links, working across the disciplines and encouraging entrepreneurship (Usher, 2002). Several initiatives were introduced to increase flexibility in choices of assessment format. For example, students were asked to present a research proposal as a one-to- one tutorial with the tutor. Students had the choice not just of the topic, but also the design and presentation format (for example, a poster or an A4 presentation pack).

Evaluation

This section presents the findings from the module evaluation carried out at the end of the academic year. The research involved the completion of module-evaluation forms and two student focus groups.

Students were asked to write about their opinions of the module in relation to the following:
- ❏ strengths, with reasons
- ❏ weaknesses, with reasons
- ❏ suggestions for improving the module.

A total of 34 students (population 140) from four different tutor groups responded, which represented a good source of reliable and useful information, summarised below:

Strengths with reasons

Students commented that the module was well structured and that it supported stu- dents' planning of personal skills development:

This module benefits 'me' as a student and has actually encouraged me to look at and work on improving my skills. This module is relevant in managing our work and study.

As previous research suggests students do not realise the value of employability skills development:

I did not realise the importance until late on in the module.

Personal skills audits and the PDAP

Students found the personal skills audit process and PDAP easy to use. One commented:

I found the skills audits and PDAP gave me an insight into my strengths and weaknesses and we got the opportunity to think about our next move like career development.

Teaching style

Tutors were asked to adopt a facilitator's role. The teaching was designed to be informal and informative. Students responded well to this:

I like the discussion technique used for teaching as it gets everyone involved and helps me understand difficult issues. Very interesting, very informative and very helpful.

Module content

Indicative content of the module received favourable comments:

The exercises; I scored 'strongly agree' and 'agree' for all statements because of the general quality of the module.

I really feel I benefited from my research proposal as it gave me an idea of a professional level of work.

I found the different managerial techniques very interesting which has helped my approach to career opportunities.

There was still an adverse opinion from HND students about the need for the inclusion of research skills designed to support students doing final-year dissertations:

The second part of the assessment seems to focus on development for Level 6.

What about those finishing at level 5 HND – maybe something to suit their needs.

Students seem to overlook the fact that research skills are life-long learning skills. Furthermore, they were encouraged to develop industry specific research proposals that could be practically applied.

Structure of module

The themed approach and progressive nature of the assignments received good comments:

Good continuous structured learning throughout the year with deadlines spread over the year.

Weaknesses with reasons

The action plan (PDAP)

Four students commented that they found the titles given to the key skills in the

PDAP document difficult to interpret:

> I found the action plan (PDAP) quite difficult in that I didn't really know what I was writing about clearly. I found some of the topics e.g. 'operational' quite difficult to comment on as I didn't really know what they meant.

There was also still some negativity towards the module's purpose from two students:

> I am slightly confused over the progress file, some of it seems pointless and repetitive.

Suggestions for next year

Module handbook

> Please explain the assessments in more depth. Maybe just have a progress file only. More managerial topics. More guest lectures (from three students). It's a good module but it seems overly complicated and the module handbook has too much information.

Employability

Four students suggested various improvements to the employability focus. These included: mock interviews, career debate workshops, workshops about students' thoughts and their ideas of future job and career opportunities.

Personal appraisals

The focus groups revealed the value of one-to-one sessions with a tutor, and participants requested more of them.

Progress files

The focus groups suggested the module should be designed around the ten key skills and we should look at and analyse one key skill each week – with homework.

They also indicated that the skills audit could be clearer and more concise; there should be more structure to the progress file and it should not be such a vague concept.

Extracts from student's progress files and reflective journals

Presented below are selected extracts from students studying PDP at Level 5. It can clearly be seen from these journals that these initiatives have helped increase motivation and engagement in the personal development process of these young people.

> This portfolio has been a great way for me to establish the weakest areas of my learning experience, enabling me to improve for the future. I feel more confident about my strengths and character. I feel that I am capable of a career in this industry and feel my approach has changed. I have become more positive and also believe that each day in industry is a learning experience and will help me grow as a person and become a better manager.

> Through the process of compiling this portfolio I have discovered that through reflection I can not only ascertain my strengths and weaknesses but also work toward improving them. Overall this module has been the most beneficial of all

those I have studied as through its efforts it has enabled me to develop many neglected and unused skills that I must certainly hold on to throughout my life beyond university.

I felt coming into Level 5 following my industrial placement year was really hard to adapt to. On returning to university I learnt a lot about myself and the way I study. Doing this action plan has made me realise my strengths and weaknesses and the areas I learn best. Studying at Level 5 has been enjoyable, but some areas I have found really difficult and had to extend the way I study from Level 4. The action plan enables me to be aware of my strengths and work on improving my weaknesses in my future studies and in the workplace.

Discussion

The most productive research method was, without doubt, that of module evaluation by students both pre- and post-module delivery. Students' experiences, views, opinions and suggestions proved a valuable source of evidence.

Four key changes had the most influence over the success of the revised module:

❑ three distinct themes
❑ the use of a personal development action plan
❑ the use of a virtual learning environment
❑ flexible choices in assessment format.

The introduction of a systematic themed approach was invaluable. This provided the module with an easy-to-follow, orderly sense of purpose for both students and tutors alike. The indicative teaching content could be seen to be clearly linked to the progressive nature of the assessments. The employability focus, in particular, gave valuable 'takeaways'.

The introduction of a PDAP booklet had the most significant impact of all the initiatives in improving engagement. The PDAP booklet provided a structured framework directly linked to the key skills. Students were able to write up their experiences in the booklet chronologically and in a systematic way. It also became easier and less time consuming for tutors to facilitate the PDP message.

The X-stream VLE meant that all supporting materials and feedback could be available 24/7. X-stream has allowed for more flexible learning approaches to support a more student-centred learning environment.

The findings of the post-module delivery survey gave some satisfying results that clearly demonstrated how dramatically engagement had improved. Students found the module well structured, beneficial and were encouraged to look at and work on developing their employability skills. The PDAP was a major vehicle in influencing a structured framework for this module. The informal teaching style and the open debates and discussions were well liked. The one-to-one appraisals made an important contribution to the quality and depth of the feedback received. Students stated that the most beneficial workshops were on research skills, management skills, employability and career planning.

A number of students did not enjoy the skills development process, finding it difficult, confusing and pointless. They saw the instructions and general concept of completing a progress file as vague. Several stated they did not realise the importance of the module until the end.

There were several useful suggestions for improving the module in the future. These included revising the PDAP to make it more user-friendly and to provide a list of 'must have' contents for the progress file. Students also suggested that the indicative teaching content should systematically map with the ten key skills outlined in the PDAP document.

The improvements made to the PPSM module handbook in 2006–07 largely created positive results for both students and teachers alike. Therefore, the key objectives, which were to improve student engagement and increase the emphasis on employability, were well met. Supporting the development of employability skills and work-related learning is critical to meeting the needs of industry and preparing graduates for their future careers. This case study has demonstrated that a stand-alone PDP module, if specifically designed, can support the aims of integrating employability skills into the curriculum.

References

Brockbank, A. & McGill, I. (1998) *Facilitating Reflective Learning in Higher Education/ SRHE.* Buckingham: Open University Press

Cranmer, S. (2006) Enhancing Graduate Employability: Best Intentions and Mixed Outcomes. *Studies in Higher Education* **31** (2) April pp 169–84

Graham, C. R. (2004) *Blended Learning Systems: Definition, Current Trends, and Future Directions.* www.uab.edu/it/instruction/technology/docs/blended_learning_systems.pdf Accessed on 01/04/06

Hind, D. (2006) *Integrating Employability and Management Skills into the tourism curriculum at Leeds Metropolitan University.* Leeds Metropolitan University

Tariq, V. (2004) Key Skills: Rhetoric, reality and reflection. *Exchange* **6** http://www.exchange.sc.uk/files/issue6.pdf Accessed 28/9/07

Usher, R. (2002) A Diversity of Doctorates: Fitness for the Knowledge Economy? *Higher Education Research and Development* **21** (2) pp 143–53

SIMON COX has worked at Leeds Metropolitan University as senior lecturer and level leader since 2003. From 1981 to 1987 he worked as an hotelier and between 1987 and 2003, for a number of leading contract-catering organisations, managing the hospitality operations of several blue-chip companies in both the private and public sector. His teaching responsibilities are mainly operations management disciplines including facilities management and food & beverage management at both undergraduate and postgraduate level. His research interests are in motivation, leadership, PDP and related employability and key skills development.

4

Enhancing enterprise, entrepreneurship and employability through PDP

Will Bowen-Jones and Karen Bill
University of Worcester

The chapter charts the progress of the University of Worcester's (UW) School of Sport and Exercise Science customised programme of Personal Development Planning (PDP) through its personal tutorial system.

PDP, in the shape of the Student Qualities Profile (SQP), was originally a university-wide initiative. However, both staff and student engagement was limited. The rationale behind the SQP was that it should support students in the development of their skills and, at the same time, act as the focus for their planning, reflection, development and recording of achievement throughout their undergraduate studies (Peters, 2001). In practice, however, the majority of students ignored what they deemed to be surplus to the mandatory requirements of their degree.

The School of Sport and Exercise Science therefore took the decision to integrate a customised version of the SQP within the personal tutorial system, creating timetabled opportunities for students to reflect, with their tutors, on their progress. It also embarked on a review of the skill set with which students were being encouraged to engage, and developed activities to support and enhance the PDP programme.

Context

The authors use the definition of PDP as indicated in the QAA guidelines:

> a structured and supported process undertaken by an individual to reflect upon their own learning, performance and / or achievement and to plan for their personal, educational and career development. (QAA, 2000: 8)

The chapter is predicated on the authors' long held belief that the relationship between PDP and student employability is a particularly strong one and that this relationship is fundamental to the development of students' ability to identify, articulate and evidence their learning and overall development. In this respect, we concur with the ESECT (Yorke & Knight, 2006: 10) definition of employability as being:

> A set of achievements, understandings and personal attributes that make individuals more likely to gain employment and be successful in their chosen occupations.

The Burgess Report (2005) reiterated that HEFCE should review current methodologies for recording student achievement and develop a more sophisticated way of measuring 'value added' – the distance travelled by the individual learner – as in the UK Government's White Paper *The Future of Higher Education*. According to Burgess:

> Many graduates cannot effectively articulate their experiences and achievements and their relevance to the post to which they are applying (curricular and extra curricular experiences) (2005: 39).

Burgess further acknowledged the importance of non-formal learning and recognised that a growing number of students and employers were beginning to accept the value of such activities. The Burgess Group's *Final Report* recommended that

> further work is done on measuring and recording the skills and achievements gained through non-formal learning and that student generated/driven information should be part of PDP (Burgess, 2007: 10).

Twenty-first-century skills for graduates

Hawkins and Winter (1995) suggest that self-reliance skills are the enabling skills which are fundamental for graduates' survival in the 21st century. They are seen as the process through which to manage a lifetime's progression in learning and work. Hawkins and Winter identify four types of skills; specialist, generalist, self-reliant and connected. It is fair to say that the sports industry 'lacks the coherence and identity of more established and mainstream industries.' (Strategic Leisure, 2004: viii) and that 'Careers are no longer like a Chinese banquet: 15 courses brought to your table one after the other. They're more like a progressive supper: bite-sized portions eaten in different places' (Association of Graduate Recruiters, 1995: 4, 16). Given that graduates are going to experience careers that are 'bite-sized' in proportion and an industry that is diverse, then justification for more entrepreneurial skills, such as networking, and more 'connected' skills is clear.

This is a call for graduates with better skills and abilities to deal with current challenges and uncertain futures. An innovative approach to problem solving, high readiness for change, self-confidence, and creativity are all attributes related to entrepreneurship. It has been maintained that 'the need for entrepreneurship education has never been greater, and the opportunities have never been so abundant.' (Henry et al, 2003: 90).

Gibb provides a pragmatic definition of entrepreneurship which is appropriate for PDP. He defines entrepreneurship as consisting of enterprising behaviours underpinned by enterprising skills and enterprising attributes. It is grounded in the proposition that these behaviours, skills and attributes are developed through a variety of enterprising experiences. These can be manifested through teaching and research, through activities outside the curriculum, and through personal skills development (1993: 14).

The challenge is clear. Higher education must aim to provide opportunities to produce graduates who are equipped to operate in a highly competitive, complex and dynamic workplace. Sleap (2005) indicates that university experiences have done little to develop entrepreneurial and business skills. The challenge in creating these opportunities is perhaps that of paying attention to the process of engagement, rather than outcome. Uddin (2008) reveals that employers feel a PDP portfolio would have little value in its own right and that they would be unlikely to use it during recruitment. However, some employers acknowledge that an eportfolio could be useful in determining the distinction between candidates of similar ability, while a significant number continue to place greater confidence in the curriculum vitae, letter of application and interviews.

Ward (2007) further advises that PDP should not only be seen as linked to extra-curricular activities, when the evidence points to the fact that PDP supports effective student learning. This support might occur either through a tutorial system based on academic development and feedback, or through credit bearing course elements.

This chapter discusses how a tutorial system was customised and implemented to provide a vehicle for personal reflection and development, while looking to increase the level of student and staff engagement with PDP. It also discusses the journey in terms of creating meaningful opportunities for students, in and out of the curriculum, to develop 21st-century employability and entrepreneurial skills.

Historical development of PDP within the school

In September 2001 the Undergraduate Modular Scheme at UW launched the Student Qualities Profile (SQP) (Peters, 2001). The rationale behind the SQP was to play an active role in the development of learning and, at the same time, be the focus for student planning, reflection, development and recording of achievement as students progressed through their undergraduate studies.

The *Student Qualities* were subject-specific and transferable skills, and personal attributes which are developed through undergraduate study. These qualities are identified by employers, universities and the government as being fundamental in the making of a graduate and what makes graduates valuable to society. If the SQP was to be successful it was important that students understood that many of the skills they would develop in their studies were transferable both within and beyond academic study. However the SQP sought to go further than this. It identified *Personal Attributes*, those personal developments which are part of educational growth as an undergraduate but which are not easily categorised as skills.

So the challenge facing academic and pastoral tutors was how to encourage the students to engage with the process of developing a *Qualities Profile*. Students, as is usual with them when embarking on a university education, tended to feel that preparing for employment was too far away to be of immediate concern and that other issues assumed a higher priority, such as learning to cope away from home for the first time, developing a new social life and coming to terms with the demands of academic work.

The SQP had the full support of the UW Students' Union. The union also sought to enhance the profile of the SQP by providing training in transferable skills, opportunities to volunteer in the union and local community, to participate in and organise sporting and non-sporting activities, in employment and in social events. The union also provided certification, called *Degree+*, for skills developed while working with the union, and which could be added to the SQP profile. The SQP would, if used to its full potential, enable students to leave Worcester not only more independent and confident, but also highly employable.

However after two years (2003), student feedback was that engagement with the SQP was very limited. The SQP had been delivered, through the Undergraduate Modular Scheme (UMS). The academic modules were assessed and contributed to the final classification of degrees, while the SQP in contrast was not assessed and so had no impact on a student's degree. It was evident that the primary reason for this lack of engagement was that there was no assessment and therefore the SQP was not perceived to be directly relevant. In addition the process of recording information was overly bureaucratic. Nevertheless, after further consultation with the careers service and the student union, the School of Sport and Exercise Science decided that the rationale behind the SQP was fundamentally sound and decided to:

❑ Customise the college SQP (See Table 1 for the Matrix of PDP skills)
❑ Incorporate the customised version of the SQP into the personal tutorial system and within relevant validation and module specifications
❑ Pilot the new system with the 2004–05 student cohorts.

The initial, customised version of the SQP identified six skill areas and did not include, for example, 'connected skills' akin to entrepreneurship. Consequently, the authors revisited the Hawkins and Winter model. While the QAA subject benchmark covers more generic and specialist skills, little recognition is given to self-reliant and connected skills. The adapted model (Figure 1) suggests how it is felt that the 21st-century sports graduate should be equipped.

Figure 1 The Complete Sports Graduate

The Complete Sports Graduate	
<u>Specialist</u>	An expert in something (e g sports physiotherapy)
<u>Generalist</u>	General skills (e g communication)
<u>Self-reliant</u>	Must be able to manage their career (e g action-planning, change, self-confidence)
<u>Connected</u>	Must be team players (e g negotiating, networking, entrepreneurship skills)

Bill & Bowen-Jones (2005), adapted from Hawkins and Winter (1995)

Table 1   Matrix of PDP Skills for Sports Graduates at UCW

Quality	D The competence to…	C The ability to…	B The capability to…	A The proficiency to…
Planning and time management	Meet imposed deadlines	Plan own time within established deadlines	Set and achieve targets over an extended period	Select, apply and defend the most appropriate time management study
Responsibility and independence	Meet imposed obligations	Be trusted and relied upon, though reliant on judgement of 'experts'	Make own judge-ments and take responsibility for self	Take responsibility for self and others
Interactive and group skills	Comprehend and respond to direct communication. Perform supervised work in a group	Assess and own and others' strengths and weaknesses. Work in a group and assimi-late own results into group project	Be able to negoti-ate and persuade. Structure teamwork, including nego-tiation of roles and responsibilities	Apply appropriate communication techniques. Co-ordi-nate group activity and carry forward an effective strategy
Problem-solving skills	Recognise and comprehend basic texts and data	Undertake a problem with initial direction	Apply an appropriate strategy to a specific problem	Evaluate and improve problem solving strat-egies independently
Reflection	Recognise external criteria	Identify own strengths and weaknesses	Self-evaluate to focus on development needs	Continually apply reflective practice for personal development
Communication and presentation skills	Comprehend and make statements of opinion. Present given information visually	Analyse and produce a structured state-ment. Apply a range of visual communica-tion techniques	Give a convincing oral presentation and field questions. Evaluate and present effective visual communication	Design and co-ordinate appropriate presentations. Design appropriate visual communication techniques
Entrepreneurship and networking skills *	Key entrepreneurial behaviours, skills and attitudes are developed.* Students understand the nature of the relationships they need to develop with key stakeholders and are familiarised with them.*	Focus on entrepre-neurial behaviour development in the context of self-employment. See all venture activities in terms of networks of *know who*	Seek opportunities Take the initiative Negotiate Take risks Make decisions Strategic orientation Autonomy Knows how to develop networks Knows how to strategically develop networks Knows how to build relationships	Demonstrates appro-priate entrepreneurial characteristics and understands their relevance to a wide range of self employ-ment, employment and social contexts Demonstrates a *'know who'* approach in relation to their particular field of study.

* from the National Council for Graduate Entrepreneurship *Learning Outcomes Framework for Higher Education*

The model drew on the National Council for Graduate Entrepreneurship learning-outcomes framework for enterprise (NCE 2003) and on Gibb's work on linking these outcomes to progression throughout the education system (2006). By embedding elements of entrepreneurship skills into the matrix of PDP skills, students were drawn to consider developing more connected skills such as networking. We recognise that not all of our students will aspire to be tomorrow's entrepreneurs, but it is undoubtedly desirable that they learn to be more creative in their chosen field of work.

One of our objectives was to create meaningful opportunities for students within and outside the curriculum. If students are to truly reflect on their experiences and gather evidence of their skill development through PDP, then these learning opportunities have to be recognised by them and embedded in all aspects of their lives, including the academic curriculum, student-union activities, work experience and careers advice and PDP. This view is supported by Tomkins (2004) who concluded that work experience (including community or live project work), practical modules and PDP were important vehicles in supporting the key skills development of students.

Curriculum development to incorporate employability

One of the outcomes of higher education is the preparation of graduates to participate fully in the world of work. As employment skills become interwoven into learning and teaching philosophies and university strategies, those creating higher education courses may need to redefine skills learning. Existing skills development should become more transparent to the students An infrastructure was developed at Worcester to give students this sort of opportunity. Business planning competitions (Bizcom) and awareness events (Enterprise Fest and commercialisation workshop developments) were incorporated across the University in partnership with internal groups such as alumni, the business partnerships office, students' services and careers.

Graduate interest in business start-up has to be cultivated and assisted to reach fruition. More opportunities and support are necessary to establish graduate small businesses. One such example at UW is a recent successful funding application to the Mercia Institute of Enterprise for £10,000 to develop technology-enhanced enterprise education (te3, 2007). The project is about 'SupPORTING ENTREPRENEURSHIP' by designing two new modules at undergraduate and postgraduate level within the Sports Studies curriculum. The focus is on developing interactive online learning materials on WebCT and holding a day long 'Sport Fest' event, similar to that of an 'Enterprise Fest.

Evaluation

Our experience is that staff engagement is fundamental for the successful implementation of the PDP programme. A significant objection raised by academics is the lack of relevance of PDP to learning in the subject curriculum as well as to life beyond higher education. However, such an undertaking is dependent on a university's vision and commitment. One of the five stated ambitions of the UW *Strategic Plan* (2007–12) is 'to produce highly employable, innovative, professional alumni'. Whichever direction we choose to take, we owe it to our students to respond to the skills agenda in order to unlock their full potential in future employment.

Our main aim was to increase the level of student and staff engagement with PDP. One way of gauging the level of student engagement has been through the monitoring of attendance at personal tutorials. In order to give the new approach the best possible chance of success, it was decided that only the incoming cohort of undergraduate degree students would be targeted. The level of attendance at personal tutorials was in excess of 80% (over 120 out of 148 students). It must be acknowledged here that a great deal of time and energy was expended by the co-ordinator, to ensure that students and staff received regular reminders and encouragement to book tutorials. Of course, attendance at tutorials is no guarantee of student or staff engagement with PDP. The personal tutorial system has existed for many years as a vehicle for pastoral care and it is perhaps inevitable that some students and, indeed, a number of staff, may well have adopted a 'normal service' approach and ignored the PDP element of the process.

From 2005–06 the school sought to keep staff records to assist in the writing of the Annual Monitoring Report. Data gathered include research and scholarly activity, publications, conference presentations, but also learning and teaching activity. It is in this section that we asked staff to record their attendance figures for personal tutorials.

The percentages for each year group show that the attendance for first years is relatively high at around 70%. This figure drops to around 40% in years two and three. Although no formal investigation has been undertaken to identify why 30% of students fail to follow up their first year tutorials, there is a substantial amount of anecdotal evidence which indicates that the optional, non-assessed nature of PDP suggests to some students that 'if it were that important it would be assessed'. Much more effort needs to be made to get the message across that going to university and coming out with a 2.1, while an achievement, is not enough to land a graduate level job. Skills and experience have to be developed. We need to continue to devote time and energy to get the message across. It is perhaps time to raise the stakes, either by making PDP related modules mandatory or by offering opportunities for students to achieve credit.

Figure 3 Tutorial attendance figures for 2005–06 and 2006–07

2005–06	Year 1	Year 2	
Totals	66.4%	39.9%	
2006–07	**Year 1**	**Year 2**	**Year 3**
Totals	71%	38.4%	41.3%

Tutors who have physical-education undergraduates among their tutees reported that there was a very high level of attendance and engagement among third year students wishing to apply for a *PGCE PE Secondary Course* place (the focus of the third-year tutorial is the drafting of a personal statement). The message here seems to be that students will engage in non-assessed and non-formalised learning provided that there is a powerful rationale for them to do so.

There is also some evidence from students to suggest that staff play a very important role in determining the level of student engagement with PDP. If a member of staff sent out a negative view of PDP at the first tutorial meeting, then not only would the student fail ever to see the value of PDP, but would also be unlikely to return to see their tutor. From a staff perspective it was apparent that some students, when reflecting on their academic and extra-curricular experiences, struggled to identify opportunities which offered them the chance to develop these skills. Students would often need examples to help them to complete the self-assessment section of the personal tutorial record sheets.

As previously stated the PDP system now includes seven customised skills:

1   Planning and time management
2   Responsibility and independence
3   Interactive and group skills
4   Problem-solving skills
5   Reflection
6   Communication and presentation skills
7   Entrepreneurship and networking skills.

Many students felt unable to record any evidence under the 'entrepreneurship' section of the record sheet. Those that did tended to record major events, such as the 'Bizcom challenge', which focused on the recognition and reward of specific business or entrepreneurial skills. While the number of students involved in these events is still relatively small, it is true to say that the benefits have been transformative and long-lasting. For example:

Figure 4   Jenny Burchill
An entrepreneurial University of Worcester Masters student won a £2,500 first prize in a prestigious West Midlands business competition for her innovative hi-tech sports analysis service. Jenny pitched her business proposal Statistical and Technical Analysis Reporting for Sport (STARS) to regional business leaders as part of Bizcom, an initiative designed to encourage entrepreneurship and business start-up within West Midlands universities.

Students have reported most difficulty in identifying evidence of the development of problem-solving, entrepreneurial and networking skills. Tutors have tried to prompt and encourage students to reflect on specific tasks undertaken both in and outside lectures. However, these remain as areas where students do not feel confident that they are making progress. There is also a significant number of students who find it difficult to recognise the development of generic skills in the curriculum. Some students tend to compartmentalise skills and focus on the specific learning outcomes of each module. When PDP is used with undergraduates on non-professional programmes specificity is difficult to establish, but those students who aspire to PGCE or other recognised career pathways quickly learn the value of developing skills which they know will be either desirable or essential.

It is probably true to say that few students who embark on an undergraduate sports degree do so in the hope or expectation that they will eventually run a business of their own. Many choose a sports degree because of their competitive success on the field of play. But should this rule out a career in the world of business? Do we, as academic staff, stifle entrepreneurship and creativity? Undoubtedly many of us lack business skills and there is little infrastructure to learn about enterprise skills. As academics we may tend to be preoccupied with subject knowledge.

Related developments
Degree+

In the original design of SQP, the Students Union provided certification, called *Degree+*, for skills developed while working with the union, which students could include in their SQP. It was felt that if this type of activity were embedded into the curriculum, it might provide a support mechanism for those students having difficulty identifying evidence of entrepreneurial skills. This development is currently under way and the aim is to work in partnership with relevant agencies across the university to develop a programme which students find accessible, while developing their employability skills and giving them work-based learning opportunities. These opportunities might be paid or voluntary work, or extra curricula activities which feed into PDP. The objectives are to:

❏ upgrade and re-launch *Degree+* through the student union
❏ embed *Degree+* within the BSc Sport Business Management degree
❏ develop support materials to enhance student development in this area, e.g. critical reflection, creativity and an on-line facility to record student experience
❏ develop a structured tutorial led approach which engages with *Degree+*.

Non-assessment (or self–assessment) of PDP
We acknowledge that the non-assessed nature of PDP needs to be addressed. It is worth noting that on many vocational programmes such as the *PGCE Secondary Course*, students are required to keep a portfolio. This is a reflective record of their development as a student teacher, in which they are required to write a series of reflective commentaries detailing their progress against the professional standards required to achieve Qualified Teacher Status (QTS). These are submitted and marked

(pass or fail) on three separate occasions. Since this is a fundamental requirement of the course, engagement with the process is altogether more immediate and the focus is maintained to the end of the course. Both staff and students recognise the value of the school's customised version of the SQP and, in particular, the process of engaging with PDP (through the personal tutorial system). Nevertheless we need to question whether this should be accredited more formally. Further development and a deeper level of engagement will only be possible if its value is formally acknowledged.

Discussion

In considering the success or otherwise of the school's PDP programme we ask ourselves the question, 'Is the glass half full or half empty'? The customised system of PDP is clearly well received by the first-year students with a 70% level of engagement. However, the percentage drop of 30% in years two and three suggests that a significant number of students are unconvinced as to the long-term value of PDP. Therefore are we to conclude that we have failed and need to come up with an alternative? That we should always consider continuous improvement goes without saying, but we cannot ignore the fact that 30% of the combined second and third year cohorts represents about 100 students. If we were to dismantle the system completely, on the grounds that a 30% 'take-up' indicates a poor return, then we would be denying a significant minority of the student body a learning opportunity which they value. The issues and action points given below are examples of those aspects which we feel have helped nurture the development and sustainability of PDP:

❑ Ensuring that all drivers at school level – learning and teaching strategy, careers, employer networks, students union, business and enterprise and curriculum development – are making valid, co-ordinated and transparent contributions to PDP opportunities

❑ Identifying and making more explicit, through module outlines and during lectures, the links between learning outcomes, learning tasks and the development of generic skills and attributes

❑ Establishing more opportunities for the students to gather evidence in support of the specific, general, self-reliant and connected skills (Hawkins & Winter 1995).

Conclusion

The challenge for us at Worcester is no different from that facing other higher education institutions. If we are to succeed in embedding PDP as a core learning process, it is vital that we promote opportunities for effective student learning both within and beyond the curriculum. Of equal importance is the need to convince academic colleagues of the key role that PDP plays in developing 21st century graduates. Furthermore, as Ward (2007: 1) acknowledges, in quoting Burgess, there is further work to be done when employers feel:

> many graduates cannot effectively articulate their experiences and achievements

and their relevance to the post for which they are applying.

References and URLs

Association of Graduate Recruiters (1995) *Skills for Graduates in the 21st Century*. Cambridge: The Association of Graduate Recruiters

Bill, K. and Bowen-Jones, W. (2005) 21st Century Skills for Sport and Recreation Graduates – Realising our Potential. *Link* **11**

Burgess, R. (2005) *Measuring and recording student achievement: Report of the Scoping Group*. At http://bookshop.universities.ac.uk/downloads/measuringachievement.pdf

Burgess, R. (2007) *Beyond the honours degree classification* The Final Report of the Burgess Group. London: Universities UK http://www.universitiesuk.ac.uk

Gibb A. A. (1993) in K. Herrmann, W. Parvin and J. O'Brian (2004) *National Council for Graduate Entrepreneurship Report*. Durham: Durham Business School

Gibb, A. A. (2006) Entrepreneurship/Enterprise Education in Schools and Colleges. Are we really building the onion or peeling it away? Paper to the ICSB World Conference. Melbourne Australia

Hawkins, P. and Winter, J. (1995) Mastering Change, Learning the Lessons of the Enterprise in Higher 74 *IETI* **37** (1)

Henry, C., Hill, F. & Leitch, C. (2003) *Entrepreneurship Education and Training*. London: Ashgate

National Commission on Entrepreneurship (NCGE) (2003) *Creating good jobs in your community*. Washington DC: NCGE. Available from http://www.ncge.com/

Peters, J. (2001) *The Student Qualities Profile*. University College Worcester

QAA (2000) Policy statement on a progress file for Higher Education. http://www.qaa.ac.uk/public/COP/COPex/contents.htm Accessed 03/11/03

Sleap, M. (2005) University Experiences and The Employment Environment. Unpublished Research Report, Higher Education Academy Network for Hospitality, Leisure, Sport and Tourism available from: http://www.hlst.heacademy.ac.uk/projects/sleap_summary.pdf

Strategic Leisure (2004) North West Development Agency Sport Business Cluster – Strategy and Action Plan

te3 (2007) http://www.te3.bham.ac.uk/MainPages/Projects_Overview.htm?code=TE3019

Tomkins, A. (2004) Best of both worlds: An exploration of key skills required for graduate work in the leisure and sport industry and links to Personal Development Planning. *Link*. **11**. Available from: http://www.hlst.heacademy.ac.uk/resources/link11/contents.html

Uddin, A. (2008) PDP and e-portfolio. *UK Newsletter* **13** February

Ward, R. (2007) PDP and e-portfolio. *UK Newsletter* **12** December

Yorke, M and Knight, P (2006) Embedding Employability into the Curriculum. *Learning and Employability Series One*. York: Higher Education Academy

WILL BOWEN-JONES is principal lecturer in the School of Sport and Exercise Science at the University of Worcester. He has responsibility for quality assurance and learning and teaching within the school. His most recent research activity is connected with inclusive practice in learning and teaching in academic departments.

KAREN BILL is associate dean in the School of Sport, Performing Arts and Leisure at the University of Wolverhampton. She has responsibility for overseeing engagement with research and applied research. Karen has recently been admitted as an entrepreneurship education fellow by the National Council for Graduate Entrepreneurship. At the time of writing this chapter, she was principal lecturer, enterprise and external relations in the School of Sport and Exercise Science at the University of Worcester.

5

Learning about me as well as the subject:
meta-learning through the use of learning inventories

John Buswell and Angela Tomkins
University of Gloucestershire

How can students be encouraged and supported to achieve deep
reflective learning and to take more responsibility for their learning through
developing greater self-awareness? Learning inventories can enable
students to acquire a language to understand the process of learning.

This chapter focuses on the use of learning inventories to assist students in developing a capacity for meta-learning (the ability to understand and manage one's own
learning). Several studies have considered the impact of self-report/assessment learning inventories on students' capacity to understand and regulate their own learning:
(Meyer & Shanahan, 2004; Muis, Winne & Jamieson-Noel, 2007; Norton, Owens
& Clark, 2004). The relationship between learning inventories and critically reflective learning is considered in this chapter.

As we will examine, a key pre-requisite of student-centred learning is self-awareness and empowerment, and this can be greatly enhanced by feedback, not simply on
performance but also on the approach to learning, and particularly what Meyer and
Shanahan refer to as 'learning engagement in context' (2004: 444). This accords with
Baxter Magolda's (1996) views on progression in how students perceive knowledge:
how we need to move students from domain one, in which knowledge is absolute,
to the fourth and final stage in which it becomes contextual (where it is constructed
by the students and related to the context in which it is studied). It is apparent from
these studies that self-regulated learners are more motivated and strategic in their
approach to their learning and perform better in their assessments. This requires
more than the standard approach to developing students' study and learning skills,
which virtually all HEIs have built into the first year of the programme. It also goes
beyond reading and responding to feedback on assessed work, important as this is.
It suggests that:

❑ students need to know and understand how they learn
❑ through this, they are more likely to take control and begin to manage and
regulate their learning.

Students are required to provide information about themselves, filling in question-naires in the learning inventories, so that they have something tangible to reflect on about their performance as a learner. The profile highlighted at the end of this process is shaped by how the student has answered the questions. It is therefore entirely their input and, of course, highly personal to each individual. We find that some students challenge their profiles and contest the validity of the exercise, but do eventually acknowledge that it reflected how they saw the questions and therefore themselves.

The key message of the case study is the belief that we need to move beyond traditional subject or content-based approaches to learning in higher education and towards context-based and student-centred approaches, involving meta-learning. The philosophy of meta-learning (Biggs, 1985; Jackson, 2004) is founded on the principles of independent and collaborative learning in which students gradually, through their programme, take responsibility for, and control of, their own learning. It encourages students to be more critical and constructivist in the way they develop their own meaning of the knowledge they are acquiring. Skills of critical thinking and independent judgement have become increasingly important in the modern world with its changing demands (Barnett, 2000; Jackson and Ward, 2004). Yet it is a world in which the individual is caught between the need for shared knowledge, interdependence and networking, and the need for individual judgement and greater flexibility and responsibility for personal and professional development. This is a fine balance to achieve, and means we should consider how we progress in encouraging independent learning skills and what Kollar and Fischer (2006) describe as 'other-regulation', where we mediate to support students in their progression towards self-empowerment and self-regulation.

We must acknowledge that not all students find it easy to develop and engage in metacognition and self-regulated learning. Indeed, Norton et al (2004) report that it is not automatic for students' reflective skills to develop through their degree and that interventions are necessary to encourage their development. Meyer and Shanahan (2004: 444) suggest that:

> meta-learning capacity requires a skill in learning that is quite different from, and superordinate to, the acquisition of other complementary learning skills (such as how to take notes, use the library and so on).

In other words, there is a clear difference between skills **for** learning and skills **in** learning. This difference lies in development of the student's self-identity and the belief that they can control and change their learning through their programme. The chapter highlights how learning inventories, and students' actions in response, can help to give them the self-awareness and strategic awareness to change their approach to learning. This was recognised by the Burgess Committee which suggested that:

> it is the graduates of our universities and colleges who will need to have the clearest idea of their skills, capabilities and achievements, both in order to 'sell

themselves' to employers and academic selectors, and to manage their own careers in increasingly less supported working environments. (Burgess, 2005: 3)

So, students need to understand their own learning in order to learn better and to enhance their personal and academic development. More attention is now being paid to students' learning experiences and opportunities (Jaros and Deakin-Crick, 2007) and their knowing how they learn and what they are capable of, as suggested by the Higher Education Academy: 'Raising self-awareness is a prerequisite to building up lifelong capabilities' (2006: 145).

Indeed, where there are opportunities for developing learning skills, the quality of students' learning improves and they experience more success. The use of learning inventories is one way of achieving this and has become more significant in the personal and academic development of students in higher education (Norton, Owens and Clark, 2004).

Context

This chapter is set in the Department of Leisure, Tourism and Hospitality Management at the University of Gloucestershire, where approximately 100 students each year undertake a 12-month paid industrial placement as part of their course. Learning and teaching practices were well established for preparing, supervising and debriefing students undertaking the industrial placement, but it was felt that even more could be done to use the learning from such rich experiences to develop critical thinking skills (especially metacognition) and lifelong learning capabilities (meta-learning).

The chapter draws on the work of the FDTL Project 'Meta: from PDP to CDP' which ran from 2005 to 2007. Its aim was to develop the criticality of students' experiential learning, particularly around industrial placements but also during other active learning such as volunteering and part-time work. The project embraced wider PDP processes and looked at how to create a progressive and structured approach to developing reflective learning and action planning skills in students. The key to this approach was the provision of a carefully structured and supported learning environment in which the development of an autonomous, empowered and self-regulated learner is an incremental and progressive process, underpinned by appropriate tools, techniques and methods. These provide students with the wherewithal to understand and manage their learning and to make sense of their experiences.

Description

Learning inventories became significant in the latter stages of the 'Meta' project as their potential to raise students' self-awareness and capacity for meta-learning emerged. The programmes outlined in the case study contain an industrial placement as the central and pivotal element of experiential learning, but the progressive and incremental approach of the placement means we need to prepare for this experience, and to fully utilise the richness of this learning environment. Learning inventories provide an important means of achieving this. The three inventories piloted were:

1   ELLI (Effective Lifelong Learning Inventory). Level 4 and beyond
2   ECI-U (Emotional Competence Inventory-University Edition). Post-placement/ Level 6, semester 1
3   TIFF (Temple Index of Functional Fluency). Level 6, semester 2. Linked to a module in mentoring practice.

Progression in the use of the learning inventories

The progression in the use of these inventories is part of the approach to developing more autonomous and empowered learners. They all appear to make a contribution to the way in which students regulate their learning and behaviour, particularly ELLI, because the 'strategic awareness' and 'changing and learning' dimensions suggest to students that they are capable of change and can adopt strategies and actions to help them achieve this.

ELLI

ELLI developed out of a research project at the University of Bristol, funded by the Lifelong Learning Foundation. The aim of this research was to identify the characteristics and qualities of effective lifelong learners and to develop resources and strategies for tracking, evaluating and recording people's growth as effective real-life learners. There were two major research strands: a scientific strand concerned with identifying the components of 'learning power' and a dynamic strand concerned with exploring how those (provisional) dimensions of 'learning power' might be useful in teaching and learning.

A national project to adapt ELLI for higher education, led by the University of Northumbria with 13 other universities, including Gloucestershire, which reported on its findings in November 2008. In 2007, Gloucestershire was the first university to pilot ELLI with a group of first-year students. A dozen personal tutors completed the questionnaire themselves and have undertaken one or two days' training in how to use and interpret ELLI.

The early study skills and pre-placement modules provided a good opportunity to introduce students to some gentle reflective learning and the concepts and dimensions of learning. This activity focuses on the concept of learning and offers students the opportunity to reflect on their approach to their studies and other areas, and to identify strategies for development in particular dimensions of learning. It is especially relevant at this stage because many students appear to find the transition from school or college into higher education challenging and mystifying. The research by the ELLI team at the University of Bristol revealed how many pupils in UK schools become less resilient as they go through the school system, and need support and guidance early on at university to encourage them to become confident, self-empowered and autonomous learners (Deakin-Crick et al, 2004). Thus students require support from their tutors and mentors in interpreting their personal ELLI profile, and this is an important step in the process of students understanding and regulating their own learning.

The ELLI questionnaire

The ELLI project trialled a mediated online learner-profiling questionnaire (ELOISE) designed to find out how learners perceive themselves in relation to seven dimensions of learning power:

- ❑ Critical curiosity
- ❑ Making meaning
- ❑ Creativity
- ❑ Changing
- ❑ Resilience
- ❑ Learning relationships
- ❑ Strategic awareness.

The ELLI questionnaire is a learning experience in itself. By visually representing a learner's profile on a histogram it demonstrates areas of strength and areas for development in learning. It challenges learners to think about various aspects of learning including some that they may not have been aware of. It also motivates them to become better learners and provides a language and set of concepts with which to reflect critically on learning experiences. ELLI may be offered for annual re-take, but there is also a progression into the ECI-U.

The ECI-U

The ECI-U was seen as an appropriate instrument to apply to learning from the placement at Level 6 semester 1 as it is more focused on self-awareness, self-management and managing relationships. This is a paper-based questionnaire and profile which facilitates feedback from someone who knows the student well (a friend perhaps). The workbook the student receives supports the process of action planning and, in the context of our model of progression, helps the student to achieve a clearer self-identity.

The students were introduced to the concept of emotional intelligence and received the following documentation:

1   The ECI-U Self-assessment questionnaire
2   The ECI-U Workbook
3   The ECI-U Feedback questionnaire.

Before students completed the questionnaire, they were asked to read sections one and two in the workbook to provide background to the questionnaire and how it might help their learning and awareness of their learning development. They then completed the self-assessment questionnaire which contains 63 statements about specific attributes or dimensions of emotional competence in four clusters of dimensions. Students had to indicate how much they thought each statement described their behaviour. There was also an opportunity to give a feedback questionnaire to someone who knew them really well to obtain an external view on the statements.

When they had plotted their profile, students were asked to turn to section four of the workbook and complete each of the 'discovery' sections. This was for the benefit of their reflective learning, but they were also asked to give us some valuable feedback on the questionnaire and its perceived relevance and usefulness.

The Temple Index of Functional Fluency (TIFF)

At Level 6 semester 2 a further instrument (TIFF) was used to enable final-year students to consider their skills, competencies and interpersonal effectiveness in the context of supporting other students in a mentoring practice module. TIFF, based on transactional analysis, focuses on learning relationships and builds on the self-identity encouraged by ELLI and, particularly, the ECI-U. At Level 6, emphasis is placed on self-regulated learning so that students feel empowered and motivated to reflect on their performance as mentors working with Level 4 students. The mentoring module therefore provided opportunities for students to develop their awareness as reflective practitioners through their active engagement in mentoring. The TIFF instrument was chosen because it provides a useful catalyst for insights into human functioning and is based on a sound, fully validated psychometric tool for personal development. For further information about TIFF see www.functionalfluency.com.

Each 'taught' session on the module was supported by a 'scaffold' of weekly activities designed to encourage students to:

❑ Build and critically evaluate knowledge and meanings about mentoring activities.
❑ Build self-awareness.
❑ Introduce a 'meaningful language' that could be used to express relationship behaviours.
❑ Identify areas that they would like to develop personalised learning.
❑ Enrich and expand on positive relationship behaviours.
❑ Transform some negative relationship behaviours.
❑ Set personal goals.

Part of the process undertaken by the students was attendance at a two-hour introductory session which explained the 'functional fluency model' underpinning the TIFF online questionnaire, a self-reporting tool that measures 'functional fluency'. On completion of the questionnaire, which provides a unique profile for each student, an individual feedback session was facilitated by a TIFF licensed 'provider'.

The results provide a profile of a person's behavioural tendencies and habits, both negative and positive, in a variety of situations and relationships. Expert feedback offers explanations of the model along with support and guidance for making use of the results. The insights gained from these discussions help to stimulate self-awareness and understanding, and encourage positive changes for increasing inter-personal effectiveness.

The feedback sessions were specifically designed to help students develop insights and increased awareness concerning their interpersonal effectiveness in their mentoring practice. As a result of these insights, students identified 'critical curiosities' so that they could undertake their mentoring sessions with greater awareness. Additionally they were able to observe and consider improving their behaviours in relationships with others which provided a useful vehicle for critical reflection, a potent tool to encourage behavioural change.

Evaluation

At the time of writing (2008), our first cohort has yet to complete the whole progression model and so we are not able to report in full its coherence and impact. We can however report on the impact of the inventories at each stage, and what we think each has contributed to in developing the capacity for self-regulation of learning and in enhancing employability skills. Student feedback has been, generally, very positive with regards to the impact on their learning and employability skills. They have found some aspects a little uncomfortable, because of what they are learning about themselves, but acknowledge the value and the benefits of the processes. In particular, they recognised the guidance and the understanding provided through engagement in learning inventories and related self-assessment.

ELLI

Reponses were mixed on the impact of ELLI, although there was a correlation between the negativity of comments and the achievement and overall approach of the student. Some students did not see the relevance or purpose of ELLI, but others offered some very insightful observations on the instrument and the process of action planning related to it, and they tended to be the better achieving students (the challenge is clearly how we can encourage the weaker students to adopt more positive attitudes to learning, although some students may not realise the value of this until much later):

> The initial endeavour with the ELLI experience was very confusing as to how it could actually be beneficial but it's much easier to follow and understand as the course has gone on.

An important observation of a number of students emphasised the importance of help by a mentor and a tutor:

> It must be said that the process can become somewhat unclear and confusing on how improvements can be made if there is no one to refer to on this matter. For example on my first ELLI profile, it was clear that I needed to improve on my 'meaning making', and after referring to a tutor I was able to clarify what this meant.

The ELLI questionnaire is easy in itself but for maximum benefit the tutors must go through the diagram with the student after the first time otherwise the whole exercise can be misunderstood and forgotten about.

Others were very clear about the benefits of completing the questionnaire and reflecting on the process and the profile generated:

My first ELLI was a learning experience in itself as I started to think more and reflect on my experiences as they happened.

Completing an ELLI profile helped me to step back and think about how I actually learn and how best to go about it.

ECI-U

The responses from students were overwhelmingly positive about this inventory and how it helped them to perceive their identities, their strengths and weaknesses and their plans for self-development. The dimensions of the inventory appeared to resonate with students and the requirement to reflect on their placement experience. It was clearly a process which they had not gone through before and the concept of emotional intelligence, as we knew, had not been previously encountered. However, students were very clear about the purpose of the inventory and its usefulness to them in developing their self-awareness and helping them to plan for the future:

I have found it to be very useful in highlighting both personal strengths and weaknesses. At university we often identify key skills for successful management; however it is rare for us to get the opportunities to participate in something like this, which will contribute to developing our skills ready for employment in the industry. I believe it will make us more aware of the need to continually develop ourselves, and to learn from situations rather than simply moving on from them, or by brushing them aside.

This emotional-competence work is something that I've never come across before so it was good to have the chance for it to be explained to me and hopefully it will be something I can use throughout my final year at university and then in my professional career.

Student response to the profile was very revealing and suggested that the inventory had caused many of them to think critically about themselves, their aspirations and self-development. A key element of the ECU-I is self-awareness, and this aligns very neatly with the focus of the model of progression adopted in encouraging greater understanding and control (action) of one's own learning:

Although I was aware of this issue, my EI profile has reiterated it for me and prompted me to do something more about it.

My feedback profile has challenged my perceptions of myself, and has allowed me to view myself as others do, not only from my individual perspective. It has enabled me to identify areas for learning, in leadership, exerting influence on others, and emotional self-awareness. This has pinpointed competencies that I wish to develop in future, to enable me to become the type of person I would like to be.

The questionnaire highlighted what I suspected anyway but now it has been shown on paper I can fully identify weaknesses and start to build on them. I also understand now why I do or don't currently achieve things in my life and that it is down to characteristics in me.

My high score in relationship management would explain my success on placement, always ensuring the staff were happy and content, finding this to be the key to a well-run business.

The EI Profile has given me an interesting insight. My good self-awareness score links with my consistent scoring in relationship management, which is why I am always happy to help others, and am particularly effective at doing so.

TIFF evaluation

All 20 mentoring students found learning about functional fluency either 'interesting' or 'insightful' or both. In module evaluations, half the group added comments expanding on their views. These comments seem to express participants' pleasurable engagement – 'really enjoyable,' and fascination with how the tool had worked to produce the relevant results.

An underlying theme in the feedback showed that the students had learned more about themselves, 'It was very useful and answered questions about myself'. Along with this were signs that some of them were taking responsibility for their experience and what they planned to do with it. Several people showed 'ownership' of their learning, 'it gave me an opportunity to find out about myself'. Usefulness was mentioned several times. The one-to-one discussions and reflection time during feedback sessions were specifically mentioned in at least four feedback comments.

More than half the students could clearly see positive changes that they would like to make in their relationship behaviours. One person went further and made explicit their awareness that it was the understanding gained that made a good foundation for change. Half of the group mentioned the actual modes of behaviour named in the functional fluency model that they planned to do 'more of' or 'less of'. There was also some evidence of putting insights about self into an action plan:

'learning to do more things for myself as well as helping others'

'be less dominant – not trying to complete a task for them because I am being too helpful'

'to be more decisive and trust my instincts'

'to try not to do the work for people'.

Another expressed an intention of achieving greater empathy through using more mature behaviour in mentoring sessions. The theme about development of self-awareness and understanding ('learning about myself') was developed in several comments as was the intention to reflect on how to use learning.

TIFF story extracts

Student A's story

The TIFF feedback inspired me to want to find a 'critical curiosity' about my relationships with others, to work on 'being myself' and to becoming more grounded. I wanted to practise this through my mentoring relationship and to take this learning into my future life. To get the most from this experience I was going to need more knowledge and practice on the skills of critical reflection and mentoring. It gave me a great boost of confidence to believe that as a mentor on this module, I could also be a learner and the learning could be lifelong and have permanence and relevance both personally and professionally. This applies not only to this module but I believe, on looking back, it has implications to learning from my entire four years at university and time before that too! These reflections gave a basis to further explore how I operated in relation to others and made me realise that no one is perfect.

Student B's story

My encounter with TIFF has taught me that I spend the majority of my time caring for the needs of others. From my TIFF feedback I developed my 'critical curiosity'; I decided to explore ways to improve my confidence in order to build my assertiveness and to allow others to take care of their own needs. TIFF identified areas of negative behaviour which I intend to work on including my tendency to over-analyse. I also want to be less submissive. TIFF has therefore expanded my horizons and helped me to learn through critical reflection. I had previously thought that to critically reflect meant to focus on the negative points about my activities. As I have now developed the skill (of critical reflection) I am able to find positive and negative points as well as new ways of doing things and thus am developing and improving my employability skills.

Student C's story

The TIFF process encourages metacognition. Moon (2006: 31) defines this as the 'ability to monitor one's current state of learning'. I feel the TIFF process has improved my metacognition and enhanced my ability to learn effectively through making me aware of my own thoughts and feelings. Reflecting on my TIFF profile I was able to make a conscious effort to address a 'critical curiosity' about myself. I wanted to focus on developing my empathetic skills through mentoring to contribute to my success in working alongside others as I believe this will be beneficial to me in my career. One way the mentoring relationship allowed me to develop my understanding of others was through enhancing my observational skills. Using a journal enabled me to reflect on mentoring sessions and to realise how the situation led me to improving myself.

Conclusions

The findings here demonstrate that to give students responsibility for managing their own learning and personal development requires a carefully planned and supported programme in which they gradually acquire the techniques and skills of reflective learning. This involves an incremental and progressive approach in which the direct support of the tutor (including the personal tutor) is reduced as the students' understanding and control of their learning develops. This student development is enhanced through the support given to students in interpreting the profiles arising from self-assessment questionnaires in learning inventories.

A key message is the need to build students' ability to be reflective and reflexive incrementally through the use of the tools and techniques (such as learning inventories). Our interventions demonstrated that most students reflect descriptively unless they are supported and encouraged to make sense of their experiences and relate these to their own learning and self-development. It is easy to assume that if students are asked to reflect on an experience, then they will be critical and will learn from it. However, it is evident that students need an understanding of learning and the concepts of learning, as well as the language with which to understand and describe their learning and some development of their skills of reflective writing if they are to engage effectively in reflective practice and in meta-learning.

At present, the validity and contribution of learning inventories to PDP and student-centred learning is contested. They are seen as 'gimmicky' and 'cosmetic' by some and, of course, some are positioned at the commercial end of learning provision. However, our experience would suggest that learning inventories enable students to assess their strengths and weaknesses in relation to their learning capabilities and emotional competence, and can help them understand the concepts and processes of learning and to acquire a language to articulate the learning that has taken place.

The three inventories used by the Meta project present a sliding scale of cost and become more expensive through the levels and as they become more specific. TIFF is a very thorough and rigorous instrument which is demanding and relatively expensive, because of the one-to-one tutorials it requires. Students clearly benefit from this and from the time and expertise of a trained tutor. However, our experience would suggest that each inventory has its merits and its place in the progression of learning throughout a programme of study.

References

Barnett, R. (2000) Supercomplexity and the Curriculum. *Studies in Higher Education* **25** (3) pp 255–67

Baxter Magolda, M. (1996) Epistemological developments in graduate and professional education. *Review of Higher Education* **19** (3) pp 283–304

Biggs, J. (1985) The role of meta-learning in study processes. *British Journal of Educational Psychology* **55** pp 185–212

Burgess, R. (2005) *Measuring and recording student achievement: Report of the Scoping Group.* At http://bookshop.universities.ac.uk/downloads/measuringachievement.pdf

Deakin-Crick, R., Broadfoot, P. and Claxton, G. (2004) Developing an effective lifelong learning inventory: the ELLI project. *Assessment in Education* **11** (3) pp 247–72

Jackson, N. (2004) Developing the concept of metalearning. *Innovations in Teaching and Learning International* **41** (4) pp 391–403

Jackson, N. & Ward, R. (2004) A fresh perspective on progress files – a way of representing complex learning and achievement in higher education. *Assessment and Evaluation in Higher Education* **29** (4)

Jackson, N. (2007) The context for immersive experiences. Presentation to the *CRA Annual Conference*, Manchester, November

Jaros, M. & Deakin-Crick, R. (2007) Personalized learning for the post-mechanical age. *Journal of Curriculum Studies* **39** (4) pp 423–40

HE Academy and Council for Industry and Higher Education (2006) *Guide on Student Employability Profiles.* York: HE Academy

Kollar, I. & Fischer, F. (2006) Supporting Self-Regulated Learners For A While and What Computers Can Contribute. *Journal of Educational Computing* **35** (4) pp 425–35

Meyer, J. & Shanahan, M. (2004) Developing meta-learning capacity in students: actionable theory and practical lessons learned in first-year economics. *Innovation in Education and Teaching International* **41** (4) November pp 443–55

Muis, K., Winne, P. & Jamieson-Noel, D. (2007) Using multi-trait multi-method analysis to examine conceptual similarities of three self-regulated learning inventories. *British Journal of Educational Psychology* **77** pp 177–95

Norton, L. Owens, T. & Clark, L. (2004) Analysing meta-learning in first-year undergraduates through their reflective discussions and writing. *Innovations in Education and Teaching International* **41** (4) November pp 423–41

JOHN BUSWELL is principal lecturer in the Department of Leisure, Tourism and Hospitality Management at the University of Gloucestershire and was, between 2004 and 2007, director of the phase 5 FDTL Project 'Meta: From PDP to CPD'. He is also Liaison Officer for Leisure for the HE Academy Subject Centre for Hospitality, Leisure, Sport and Tourism, based at Oxford Brookes University. He is a member of the Open University Validation and Awards Committees. His research interests and publications are in pedagogy and in the area of service quality in leisure, tourism and sport.

ANGELA TOMKINS is a senior lecturer at the University of Gloucestershire. She supports students in career planning through designing personalised and innovative techniques which stimulate and engage them in meaningful activities, building knowledge and enhancing self-confidence. She has developed and made extensive use of tools and techniques to support the development of skills in critical reflection, primarily through the use of narrative techniques combined with cross level peer-supported mentoring.

6

How SAPHE are your students?
Student awareness of personal finance in higher education

Pru Marriott *Winchester Business School*

One of the main transitional problems facing undergraduate students is the challenge of financing their period in higher education. This chapter looks at a web-based diagnostic study of the financial awareness and budgeting capabilities of first-experience business studies undergraduates

Student debt is now an expected outcome of attending university. Apart from the negative consequences debt may have on participation in HE, it can have a detrimental impact on the academic performance and psychological well-being of students as they strive to fund their education and reduce their debt through part-time working patterns. Poor financial-literacy awareness, understanding, capability or whatever term is used to describe young people's knowledge of financial matters is a global problem. In the UK the various initiatives that have been introduced in schools to increase the financial awareness of young adults must therefore be applauded. We need to explore how effective these financial literacy initiatives are in raising levels of financial awareness.

This study reveals serious gaps in students' personal financial knowledge across themes linked to student fees and loans, employment, banking and general expenditure. It is evident that the lessons students receive in school are not targeting the issues that are relevant for a period in higher education. Many students enter university with existing debts and yet lack the budgeting skills necessary to deal with the severe cash restrictions they will encounter there.

The use of a web-based diagnostic and support tool, now available to students at HE institutions across the UK, will help students raise their personal financial awareness, aid their understanding of personal finance matters and improve their ability to cope with their finances while at university.

Objectives
BMAF sponsored the development of an on-line instrument targeted at Students' Awareness of Personal Finances in Higher Education (SAPHE). The aim of this

project was to undertake a survey of undergraduates that would:

❑ Identify gaps in students' financial awareness as a result of ineffective preparation for HE.

❑ Help students raise their personal financial awareness, aid their understanding of personal finance matters and improve their ability to cope with their finances while at university.

❑ Improve the money management skills of university students which could result in less reliance on debt finance and part-time work to fund their studies.

❑ Give students transferable skills with long-term added value.

❑ Use an innovative combination of blended learning consisting of web-based diagnostics and on-line support material.

Rationale

Academic institutions have a responsibility to provide the help and advice that students need to cope with the financial implications of attending university. Raising students' awareness of personal finances and providing support and guidance could enhance retention and progression within the context of a university's widening participation agenda. Students' money management skills could be improved which might result in less reliance on debt finance and part-time work to fund their studies. This could help to improve the educational experience of first-experience students and have a beneficial effect on their academic performance, self-esteem and achievement and could also help improve retention.

The skills gained from the overall exercise are transferable skills, with long-term added value for the students. The diagnostic and support package could form part of student PDP portfolios and have a positive impact on employability.

There are also policy implications for government especially if it is serious about improving the level of basic skills across the UK (Leitch, 2006) and its commitment to a widening access agenda (HEFCE, 2003; HEFCW, 2005). The government has long-term aspirations for improving the level of financial literacy across the UK and in its recent publication *Financial Capability: the government's long-term approach* recognises that children and young people should

> have access to a planned and coherent programme of personal finance education so that they leave school with the skills and confidence to manage their money well.
> (HM Treasury, 2007)

Banks, charitable organisations, professional bodies and the government have undertaken numerous initiatives to increase the level of financial literacy of students across the UK. But how effective are they at increasing undergraduate awareness of their personal financial issues and preparing them for life at university?

Through the use of a web-based diagnostic tool, accessible by students at the University of Glamorgan, areas of weakness in students' personal financial awareness have been highlighted which call into question the effectiveness of the various initiatives in schools to improve financial awareness.

Context

There have been a number of significant changes to the financial support for higher education students in the UK in recent years following the replacement of maintenance grants with student loans and the introduction of repayable tuition fees (HM Government, 2004). Furthermore, the government expects universities to widen access to their courses to increase participation rates and this is attracting students from less 'well-off' backgrounds (HEFCE, 2003; HEFCW, 2005).

While students have always found balancing their finances difficult, the current generation is faced with unprecedented debt burdens during and on completion of their studies. Low levels of financial understanding in the UK (Egg, 2005) have been reported and a worrying knowledge gap concerning personal finance amongst young adults has been reported (RBS, 2004; Thomas, 2004). Part of the problem is the low profile of personal finance education (PFE) in the school curriculum, even though it is seen as an area of high importance (FSA, 2006). PFE is currently taught in UK schools as part of the personal, social and health education lessons but the 'relatively narrow range of topics covered and the infrequency and inconsistency with which they are delivered, are areas for concern' (FSA, 2006: 7). Marriott identified serious gaps in first-year undergraduate students' personal-financial knowledge in areas linked to the student fees and loans system, employment, banking and general expenditure, and concludes that

> students are entering a critical stage of their lives ill-equipped to cope with the severe cash restrictions they will encounter. (Marriott, 2007: 25)

Research undertaken by Pure Potential (2007), an independent campaign group which aims to increase access to university, reports that school leavers are just as anxious and uninformed about the higher education choices available to them as pupils were 12 months ago: 75% of school leavers do not understand university tuition fees, and 93% know little or nothing about the financial support available at university. The survey of 3,000 lower-sixth pupils across the UK reveals that school pupils are still being 'put off going to university'.

For those students who choose to attend university, student debt is now expected and, apart from the negative consequences it may have on participation in HE (Connor & Dawson, 2001; Archer et al, 2003; Callender, 2003; Callender and Jackson, 2004), it can have a detrimental impact on academic performance (Hobbs and McKechnie, 1997; Metcalf, 2001; Payne, 2002; McKechnie et al, 2002; Purcell et al, 2005) and the psychological wellbeing of students (Scott et al, 2001; Stradling, 2001; Cooke et al, 2004) as they strive to fund their education and reduce their debt through part-time work.

The available research suggests that first-year students are likely to lack financial awareness. However, much of the work undertaken in the UK in the area of financial literacy and awareness has been either through government initiatives in schools or through studies sponsored by the financial services industry. This project is targeted at higher education students and investigates the personal-financial awareness and attitude to debt of first-experience undergraduate students.

Description

A questionnaire instrument was developed with 34 multiple-choice questions targeted specifically at the personal financial skills of undergraduates. The instrument asked questions about students' ability and intention to budget and their attitude towards budgeting, as well as gathering background variables including the amount and type of part-time work undertaken, their motivations for working part-time, their level of indebtedness at the start of their studies and whether they had received lessons on personal finance at school. The questionnaire also included Callender's (2003) attitude-to-debt measure. The instrument consists of 10 statements measured on a five-point Likert scale where the mean scores, ranging from one to five, are calculated and plotted on a continuum. At one extreme there is strong debt aversion and at the other a tolerant attitude to debt, characterised respectively by a belief that owing money is basically wrong and an attitude that considers debt to be a normal part of today's lifestyle. A score of four or five indicates a more tolerant stance towards debt and a score of one or two suggests an intolerant position.

The multiple-choice test of financial knowledge included questions that students should reasonably be expected to answer rather than questions of a general financial-IQ nature. The questions asked were grouped around four main themes: student fees and loans (for example, amounts payable and available, repayment rates), employment (for example, minimum wage, tax allowance, income tax rates, terminology), banking and finance and general expenditure. The reported scores of the multiple-choice test section represent the percentage of correct answers.

A paper-based version of the instrument was piloted at the University of Glamorgan at the start of academic year 2005–06. In the following two academic years, 2006–07 and 2007–08, an on-line version was used. The exercise was undertaken during the induction week of each year to all first-year UK status business school undergraduates. The number of participants and their profile are presented in Table 1.

Table 1   Respondents and profile

	2005–06	2006–07	2007–08
Participants	149	220	146
Male	58%	58%	54%
Female	42%	42%	46%
Average age	19.5	20.5	19.5

Evaluation

Across all academic years a high percentage of students indicated an intention to work part-time (Table 2) during their period at university. This high level of part-time working supports the findings of Callender and Kemp (2000), Metcalf (2001) and Carney et al. (2005).

Table 2   Intention to work part-time

	2005–06	2006–07	2007–08
Working part-time	81%	73%	73%
Mean weekly hours	15	17	17

The main occupations were bar and shop work, but there were some relatively unexpected part-time jobs including a care worker, lifeguard, mechanic and labourer. However, all of these jobs are relatively low-paid. This means that the number of hours that students need to work to generate the funds required to finance their time at university is greatly increased.

For all three years, just under half the students were entering HE with debt (Table 3) which may be a contributory factor in the need to work part-time. However, term-time working is not restricted to those with prior indebtedness. It seems that students are either working to avoid debt or to help manage the level of debt they have.

Table 3   Levels of debt on entering HE

Year	No debt	Debt			
2005–06	58% (n=86)	42% (n=63)			n=149
		Level of debt			
		£1–£1,000	£1,001–£2,000	£2,001+	n=63
		35%	25%	40%	
2006–07	52% (n=113)	42% (n=107)			n=220
		Level of debt			
		£1–£1,000	£1001–£2,000	£2,001+	n=107
		44%	22%	34%	
2007–08	58% (n=85)	42% (n=61)			n=146
		Level of debt			
		£1-£1,000	£1001-£2,000	£2,001+	n=61
		52%	23%	25%	

In terms of students' budgeting capabilities and intention to budget (Table 4) it was pleasing to see that over 60% of students across the three years indicated that they had an awareness of budgeting. However, not all students intended to use this skill at university and if they did, the frequency of their budgeting activity was restricted to once a month.

In the first two years of the study students' knowledge of budgeting seemed to be intuitive and self-taught rather than being obtained through school lessons. The third year of the study revealed an increase in the number of students receiving lessons in school, although the percentage of students indicating an ability to budget was lower than previous years. It appears that the government's initiative to raise the level of financial awareness of young people is being promoted in schools but its effectiveness may still be questionable. This supports the finding of Thomas (2004) that the extent and quality of financial literacy teaching in schools varies greatly. Across all three years, over 80% of students felt that lessons on personal finance should be provided at university.

Table 4 Budgeting capabilities and intention to budget

	2005–06 n=149	2006–07 n = 220	2007–08 n=146
Budgeting capabilities	70%	66%	62%
Intention to budget (students with budgeting capabilities)	60%	40%	41%
Lessons on personal finance at school	21%	16%	82%
Lessons on personal finance should be provided at university	80%	89%	90%

The study has identified significant weaknesses in student understanding of personal financial matters. Answers to questions relating to student fees and loans, employment issues (such as the minimum wage, tax rate, national insurance), and banking and finance matters reveal low levels of financial awareness amongst first year business studies undergraduates.

The results of the multiple-choice section produced some interesting, but rather worrying, results across all four question groupings and all three years. The mean percentage mark obtained in the tests was below 39% in all cases although performance varied according to the theme of the questions (Table 5).

Table 5 Results of the multiple-choice questions
(Blank boxes indicate the absence of the question from the test)

	2005–06 n=149	2006–07 n = 220	2007–08 n=146
Overall mean percentage	32%	38%	35%
Tuition fees and Loans	% correct (of students with fees and loans)		
1 How much are your tuition fees? (all)	70%	84%	48%
2 Student loan repayment threshold	59%	91%	82%
3 Interest charged on loan	15%	12%	38%
4 Percentage of chargeable income for repayments	19%	14%	9%
5 Student loans deduction example	7%	16%	21%
6 Collection method of loan repayment	39%	58%	24%
7 Amount of student loan (independent of parent income)	18%	12%	
8 How will you receive your maintenance loan?		79%	66%
9 How will you receive your tuition fee?			88%
10 Chargeable income example			14%

Table 5   Results of the multiple-choice questions continued

Employment	% correct (of students intending to work)		
1 What is the minimum wage?	14%	19%	23%
2 Income tax earnings threshold	8%	29%	21%
3 What is taxable income threshold?	9%	10%	12%
4 What does PAYE stand for?	49%	58%	53%
5 What does NIC stand for?	65%	68%	74%
6 NIC is calculated as a % of what?	8%	14%	16%
7 What is the NIC % rate?	1%	6%	8%
8 What is the basic rate of income tax?		22%	27%
9 Taxable income example when earning £10,000?		22%	22%

Banking and Finance	% correct (all students)		
1 Definition of debit card	84%	90%	87%
2 Direct debit vs standing order	24%	26%	29%
3 Meaning of CPI	31%	42%	
4 Current rate of inflation	22%	16%	12%
5 Current Euros to £ exchange rate	71%	76%	70%
6 Meaning of base rate	19%	40%	40%
7 Current base rate %	5%	8%	22%
8 When to save for pension?	41%		
9 Description of an asset	85%	87%	
10 Meaning of liquidity	15%	17%	22%
11 Definition of inflation	46%	43%	49%
12 Meaning of APR	64%	64%	65%
13 When to save?	49%	47%	53%

General Expenditure	% correct (all students)		
1 Cost of TV licence	28%	37%	30%
2 Amount of the fine for not having a TV licence	66%	68%	76%
3 VAT calculation	62%	61%	65%
4 UK debt level	11%	9%	
5 Credit card calculation 1 – how long to repay?	19%	18%	13%
6 Credit card calculation 2 – how much interest?	9%	16%	14%
7 VAT rate			86%
8 VAT not applicable			13%
9 VAT rate on domestic supplies			14%

Students were asked to comment on the usefulness of the exercise. Not all students valued the activity but the majority (68% and above) in all three years found the exercise useful (Table 6).

Table 6   Students' rating of the exercise

	2005–06 n=149	2006–07 n = 220	2007–08 n=146
Very useful	12%	21%	16%
Useful	56%	51%	53%
Neither useful nor useless	28%	23%	27%
Useless	1%	2%	2%
Waste of time	3%	3%	1%

Of the students who responded to the invitation to comment on the questionnaire, the most frequently requested information was linked to help and advice on budgeting. For example,

'How to budget your money as a lot of students go mental with spending because the money's there.' [19 year old, male]

'Budgeting lessons would have been useful.' [21 year old, male]

'Just how to manage your budget. It should be provided at school also.' [18 year old, female]

'I believe financial advice, i.e. budgeting, should have been offered by the university to try and prevent debt. Also any information would have been useful on how to manage your time while at university.' [19 year old, male]

'I feel that I should have been helped with my finances because I'm not sure really how much I can afford to spend every week.' [18 year old, female]

'Not personally but I know several other people who have already spent their loan this term and are already eating into an overdraft – after 6 weeks! What happens if they get a credit card?' [19 year old, male]

'Kindly please tell me where can I get any financial support. I need a scholarship or any sort of reduction in fees. Kindly please tell me what I should do'. [18 year old, female student]

The final comment sums up what one student said about the whole exercise:

I have found this exercise extremely useful. I now realise how little I know about the things I really need to know something about. Thank you. [18 year old, female]

Discussion

The picture that emerges of the 'typical' first-year undergraduate student is one of school leaving age, relying on low-paid part-time work to finance their period in higher education. The mean test performances in 2005–06, 2006–07 and 2007–08 of 32%, 38% and 35% respectively, indicate that there are serious gaps in students' personal financial knowledge in all areas, and in particular in their basic understanding of the student-loan system and part-time work. It is evident that the lessons students receive in school are not targeting the issues that are relevant for a period in higher education.

It seems that these students are entering a critical stage of their lives ill- equipped to cope with the severe cash restrictions they will encounter. It is encouraging that over 60% of students in the study possess budgeting capabilities but worrying that they do not intend to use these skills appropriately, particularly when many students are entering university with existing debt.

The comments received from students, together with the overall analysis of results, demonstrate that there are serious deficiencies in the personal financial awareness of these undergraduate business school students and they are a strong endorsement for the provision of lessons in personal finance at school and university.

The study reports the results of business studies undergraduates at one HE institution and it may not be reasonable to extrapolate these results to other students at the same university, or to students studying at other institutions. However, it is worrying to see such low financial awareness among students studying business related subjects, and raises the question of how well non-business school undergraduates might perform.

Through the use of a web-based diagnostic tool, accessible by students at other HE institutions across the UK, future research will identify whether poor financial awareness of students is a national issue. (http://saphe.glam.ac.uk). The skills obtained from the overall exercise are transferable skills, with long-term added value for the students, and the diagnostic and support package developed could form part of students' PDP portfolios and have a positive impact on employability.

References

Archer, L., Hutchins, M. and Ross, A. (2003) *Higher Education and Social Class*. London, Routledge Falmer

Callender, C. (2003) Attitudes to debt: school leavers' and further educations students' attitudes to debt and their impact on participation in higher education. Universities UK, London

Callender, C. and Jackson, J. (2004) *Fear of debt and Higher Education participation, Families and Social Capital*. ESRC Research Group, London South Bank University

Callender, C. and Kemp, M. (2000) Changing student finances: Income, expenditure and the take up of student loans among full and part-time higher education students in 1998/1999. Research Report **213**. London, DfEE

Carney, C., McNeish, S. and McColl, J. (2005) The impact of part-time employment on students' health and academic performance: a Scottish perspective. *Journal of Further and Higher Education* **29** (4) November pp 307–19

Connor, H. and Dawson, S. (2001) with Tyers, C., Eccles, J., Regan, J. and Aston, J. *Social Class and Higher Education: issues affecting decisions on participation by lower social class groups*. Research Report **267**. London, DfEE

Cooke, R., Barkham, M., Audin, K., Bradley, M. & Davy, J. (2004) Student debt and its relation to student mental health. *Journal of Further and Higher Education* **28** (1) pp 53–66

Egg (2006) http://www.financial-iq.co.uk/home.html, last accessed 14 April 2005

Financial Services Authority (2006) *Personal finance education in schools: a UK benchmark study*. June http://www.fsa.gov.uk/Pages/Library/Other_publications/Consumer/index.shtml, last accessed 9 November 2006

Higher Education Funding Council for England (HEFCE) (2003) *Strategic Plan 2003-08* http://www.hefce.ac.uk/pubs/hefce/2003/03_35/03_35.doc, last accessed 1 April 2006

Higher Education Funding Council for Wales (HEFCW) (2005) *'Reaching Higher', Target for Widening Access* http://www.hefcw.ac.uk/Sector_Management/access_target.htm, last accessed 1 April 2006

Her Majesty's Government (2004) *Higher Education Bill*. January 2004, London: HMSO

HM Treasury (2007) *Financial capability: the Government's long term approach*. HMSO, http://www.hm-treasury.gov.uk/media/1/F/fincap_150107. pdf _07_04.cfm, last accessed 7 May 2008

Hobbs, S. and McKechnie, J. (1997) *Child employment in Britain: A social and psychological analysis*. Edinburgh, The Stationery Office

Leitch, S. (2006) Prosperity for all in the global economy – World class skills, Leitch Review of Skills, December, http:/hm-treasury.gov.uk/leitch, last accessed 20 January 2007

Marriott, P. (2007) An analysis of first experience students' financial awareness and attitude to debt in a post-1992 UK university. *Higher Education Quarterly* **61** (4) pp 498–519

McKechnie, J., Hill, S. and Hobbs, S. (2002) *Work and school: Part-time employment amongst senior school students*. Paisley, University of Paisley

Metcalf, H. (2001) *Increasing inequality in higher education: the role of term time working*. London, National Institute of Economic and Social Research

Payne, J. (2002) Post-16 students and part-time jobs: Patterns and effect – a report based on the England and Wales Youth Cohort Study. *Labour Trends* March 159–60

Purcell, K., Elias, P., Davies, R., & Wilton, N. (2005) *The Class of '99: A study of the early labour market experience of recent graduates*. Summary Report. Sheffield, Department for Education and Skills

Pure Potential (2007) *2007 Events Report* (Annual Survey). London: Pure Potential

RBS (2004) Financial Future of UK's Cash-Rich Kids Hangs in the Balance. Press Release, http://www.rbs.com/media03.asp, accessed 01.01.07

Scott, A. J., Lewis, A. and Lea S. E. G. (eds) (2001) *Student debt: the causes and consequences of undergraduate borrowing in the UK*. Bristol, The Policy Press

Stradling, S. (2001) The psychological effects of student debt. In A. J. Scott, A Lewis and S. E. G. Lea (eds) *Student debt: the causes and consequences of undergraduate borrowing in the UK* Bristol, The Policy Press pp 59–74)

Thomas, L. (2004) Evaluation of the pfeg Excellence and Access programme. London, Brunel University

PRU MARRIOTT is head of Accounting, Economics and Finance at the Winchester Business School. She is an active researcher in accounting education investigating the factors that affect the learning experiences of students in higher education including studies into student learning styles and learning approaches, students' attitudes towards information and communication technology and the accounting profession. Research contributions include the CAMEL Tangible Benefits of E-Learning Project (JISC) and *Practice which Works: a snapshot of assessment practice in Wales* (HEA). She is a member of the editorial board of *The Journal of Accounting Education* is an active member of the British Accounting Association (BAA), the BAA Accounting Education Special Interest Group (BAA-AE).

7

Student engagement with feedback

Jacqueline Lynch
University of Westminster

This chapter investigates student perceptions of feedback and how students used the feedback on an undergraduate business programme at the University of Westminster. In particular, it discusses the links students make between the mark and any written comments and assesses how students use feedback to improve and develop

The principles of 'good' feedback are well documented (cf. Gibbs, 1999; Black and William, 1998; Boud, 2000; Nicol and Macfarlane-Dick, 2004; www.heacademy. ac.uk/ourwork/learning/assessment/senlef). Why is it then that we seem unable to deliver 'good' feedback? We all know the issues. So why do I hear students say time and time again 'Why didn't I get a better mark?' The obvious response is 'have you read the feedback?' The conversation continues with the student proclaiming that they have, but still do not understand the mark.

The starting point for trying to resolve this apparent impasse is 'I give good feedback' – but do I? What did I really know? I too had a number of questions – Why don't students read the feedback? Why do they make the same mistakes? Why don't they collect their assignments? Students only appear to be emotionally fixated on the mark, which for them is the 'real' feedback.

In order to understand the issues, research was carried out with all undergraduate students on a business degree within Harrow Business School, University of Westminster. The case study reviews the findings of research which investigated student perceptions of feedback and how they used feedback on an undergraduate business programme. It identifies two key areas for further development and finishes with suggestions for developing practice.

Rationale

Student feedback

A number of themes can be identified in the literature: the purpose of feedback, its timeliness, different approaches depending on the discipline and student views (ranging from language issues to messages about themselves).

Purpose of feedback

Brown & Knight (1995) suggest that students want and expect feedback to help them develop and to be an aid to learning. As academics we all know that feedback helps to reduce mistakes, enables grading and is a performance indicator for both students and the course. It is widely acknowledged that most of us try to give good, timely, effective feedback. In his study Mutch (2003: 24) acknowledged that 'most academics were trying their best... to give helpful feedback to their students'.

Student views of feedback

Feedback implies messages about the students themselves (Stierer, 2000), about the function of academic writing and the values and beliefs underpinning the institution (Ivanic et al, 2000). Nicol and MacFarlane-Dick (2004) report that until recently lecturers 'transmitted' feedback to students which were about the strength and weaknesses of their work which the students then decoded and incorporated into their learning. However, later work suggests that this is more complex than it seems at first.

Language

The language of feedback can pose a problem and students may feel unsure or confused about what they have done wrong. This poses the question, 'Who are we writing the feedback for?' In addition, different disciplines emphasise different skills and place different degrees of importance on approaches to student writing. Similarly, different approaches and inconsistency between tutors lead to confusion: 'everybody seems to want something different' (Stierer, 2000: 40).

Length of feedback

Quantity depends on how much time is available and the beliefs of the tutors (Ivanic et al, 2000) with fewer comments given to better final-year students:

> Given the plethora of ideas, emphasis and approach, is it surprising that students may not read the written feedback or that they may interpret a different message from the feedback from that which the member of staff intended to convey. (Mutch, 2003: 25)

Context

The research was carried out with all undergraduate students on the BA Business programme across all three years.

It was known that innovative practices and good feedback approaches were being used, but it was felt that there might be inconsistencies in the approaches adopted by teaching staff, for a variety of reasons. There was a policy for return of work within the school with suggestions for good practice.

Anecdotally, comments from the student body centred around the emotional response of not liking the mark that they had received in terms of the amount of effort that they had put in. They felt that they had not been adequately rewarded or they did not understand the comments. In some case students indicated that the marker 'did not care' as there were not many comments or that they had not had feedback.

In order to substantiate the reality, research was undertaken to assess student perceptions of feedback on an undergraduate business programme, which included a number of specialist pathways. In this way we could bring what we know from the outside environment and compare it with the findings of our own student body to establish the benchmark. We wanted to understand exactly where our students were in the feedback debate if we were to develop a feedback strategy for the course and identify areas of best practice. A further output would be to develop principles of best practice, identify staff development needs and ultimately develop a feedback strategy for the School.

Objectives and methodology

The exploratory research adopted both a quantitative and qualitative approach using focus groups and a questionnaire.

The research objectives were:
❑ To understand student perceptions of feedback
❑ To understand the links they make between the mark and the written comments
❑ To assess how students use feedback to improve and develop.

Data collection

The research was carried out in two stages. The first stage involved the completion of six focus groups with Level 4, 5, and 6 students on the BA business programme to identify key issues for further investigation. Students were recruited in the early part of the year and invited to participate in focus groups, which lasted about 90 minutes. The data was collected using a discussion guide to generate discussion and all groups were tape recorded and transcribed for ease of analysis. Examples of written feedback were presented as stimulus materials along with the suggestion of different methods of assessment e.g. peer assessment.

A number of key research themes arose which were then used to develop the questionnaire.

Later in the year a postal questionnaire was sent to all full and part-time students on the course. This comprised a three-stage mailing over a period of a month. The first questionnaires were sent at the beginning of June and then two reminders were sent at two-week intervals. To increase the response rates a prize draw was used. In total 176 responses were usable which represented a 39% response rate.

Main findings

The main findings can be subdivided into four main themes.

1   Perception of feedback

The qualitative research suggested that students saw feedback as the written comments associated with a marked assignment that form part of the overall assessment for a module.

'feedback ...always has a mark with it.'

'is associated with a project or assignment.'

This was borne out by the quantitative findings where students indicated that feedback should always be written down (87%) and have a mark attached (74%). The exception to written feedback was verbal (in-class) feedback given in relation to assessed presentations.

Generally, students understood the feedback they received (76%) and understood it to be an important part of their learning (77%). However, there were a number of cases mentioned where there were problems related to the use of language – as Stierer (2000) suggests – or inability to read the handwriting of the lecturer. Interestingly, there was little recognition of feedback happening in seminars. The link between the student perception of feedback only being associated with a mark and an assignment is evident and they did not appear to see feedback outside these parameters.

On further analysis, there was evidence that students did acknowledge peer assessment and self-assessment (see student engagement below) but they had reservations about their usage.

Consistency of feedback

Students felt there was a lack of consistency between lecturers, seminar leaders, and between modules and that feedback varied in terms of content and quality depending on who wrote it.

'... it [feedback] varies between tutors.'

This is supported by the quantitative findings as students overwhelmingly indicated that feedback varied across modules. Interestingly, consistency appeared to be a significant factor in the second year. One explanation of this finding is that students' marks count towards their degree in the second year and students start to take more notice of the feedback and its importance to them increases.

Quality of feedback

For many students quantity appeared to equate to quality (82%). This result also has implications for the relationship between assessment, the mark and written comments which will be discussed below. Comments regarding effort arose spontaneously in the focus groups, where students felt that the volume of feedback did not adequately reflect the effort they had put into the assignment.

'I put so much effort in doing it; but why doesn't the tutor put effort in reading it?'

On probing 'effort', the comments were in relation to situations where feedback had been given but only a few lines of feedback had been written. Either it did not appear to matter whether the mark was high or low in these instances. For example, a student with 65% was just as likely to say it as a student with a mark of 50%. When this element was investigated further, 44% of students indicated that feedback did not reflect the effort that they had put in.

Students were asked to define what 'good' feedback meant to them. Students suggested that 'good' feedback should indicate ways to improve, indicate strengths and weaknesses, be understandable and clear, using simple language. They also felt that feedback was used to justify or explain the mark. Again this has implications for the relationship between the mark and written comments. Generally students were happy with timeliness of feedback (75%).

2 Purpose of feedback
Students recognised that feedback was to help them identify areas for improvement, help understand where they went wrong and was an explanation of the mark.

Change of feedback over time
There was little evidence to suggest that feedback changes over time, but interestingly, results change slightly at Level 4. Students at Levels 5 and 6 suggested that it was easier to approach lecturers later in the course as they felt they knew them better and the students had more confidence to ask when they were not satisfied with their feedback. Students felt that the feedback they received did not change significantly over time, but felt better equipped to ask questions.

3 Relationship between mark and written comment
The quantitative results suggested that students read the comments regardless of the mark that they received and 90% of students indicated they use feedback to improve work next time. The findings from the quantitative and qualitative research differ here as evidence from the focus groups appears 'more honest' where students admitted that sometimes they do not read the comments and therefore do not use the feedback.

'When you get your work back you look at the grade – maybe I'd read it later on.'
Some students felt that if a mark seemed poor and the feedback was limited then they would be less likely to use it or to seek further feedback from the marker. This was a significant issue for first-year students. There was also some evidence that some students see the mark itself as being more important to them than the feedback.

'Use [feedback] to justify my grade only as I'm not re-taking any modules'.
There was acknowledgement in the focus groups (although not substantiated in the quantitative research) that when students are being strategic in their assignments their expectations of feedback are low.

'If I do a piece of work at the last minute and I just aim to pass, then I look at the mark to see if I pass. I don't read the comments because I know the work is not good.'

Frustration is felt at feedback that does not adequately (in the student's view) explain why a mark was given and what would be required to score more highly. Even if the mark is seen as good, there is still an expectation of comment on how to improve.

'I got 60 and well, it's not good is it? But my supervisor says 'you did well'.

'but why do we get a 60? …[without comments for improvement] I can't use that, it doesn't help me at all.'

There were indications that perceptions of a glass ceiling existed. The absence of feedback about how to improve an assignment with high marks (around 70+) gives a perception among students of an artificial ceiling on the maximum mark that can be achieved.

'I've found it really frustrating – sometimes it says excellent work and you've done really well, but no improvement points… it's very hard to get above 70.'

Separating feedback and marks

As an experiment, feedback was given to a group of students without the marks attached. General feedback for the assignment was made available via Blackboard, it was reiterated in class both verbally and visually using PowerPoint and then individual pieces of work with individual comments were returned to the students. The students were asked to judge their own work and assign a mark to it. The actual marks were given to students a week later. A number of interesting observations arose:

❏ Students appeared to focus on the feedback and comments
❏ When the students received their marks they appeared either pleasantly surprised or the result was what they expected
❏ There were fewer student queries about how they could improve.

The emotional attachment to the mark had been removed and the students focused on assessing their performance in relation to the feedback about their work, and they rated themselves about right or slightly lower than their actual grade.

4 Student engagement

Student involvement in feedback was explored in the focus groups. Students appeared to be unsure about what would motivate them to become more involved in the feedback process. It was difficult to get them to think beyond how they are currently involved. This was further explored via the questionnaire by attitudinal statements such as 'Feedback is a two way process in which I am involved'. Interestingly only 50% of students indicated that they felt involvement. Students may not have grasped that feedback is about what they do with it and their participation to engage in the process. In order to try and encourage students to think about other issues surrounding their involvement, the ideas of peer assessment and self-assessment were explored.

The idea of assessment and feedback by peers was met with very mixed views.

There was a perceived risk of favouritism among friends and the existence of personal dislikes affecting results. However, peer-group feedback for presentations appeared to be more acceptable for some students although they felt that the work should still be awarded a mark by seminar leaders.

> 'I think this [peer assessment] is a really big waste of time. With the same academic background, how are they qualified to judge you?' Perhaps for presentation – for entertainment value only, not content.'

> 'Good for presentations – [referring to an actual occasion] all present said one good point and then one bad point. Also all gave a grade and the marker formulated an average grade – good but care is needed.'

This mixed view appeared to be borne out by the quantitative findings where only 54% of students agreed with the statement that peer assessment helps to improve their work.

Again this idea produced mixed views with some suggesting that it is unrealistic to self-assess while others see it as useful in stimulating thinking about their own work.

> 'It's just a waste of time if you ask me. I wouldn't sit down and start self-assessing myself after I've done a 4,000 word essay – no way.'

> 'I like self assessing – makes you view it [the assignment] critically.'

There was also comment that a lack of student motivation to use feedback might affect the marker's likelihood of giving detailed feedback.

> 'Is it worth the teacher having to write down all this information if the person who is going to be receiving the grade doesn't really care what you think anyway.'

When students were asked about suggestions for improvement to the feedback process in general, they called for more personal, face-to-face feedback. However, there was some recognition of the possible workload this could impose on markers and the possibility that some students would not take advantage of this opportunity.

Discussion

This case study has highlighted research findings which investigated student perceptions of feedback and how they used the feedback on an undergraduate business programme at the University of Westminster. In particular, the links students make between the mark and the written comments and how students use feedback has been reviewed.

So what have we learned?

1   The students' view of good quality feedback equated to volume.
2   In reality students receive a lot of feedback but they do not appear to recognise it as such e.g. work in seminars, comments from their peers (peer feedback). Even general feedback did not appear to be recognised as it was not specific to the individual. It was not until certain individuals received their work that they

claimed that they had had feedback. It was interesting that they did not assess their performance against the general hints for improvement.

3   Students did not understand their role in the feedback process, which seemed to indicate that feedback was something 'done to them' rather than them being active in the process. This point gives weight to the comment above.

4   Separation of the mark and feedback meant that students focused on learning. Once the emotional attachment to the mark had been removed they focused on assessing their performance in relation to the feedback about their work.

5   Many lecturers spend a lot of time writing what they think is good feedback. However, is it written in a language which students understand? For example – 'You need to structure your argument'. The question that needs to be asked is who are we writing the feedback for? Students? Ourselves to justify our marking? The external examiner?

6   Students admitted that some of them are not motivated to read the feedback. For them the mark is the only thing that matters. This approach severely hampers their learning because comments which are not read cannot be used to improve their next piece of work. They take the view that as they will never sit the module again 'What's the point?' However, in many instances the types of error that are commented on are similar in different pieces of work – style of writing, typographical errors, lack of attention to detail – which may not be related to content.

7   There was a reticence about adopting peer assessment. Initially students find peer assessment daunting and some may be resistant to it. However, the reality of the situation is that with guidance they are able to assess the work of others and the judgements they make are fairly accurate.

8   Better students are entitled to receive feedback on how to improve. If substantive comments on improvement cannot be made, are they entitled to a mark closer to 100% rather than say 72%?

Development of practice

The results of this research have led to changes in teaching practice and the study has been further used to manage student expectations about feedback, encourage and develop their role in the process and change the way that the school views feedback.

Examples of practices that have changed include:

❑   compulsory team briefings to agree the marking and feedback approach
❑   typed sheets indicating criteria, weighting and mark to overcome handwriting issues
❑   visual, verbal, written feedback with examples
❑   pre-assignment guidance
❑   increased use of peer and self-assessment (Gibbs, 1999; Boud, 2000) and feedback
❑   messages about what constitutes feedback explained in lectures and using very

simple words to focus student attention – 'You could improve your work by…'

What challenges do we still face?

Teaching practice is still developing with colleagues looking at automated feedback systems and more 'quick and dirty' feedback. However, there are still a few challenges that we face:

1 Setting student expectations about what feedback means, how they might use it and their role in the process.
2 How to engage the students more deeply with the feedback so that they understand their role in the process and engage in deep learning to overcome motivational issues?
3 Unless we move away from the lecturer being in 'control' of feedback, student behaviour will never change (Black and Williams 1998; Boud, 2000)
4 How do we overcome the mechanistic approach to just doing what has been done before? For instance, copying exemplars but with no depth of understanding.

   How do we engage the hearts and minds of our well intentioned colleagues so that the overall approach becomes consistent?

   We are still not there yet!

References and URLs

Black and William (1998) Assessment and classroom learning. *Assessment in Education* 5 (1) p 54

Boud, D. (2000) Sustainable assessment: rethinking assessment for the learning society *Studies in Continuing Education* 22 (2) pp. 151–67

Brown, S. & Knight, P. (1995) *Assessing learners in Higher Education*. London, Kogan Page

Gibbs, G. (1999), Using Assessment strategically to change the way students learn. In Brown S. and Glasner A. (eds) *Assessment matters in Higher Education: Choosing and Using Diverse Approaches.* Buckingham, SRHE/Open University

Ivanic, R., Clarke, R. & Rimmershaw, R. (2000) 'What am I Supposed to Make of This?' The Messages Conveyed to Students by Tutors' Written Comments. In Lea, M. & Stierer, B. (eds) (2000) *Student Writing in Higher Education New Contexts*. Buckingham, Open University Press/SRHE

Mutch, A. (2003) 'Exploring the practice of feedback to students', *Active Learning in Higher Education* 4 (1) pp 24–38

Nicol, D. and MacFarlane-Dick, D. (2004) Rethinking formative assessment in HE: a theoretical model and seven principles of good feedback practice. In Juwah, C., Macfarlane-Dick, D., Matthew, B., Nicol, D. and Smith, B. (2004) *Enhancing student learning through effective formative feedback*. [online]. The Higher Education Academy. Available from www.ltsn.ac.uk/genericcentre [Accessed 25 January 2008]

Rust, C. (2002) The Impact of Assessment on Student Learning: How Can Research Literature Practically Help to Inform the Development of Departmental Assessment Strategies and Learner-Centred Assessment Practices? *Active Learning in Higher Education* 3 (2) pp 145–58

Stierer, B. (2000) Schoolteachers as Students: Academic Literacy and the Construction of Professional Courses in Education. In Lea, M. & Stierer, B. (eds) (2000) *Student Writing in Higher Education: New Contexts*. Buckingham: Open University Press/SRHE pp 179–95

www.heacademy.ac.uk/ourwork/learning/assessment/senlef

www.mw.brookes.ac.uk/display/eswaf/home

JACQUELINE LYNCH is a principal lecturer and subject leader in marketing and was one of the first teaching fellows to be appointed by the University of Westminster. She is also a chartered marketer and member of the Chartered Institute of Marketing, the Institute of Direct Marketing and the Higher Education Academy.

She has a passion for learning and teaching and her teaching research interests are in feedback to students, managing student expectations, internationalisation of the curriculum, marketing education, graduate employment in marketing, marketing and logistics, and creativity.

8

'Is that your final answer?
Encouraging student participation using a personal response system

Wendy Beekes
Lancaster University Management School

Using the radio frequency Personal Response System (PRS) to ask multiple-choice, true/false and answer-series questions has produced high levels of engagement from students who receive real-time feedback on their understanding of key topics.

Introduction

In order to increase the level of student participation and engagement during lectures, I introduced the Personal Response System (PRS) into my classes. The radio frequency PRS is an electronic teaching resource which provides an experience similar to 'Ask the Audience' on the television programme *Who Wants to Be a Millionaire?* During the session, students are equipped with a handset to vote on the questions and the system collates all the votes. Following voting, a graphic is shown on screen, detailing the student responses to a particular question. Lancaster University has used an infrared PRS since academic year 2000–01, although the system is not very flexible and unsuitable for use with larger classes. The increases in class size at the undergraduate level and the desire to provide more feedback on an individual basis led to grants being placed to purchase a radio frequency PRS. The new radio frequency PRS overcomes the limitations of the infrared PRS; it is quick to set up, offers a number of different question formats and is only constrained by the number of handsets.

This case study outlines the use of the radio frequency PRS in my second-year introductory-level *Management Accounting* course. The use of the PRS for regular testing was intended to provide a more engaging and active learning approach for students in lectures, as well as providing timely feedback to students on a regular basis on their understanding. In addition, this was intended to provide incentives for students to keep up to date with course materials throughout the term. The students have responded positively to the use of the PRS in my classes in the current academic year 2007–08 and many have commented that it was a 'fun' and helpful resource.

Why use the Personal Response System?

The radio frequency PRS is an electronic teaching resource which enables the lecturer to ask the class a variety of questions including true/false, multiple choice, numerical reasoning or answer series. The system may be used anonymously by students if the lecturer wishes to gauge the students' understanding. Alternatively, if the lecturer wishes to use the system for class testing or collecting homework, this is also possible. To use the system for testing, the students log in to the system using an identification number, and responses from individual students can then be identified. The system will grade students' responses after the session according to certain criteria which the lecturer can amend according to course benchmarks (Beekes, 2008a). The PRS can also be used for attendance monitoring as class lists may be uploaded in advance of the class and students who are absent are identified by the reports produced by the PRS software.

During the session, students can vote for their chosen answer with a handset which has both numerical and alphabetical buttons. As can be seen from Figure 1, the handset is almost like a pocket calculator with buttons for true/false, 1 to 9 and text entry. The handset can also tell the user how much battery life is left, a useful feature if this is to be used for testing in classes. The responses are collected wirelessly by a small box which is connected to the computer by a USB cable.[1] The PRS software is easy to use for writing questions; it is very similar to a word processor and the questions may also be entered into the lecturer's PowerPoint presentation for the class. There is no limit to the number of questions which can be stored on the system and it is simple to copy the questions from one folder to another folder in the questions directory. This makes setting up a bank of questions and selecting particular questions for a class test an easy task.

Figure 1   The radio frequency
Interwrite PRS handset
Source   Interwrite Learning (2008)

When running a PRS session, everyone is provided with a handset to vote. After everyone has logged in, the lecturer starts the session, and the question and possible answers are shown on screen. The lecturer determines the amount of time for each question and after the clock has been started, the amount of time left to answer

1   The radio frequency PRS is much easier to set up than infrared PRS technology which Lancaster University has used since academic year 2000/2001. The new PRS uses radio waves and so does not require receivers to be distributed around a teaching room, connected with wires which are then connected to a computer. This means that the system is more reliable and does not require additional support from Audio Visual Services at the University to set up the system.

a question is displayed on screen. In addition, the display also shows the number of students who have voted. The time for a given question may be altered by the lecturer during the session as necessary. For example, if students appear to find a particular question tricky, the lecturer can extend the amount of time while voting is taking place. Alternatively, if everyone in the class has answered the question, the lecturer can stop the clock. The lecturer may also vary the number of times students can answer a particular question, allowing them to re-think and change their answer. Naturally for class testing, this feature may be turned off.

After time is up for voting on a question, the system collates all votes and displays a graphic on screen showing how the students have voted. Instantly the students get feedback on their understanding of the key concepts reviewed. It also enables the lecturer to explain the rationale for the correct answer and in addition to providing quick feedback to the student group, it also helps the lecturer see what the class does (and in some cases does not!) understand well which can help curriculum development for the future. As Draper et al (2002) suggest, this can also provide the lecturer with useful feedback on the students' understanding of key topic areas. In addition, this could be useful to the lecturer in deciding on additional problems or reading materials to help students on the course.

The course context

The PRS has been integrated into my second year undergraduate *Management Accounting* class for the first time during the current academic year, 2007–08. This 10-week course runs twice a year in both the first and second terms and typically has approximately 350 students per year, split across the two terms. The course is compulsory for a number of students in the management school (including accounting and finance, and some business studies students). Although this is a second-year course, it is at an introductory level, but students will have studied financial accounting and book-keeping previously. Even before they start the course, some students have pre-conceived ideas about what accounting is all about from previous courses; often students believe that accounting is primarily about 'number crunching', and employing rules and regulations to financial information. *Management Accounting* in contrast is about meeting the needs of managers; although there are some techniques involving calculations, the course is primarily about decision-making, planning and control which can involve a significant amount of discussion. Therefore a key aim of introducing the PRS is to encourage students to overcome these misconceptions and broaden their awareness of the key topic areas. Earlier research has found that students are more likely to retain the key concepts learned if a more 'fun' way to learn is adopted (Marston, 2003), and I hope through using the PRS students enjoy the classes and engage with the subject more fully during class time than might otherwise be the case. Figure 2 shows the students using the system in my course.

Figure 2   Students on my Introductory Management Accounting Course using the PRS

A key aim of using the PRS was to improve the timeliness of feedback to students on their understanding of course topics. Last year, the course was assessed by a take-home report (25%), with an end of the term deadline and an end of year examination (75%). This meant that students did not get feedback on their assessed course-work until after the course had been completed. Therefore, the only regular feedback mechanism was the weekly tutorial sessions, which although vital to the course and student understanding, did not appear to be meeting students' needs for regular feedback. Departmental feedback student questionnaires from this course last year commented on the students' desire for additional feedback during term-time as the course progresses. In addition, results in the 2007 National Student Survey showed that generally in Business and Management subject areas, courses were quite poor in their ability to provide timely and regular feedback on student progress (HEFCE, 2007).

Following the course feedback last year, several funding bids to purchase a new PRS system suitable for use in larger classes were submitted. Bids to the school IT Committee and Lancaster University Friends Programme were successful and the radio frequency PRS was purchased in 2007. To incorporate the PRS into my lectures I re-structured my course to include regular testing using the PRS each week during lectures. This attempted to address student desire for additional feedback, and although I do not include this in the summative assessment for the course, students do receive informal feedback on their progress on a weekly basis.

Aims of using the Personal Response System

The use of the PRS in class time encourages active learning to take place and prevents the passive approach, often typical of lectures (Snyder, 2003). The PRS sessions try to achieve active engagement of all class attendees, irrespective of their background and knowledge level. Admittedly, the use of multiple-choice questions in lectures to encourage students to take an active approach to learning is not new (see Harden et al, 1968; Dunn, 1969). However, asking students to raise their hand in response to the answer they think is correct is problematic and in my experience does not work successfully. When I have done this in my classes, I have typically found that Asian students in particular, and also some British students, are less likely to participate in answering questions during lectures for fear of 'loss of face' in front of their colleagues if they vote for an incorrect answer (as discussed by Beekes, 2006). The advantage of using PRS is that it collects responses anonymously, or by student identification number, so that the individual's identity is protected when answering the question posed. This means that the lecturer can get 100 per cent participation in classes when asking questions, something which I have previously been unable to achieve when asking students to raise their hands to vote for the correct answer. By using the PRS the lecturer therefore gets a more accurate representation of the students' understanding than has previously been the case when asking multiple-choice questions in class.

In addition to increasing the level of participation in classes during class time and providing timely feedback, the use of regular testing with the PRS gives students an incentive to keep up-to-date with course materials. The weekly questions were staged so that some were relevant to the previous week's lectures and some to the current week's work. This provides the incentive for students to keep up-to-date with the reading and problems set for classes. It also provides feedback to students as the course progresses and highlights areas of weakness to students (Liebler, 2003) or where preparatory reading has not been completed in sufficient depth.

Is the Personal Response System effective?

Using the Personal Response System

The main features of this approach involve asking a series of questions during the sessions. The format is very flexible and I tend to use a number of formats including multiple choice, answer series and true/false type of questions. The system may also be used for text-entry and survey questions, although I have yet to use these features in my classes, but intend to do so next year. During the session, each student 'logs in' to the system using their student-identification number which enables the responses to be tracked to a particular individual. There is a set time for questions to be answered, which I adjust as necessary, to ensure everyone has a chance to vote.

After the voting time is over, a graphical summary of the overall class voting is displayed on screen. This bar chart of voting creates a 'wow' factor, particularly if a large number of students vote for an incorrect answer (which happens from time to time). This active approach may encourage students to retain knowledge of the key concepts of the course (Cue, 1998). I have found that many of the students score well on these PRS sessions and I hope that this will also be reflected in their coursework and examination performance. For those that do not score well, I hope it provides them with useful feedback on where they need to focus their studies.

At the end of each session, the PRS software can be used to generate summary reports. These reports are available from the PRS software as file downloads either in .csv or .pdf formats. The reports compiled by the PRS software include a detailed student-by-student report which shows the average for the class (to enable students to benchmark relative to their peers), the student's vote, and the correct answer. In addition, there are summaries of the student votes by individual student and the class as a whole, so students can benchmark themselves against their colleagues. I place all of the detailed and summary reports on the VLE immediately after the class. I also create a document summary showing a running total of the scores from the PRS sessions and upload this on the VLE. This all typically takes about 10 to 15 minutes to complete after the class as each report is compiled separately by the software. This real-time feedback enables students' to track their progress week by week, focus their self-study, and seek further clarification of aspects that are not understood well.

Student feedback on using the Personal Response System

I have found that the PRS is very effective at encouraging class participation. It engages the class during the lecture time and is fun to use for both the lecturer and student group. Comments from the departmental feedback questionnaires and the course VLE are positive; they say that students have found the PRS sessions 'helpful' and 'very good fun!' One student commented: 'The weekly revision parts of the lecture using the [PRS] were useful.' Another student commented that the PRS was the best part of lectures:

> I think the introduction of the PRS is a new way of teaching and also learning and therefore engages more people, due to providing some variety. I have enjoyed using and learning from this system.

These comments demonstrate students' enthusiasm for using the system and they have been echoed in feedback from staff-student forums.

A student feedback questionnaire was conducted shortly before the end of the course and 117 student responses were collected. Students were asked to respond on a scale of 1 to 5 (where 1 is strongly disagree and 5 is strongly agree) to a series of statements used in prior research into the PRS (Elliott, 2003). The results are shown in Table 1. The student responses to statement 1 suggest most of them found the system easy to use. Once the students have logged into the system, answering the questions through pressing the appropriate buttons (true/false, 1 to 9 or A to E) is a straightforward task. The students voted with mean 3.8 and median 4.0 to

Table 1   Results of the PRS Questionnaire

		Average	Std. dev	Median
1	The PRS is easy to use	3.8	1.0	4.0
2	Using the PRS has increased my enjoyment of lectures	3.6	1.2	4.0
3	Using the PRS has encouraged me to attend lectures	3.3	1.3	3.0
4	Using the PRS has helped my concentration levels in lectures	3.1	1.1	3.0
5	Using the PRS has increased my confidence on this course	2.8	1.0	3.0

Source of PRS questions: Elliott (2003)

the statement that the PRS increased their enjoyment of lectures. This is echoed in comments received from students about the system. One student commented: 'I liked the electronic quiz things we did as it gives you an idea of how you are doing and it makes the lectures interesting.' In terms of the level of lecture attendance, students voted with mean 3.3 and median 3.0 to the statement that the PRS encouraged them to attend lectures. On average students tended to agree with the statement, and anecdotal evidence from the University of Aberdeen (2005) and other colleagues in the Management School at Lancaster suggests that the PRS has a positive impact in terms of encouraging attendance at lectures.

Students provided less favourable responses to the statement relating to concentration levels in lectures: they voted with mean 3.1 and median 3.0. This was perhaps because students felt that they would be concentrating in lectures anyway irrespective of whether the PRS was used. In addition, students voted with mean 2.8 and median 3.0 to the statement that the PRS had increased their confidence on the course. Again, there could be a number of reasons for this which relate to the fact that students felt quite confident on this particular course as it covers introductory material. A few students commented on the feedback questionnaires that they would have preferred to have spent additional time on lecture material and more examples, rather than completing the PRS sessions. Other students suggested that the sessions did provide useful feedback on the course as it progresses and it was helpful to clarify their understanding. However, as with any teaching method, you cannot please all students all the time, but these PRS sessions have been a fun and engaging way for students to track their progress and keep up-to-date with the course materials.

At this stage it is too soon to track the students' progress on the PRS and the final mark awarded for the course as the examinations for both cohorts have not taken place. However it will be interesting to relate the marks on weekly PRS sessions and the final marks to see whether it does provide an indicative result of a student's final mark for the course.

Problems faced and lessons learned in implementation

How did the Personal Response System technology work?

Introducing new technology into classes always has a certain risk element for the lecturer as you are never quite sure of two things. First, whether the technology will be easy to set up and will work during the class, and secondly, how the students will respond to it. At Lancaster University we had experience of using an older version of the PRS technology which used infrared handsets (as discussed by Beekes, 2006; Elliott, 2001, 2003). However this PRS was frequently unreliable due to the large number of wires connecting the receivers to the system.

The infrared PRS was not always straightforward to set up, unlike the radio frequency PRS which is easy to use and takes only a couple of minutes to set up for a large class. In addition, the infrared PRS was not suitable for use with larger groups of students due to the number of receivers required to record the handset responses, whereas the only constraint with the new system is the availability of handsets. The other problem with the infrared PRS is that it is only suitable for use with multiple-choice questions. The radio frequency PRS is more flexible and I intend to use a greater variety of question formats next year. In addition, the infrared PRS software did not show the questions on screen while the clock was running. Since the questions were not directly entered into the system, I displayed the questions on transparencies, and the PRS software was projected onto another screen at the same time. This obviously limited my ability to use the PRS in certain classes, as not all rooms had two screens. These problems have all been overcome with the new radio frequency PRS which can be run anywhere on campus, subject to computer-hardware availability.

From my previous experience of using the infrared PRS in *ad hoc* sessions with postgraduate and undergraduate students, I was fairly confident that the students would react well to receiving additional feedback and using the PRS in classes. However, using the PRS on a weekly basis throughout the term had not been done before at the school and I was not sure how the students would respond to this. In addition, the infrared PRS had never been used in named mode for testing during the class, and so I was breaking new ground with the new system. To familiarise myself with the new system and using it for informal testing, I spent time practising with the technology and learning what types of questions would work well by testing them out on colleagues. This was very fruitful as I received useful feedback which helped me to design the sessions for students.

To enable regular PRS sessions to take place, my introductory *Management Accounting* course was re-designed during the summer break in 2007. I usually allow about 20–25 minutes per week in my lectures to do the PRS sessions, depending on the week's lecture coverage. This did involve some reduction in topic coverage from the syllabus. However, I believe the benefits in terms of greater course participation and involvement make this worthwhile. Students can see their overall progress throughout the term as I place an updated total on the VLE for the course after the lecture on a weekly basis. Students also particularly like to learn who was the 'fastest finger first' (i.e. the student who got to the correct answer in the fastest time and I place the library card number of the relevant student on the VLE and the time taken to answer the question.) It is a simple matter to retrieve this information from the system output and creates a fun element to the answer-series type of questions.

In addition to time re-designing my course, there was also time required to write the questions, and compile the reports after each session where the PRS was used. Writing the questions was not too time consuming, although at the start, I found I vastly over-estimated the number of questions that could be completed during a session. I also hadn't always given sufficient time on the clock to enable students to answer the questions, but this was a simple matter to amend during the session. I found that the most effective order is to start with a few true/false questions to get the session started and then move on to multiple-choice and answer-series questions which take longer to answer. I learnt a lot in the first couple of classes about the appropriate amount of time for each of the question types and which questions work well, largely through trial and error.

Challenges faced in introducing the Personal Response System

One of the major hurdles faced was to familiarise myself with the technology and getting it all to work successfully during the class. The PRS manuals that came with the system were not as helpful as they might have been, and I ended up playing with the system at the weekend to find out how it worked. After a bit of trial and error, I got the system working successfully. Once I had familiarised myself with the system, setting it up took just a few minutes at the start of the class. From my experiences, I created a guide of how to use the PRS to help other colleagues.[2] Subsequently I have also given presentations to colleagues at Lancaster University to share my knowledge and experience.

One thing that had not been considered in purchasing the new PRS was the practicality of keeping the handsets and transporting them to the lecture theatre. It is a major challenge to get the system to the lecture theatre as the PRS bags contain only 32 handsets each! This has practical implications for the lecturer, but I have been able to purchase a couple of trolleys and postgraduate students help me with them to the lecture theatre each week, so this was fairly easily overcome. Clearly with larger classes, transporting the system around campus could be problematic if the campus is not accessible and assistance is not available. However once in the lecture theatre, it is a simple task to set up the system; there are just two wires to connect to a receiver box and the computer. All that remains to be done when the software is started is to ensure all students log in correctly during the session using their library card identification number. On reflection, compared to the infrared PRS, the radio frequency PRS has been a significant step forward for the lecturer in terms of ease of use, and encouraging learning and greater participation during lecture time for classes of all sizes.

Conclusions

Using new technology is often perceived as a risky strategy by colleagues and many will shy away from using such resources in their teaching. However I have shown that if you adapt your teaching and embrace technology, it can be used effectively to improve the level of feedback we give our students, and make learning fun and more interactive. I am happy to admit that using the PRS has not been without challenges: getting the money to fund the system in the first place, learning about the system and the practical issue of getting it into the teaching room. The system is not cheap to

2   Further information about using the PRS is available to download from my webpage: www.lancs. ac.uk/staff/beekes/Personal_response_system.htm

purchase – our system for 350 students cost in the region of £15,000 and the cost seems to vary significantly from supplier to supplier.[3] The main hub and software to run the questions cost in the region of £200, but handsets will cost approximately £40 each, depending on order size. However, despite the large upfront investment, I think it has all been worthwhile; the students have found it a fun and engaging method of teaching. I think it has also encouraged students to take a more positive attitude towards my course. The PRS technology is suitable for most, if not all courses, as the format of the questions can be chosen to suit the particular topic area. I have found that my course is very easy to adapt to a number of different question formats and I am planning to use the text-entry next year, in addition to numerical reasoning.

As is the case with most types of learning technology, now that I have successfully used the system, others have become keen to use this on their courses. I have given seminars at the school, showing colleagues how to use the system and suggested how they can avoid some of the set-up costs I have incurred. As a result the system is now being regularly used in the Economics and Management Science departments, as well as in Accounting and Finance. Colleagues have commented that as a result of using the PRS attendance at their lectures has improved, as well the level of engagement with the course as a whole.

Acknowledgements

Dr Caroline Elliott (Department of Economics, Lancaster University) and I have been fortunate to receive sufficient funding to enable equipment to be purchased to enable the PRS to be run with any course in the Lancaster University Management School at the undergraduate or postgraduate level. We would like to thank the Lancaster University Management School IT Committee and the Lancaster Friends' Programme for their generous funding to enable us to purchase this great system. The author would also like to thank Dr K. T. Soo for reading through drafts of this piece.

---

3 Our PRS was purchased from Universal AV Services Ltd, www.uniav.com, although there are many suppliers of this type of system.

References

Beekes, W. A. (2006) The 'Millionaire' Method for Encouraging Participation. *Active Learning in Higher Education* **7** (1) pp 25–36

Beekes, W. A. (2008a) Ask the Audience in Lectures. Increasing Participation and Improving the Timeliness of Feedback. *Business Management Accountancy and Finance Magazine* Higher Education Academy **4** pp 3–4

Beekes, W. A. (2008b) Personal Response System. Ask the Audience in Your Lectures. http://www.lancs.ac.uk/staff/beekes/Personal_response_system.htm [accessed 12 March 2008].

Cue, N. (1998) A Universal Learning Tool for Classrooms? Paper presented at the First Quality in Teaching and Learning Conference, Hong Kong International Trade and Exhibition Centre, Hong Kong, December 10–12. http://celt.ust.hk/ideas/prs/pdf/Nelsoncue.pdf [accessed 12 March 2008]

Draper, S. W., Cargill, J. & Cutts, Q. (2002) Electronically Enhanced Classroom Interaction. *Australian Journal of Education Technology* **18** (1) pp 13–23

Dunn, W. R. (1969) Programmed Learning News, Feedback Devices in University Lectures. *New University* **3** (4) pp 21–22

Elliott, C. (2001) Case Study: Economic Lectures Using a Personal Response System. *Economics Learning, Support and Teaching Network.* http://www.economicsnetwork.ac.uk/showcase/elliott_prs.htm [accessed 12 March 2008].

Elliott, C. (2003) Using a Personal Response System in Economics Teaching. *International Review of Economics Education* **1** pp 80–86. Also available at http://www.economicsnetwork.ac.uk/iree/i1/elliott.htm [accessed 12 March 2008].

Harden, McG. R., Wayne, Sir E. & Donald, G. (1968) An Audio-visual Technique for Medical Teaching. *Journal of Medical and Biological Illustration* **18** (1) pp 29–32

HEFCE (2007) *The National Student Survey 2007.* (Higher Education Funding Council for England) http://www.hefce.ac.uk/learning/nss/data/2007/files2007/NSS2007SummaryData.xls [accessed 20 October 2007]

Interwrite Learning (2008) *PRS RF.* http://www.interwritelearning.com/products/prs/radio/detail.html [accessed 12 March 2008]

Liebler, R. J. (2003) The Five-Minute Quiz. *Journal of Accounting Education* **21** (3) pp 261–65

Marston, P. (2003) Strategies for Developing Interactive Teaching Resources. Mini-Paper: What is the PRS and How Might it be Used? http://www.abdn.ac.uk/diss/ltu/pmarston/prs/mini-paper.hti [accessed 26 July 2004]

Snyder, K. D. (2003) Ropes, Poles and Space. *Active Learning in Higher Education* **4** (2) pp 159–67

University of Aberdeen (2005) Using Personal Response Systems (PRS) to Introduce Interactivity to Your Lectures and Tutorials. http://www.abdn.ac.uk/~clt011/prs/ [accessed 12 March 2008].

WENDY BEEKES is the director of first year undergraduate studies in accounting and finance at Lancaster University Management School. Since April 2000 she has lectured and tutored on various undergraduate and postgraduate programmes offered by the School, and has also been involved in MBA project and PhD supervision.

She has teaching responsibility for introductory accounting at the undergraduate level to first and second year students, with particular focus on management accounting and financial statement analysis. She is a fellow of the Higher Education Academy and an active researcher who makes regular presentations at the American, British and European Accounting Association annual conferences. In addition to her own research, she is also currently supervising doctoral students in the research areas of corporate governance and the link to earnings timeliness, and analyst forecast accuracy.

9

Using eportfolio on two versions of an employability skills module

Peter Robinson, Crispin Dale and Debra Wale
University of Wolverhampton

This chapter compares an employability skills module taught in a traditional environment with delivery through the PebblePad eportfolio to work-based learners and discusses how we overcame the challenges that were encountered.

This study is a critical comparison of the use of eportfolio for teaching and reflective student-centred assessment across two iterations of the same module. The first, *Employability Skills* (LI1011), is a traditional module taught in a lecture theatre, but requiring students to use eportfolio to submit a reflective personal development planning portfolio. The second, *Employability Skills for Travel Operations Management* (FDa LI1015), is delivered online for a specific course with learners, so while assessment is the same in both iterations, in the latter eportfolio is also used as a teaching mechanism. Both modules have been designed to enable the student to assess and develop a range of professional and personal skills to promote future personal and career development. The modules give consideration to research skills, report and essay writing, critical thinking and group work. The module objectives include: an ability to take responsibility for learning and personal development; evaluate progress and achievement of personal development and specify targets; development of a range of interpersonal and transferable skills; and self managed learning in a professional context.

Introduction

Rationale

The purpose of this chapter is to illustrate the impact of eportfolio on student learning, and in particular on reflective practice and personal development planning, and to compare different applications of eportfolio for different user needs. It is a critical comparison that investigates and questions the approaches taken and strives to inform best practice in the use of eportfolio for this type of learning. Of course there are weaknesses in this approach, not least the fact that the mature students on the distance-learning course are more familiar with PDP as a routine part of their progression in employment. The context of the eportfolio system at the University of Wolverhampton (UoW) is discussed before going on to evaluate its application to the two employability modules.

PebblePad as an eportfolio

The development of PDP has been a key focus of UoW's learning and teaching strategies since 2002. The central underpinning for the development of PDP in the strategy has been the Personal, Academic, Careers and Employment initiative (PACE). The PACE initiative takes a structured approach to the development of a student's reflective skills during the course of their studies and beyond. This process was initially supported through a paper-based system but this had a number of noticeable drawbacks including a lack of flexibility and consistency across subject areas. An eportfolio system, known as PebblePad, was developed by Pebble Learning in collaboration with the university to meet the needs of the reflective learning process and tap into contemporary methods of communicating such as social networking which has been so rapidly adopted in the student community. PebblePad supports work on the development of personal 'assets' that drive the process of reflection. This may include work-related experiences, achievements, thoughts and action plans. The development of personal assets is based on the principles of Kolb's learning cycle – experience, reflection, theorising and action (Moon, 2004) – and SWOT analysis (strengths, weaknesses, opportunities and threats). Once created, the assets are logged in the user's 'asset store' and can be drawn on for further reflection and discussion.

The assets can also be used as part of the development of a user's webfolio. This is a personal website in which assets, files, images and weblinks can be attached. As an e-submission facility, Webfolios can be uploaded onto the gateway for tutor comment and feedback. PebblePad also enables the creation of blogs where students can further reflect on their own experiences or discuss issues as directed by the tutor. PebblePad is essentially a personal and private space, although in common with the ethos of social networking, assets, webfolios and blogs can be shared with others as part of the development of a wider reflective learning community.

The rationale for using PebblePad as the delivery mechanism for supporting the modules has a number of components.

1   The modules are geared to the needs of students reflecting on their experiences in a work-based and/or academic context. Students, therefore, require a system that enables them to structure their reflections coherently while also offering the potential to share these with other users.

2   The modules require students to have access to an electronic system that enables them to record reflections and experiences as and when they occur. The flexibility and accessibility of the PebblePad system offers the potential for students to engage with their studies, any time, any place, anywhere.

3   Students in the Travel Operations Management Foundation degree (FDa) are required to engage with materials as part of a distance-learning programme. As the case study illustrates, PebblePad has been effectively used to put the learning materials into a distance-learning format.

4   It was necessary to enable students to gain online feedback from module tutors. The use of PebblePad to support the delivery and assessment of the two employability modules is now discussed.

Employability Skills (LI1011)

The taught version (LI1011) combines classroom and multi-media teaching and assessment methods through a student-centred approach to learning. The module covers the necessary professional and personal skills: report writing, referencing, presentation skills and relevant development theories to reflect on and underpin learning. Delivered in the first semester, the module enables the students to build their professional and personal skills, and is assessed through submission of a reflective portfolio.

The module is delivered as a series of lectures in the classroom. Lecture materials are posted onto the UoW's virtual learning environment (WOLF) prior to each session enabling students to print, review and bring the materials to taught sessions. For their summative assessment, students submit a portfolio of work in hard copy. The portfolio contains six formative tasks directly linked to the 12 taught sessions. Two of the tasks are completed on-line using PebblePad. At present students are required to print these to add to the portfolio. It is proposed that the portfolio will be changed to electronic format in the future to simplify the assessment process for students (this was successfully trialled in the on-line version LI1015) and to move to meeting the UoW's teaching and learning strategy for online assessment by 2012.

A deepening of the students' learning process is facilitated by the student-centred teaching and learning methods used to deliver this module. These are based on Kolb's learning cycle in which concrete experience is followed by reflection, and encompass the principles of cognitive-learning theory (Biggs, 2003). The premise of cognitive theory is that covering information is not the same as engendering the relevant knowledge in the minds of the students, as Brown and Race highlight – 'more important than mere coverage is providing time to reflect and digest theory' (2002: 51).

Student experience

Materials are posted on to WOLF prior to each session to enable students to carry out any suggested preparation prior to each taught session and to begin the process of deeper learning. Students are then taught the concepts and theories. Seminars following lectures provide the opportunity for students to consolidate the learning:

> [the best thing about the module has been] the seminar activities because it is more enjoyable when I am taking part in the learning, it helps me to remember

information easier. (student feedback LI1011)

Using group activities in the seminar sessions encourages students to put taught material into practice, offering them the opportunity to reflect on the application of theory to practice. For example, the use of the Belbin test offers each student the opportunity to assess themselves in the lecture, and then to test out the result through a group activity in the seminar.

Building in some means of checking students' understanding of key concepts and ideas in the lecture can be invaluable (Brown & Race, 2002). It also provides the opportunity for information to be absorbed in parts of the brain where information to be remembered is stored. Each session provides students with the opportunity to gain confidence in their presentation skills. In their groups, students are required to present the results of the seminar tasks. This provides the opportunity for tutors to check that learning has taken place and to provide immediate constructive feedback which in turn enables students to clarify understanding in preparation for completion of the related formative task. Brown & Race suggest:

> It's only when the students have applied, extended, compared, evaluated, argued with, summarised, contested and played around with the information… that it becomes their knowledge. (2002: 59)

Assessment and achievement

The summative assessment is a portfolio containing six formative tasks, including a blog requiring reflection on their own learning styles and PDP with an action plan for the next semester which draws on all the taught material. Higher-grade achievers demonstrated analysis of their PDP skills with appropriate reflection on and application of taught theories such as Honey and Mumford's learning styles (1982). The results are spread across the grade range with a high number of students around B, C and D grades. This is a very different profile to the achievement of students in LI1015.

Employability Skills for Travel Operations Management (LI1015)

This module is part of a foundation degree in Travel Operations Management, which was developed as part of the university's response to the government drive for new awards at sub-degree level. The outcome has been a sector-specific FDa (Arts) delivered equally by three higher education institutions, Coventry University, University College Birmingham and the University of Wolverhampton (Robinson et al, 2007). The first pilot cohort comprises 61 staff from a major UK employer. Most had left formal education at 16 or 18 and have progressed their career in the company.

From the start of the programme development the learner was placed at the centre of planning and key to this was the use of an e-learning platform. Both hardware and software considerations were linked with debate on how much time would be given by the employer for learning (Lewis and Whitlock, 2003). All the reading materials, journals and books are available electronically. PebblePad is used for all learning materials and for submission of student work.

To reduce the risk of students losing touch with the techniques there has to be an appropriate lesson format (Robinson et al, 2007). The content is broken down into lesson-size 'chunks' of 12 sessions per module with formative tasks, plus an introductory section with assessments for download. In addition the course introduction on the PebblePad gateway links to all course documentation, online reading lists, contact details and useful websites.

Woodley advises (2001, cited in Biggs 2003, p 218) that online teaching is 'not about one-way delivery, putting your notes on the web' but about reconfiguring the notes so

> the content (is) interactive (and) also ensures that students are not working in isolation ... interaction is vital to learning and we will need to explore the ways in which the type of interaction that takes place in the classroom can be emulated online.

In this module initially this has been tried through the use of blogs.

Lessons develop in difficulty as students build up knowledge of relevant theories and concepts and start to acquire the necessary research and writing skills. All tasks are structured to ensure students are aware of how long should be spent on each session with guideline times or word lengths. This has proved a valuable way of ensuring students do not waste unnecessary time on the set activities.

Students are able to progress through the course materials at their own pace, with only two assessment deadlines, which appears to support Biggs' view that 'asynchronous (learning) is in principle little different from on-campus teaching using ET (educational technology)' (2003: 224).

A number of potential barriers were recognised before the programme commenced and strategies developed to cope with them. These concerns included:

❑ the risk of students feeling lonely and disengaged when sitting at home working on their course
❑ potential IT-access issues because of location, job role or employer-IT systems
❑ the challenges presented by returning to education and using unfamiliar technologies.

Induction

The course team, along with the employer, decided a face-to-face induction to the systems and materials would enable learners to meet each other, interact with the technology and 'experience' university (Robinson et al, 2007). A two-day induction was planned to introduce students to studying in HE, explain procedures, introduce the content of the Year 5 modules and assessment, ensure students could meet their personal tutors and course staff, and provide training on PebblePad and electronic resources. The induction was made compulsory by the employer and this ensured that all students received training, which helped to overcome a risk discussed by Moron-Garcia where lecturers

> were concerned about the inadequate and voluntary nature of most induction sessions which meant many students missed out and put an increasing burden on (lecturers) to provide this support. (Moron-Garcia, 2006: 20)

This also

> ensured problems caused by registration and passwords were combatted through orientation sessions to ensure all students were issued with passwords, knew how to log on, and could access the VLE. (Moron-Garcia, 2006: 20)

Student support

Each student has a personal tutor. A proactive approach is adopted with tutors emailing their students on a minimum of a monthly basis in order to support retention. This is being closely monitored to evaluate its effectiveness. Phone appointments and face-to-face meetings have also proved invaluable where students have needed step-by-step help.

Outside the university structures, a number of students have got together in the pub or over lunchtime to work through tasks and support each other. As a result, study days have been offered to cover areas of concern and to deliver assessment surgeries. These days were not accessible to all students so the sessions were recorded and distributed on DVD and through YouTube, and linked to the course materials in PebblePad. An on-line student forum has also been set up which relates issues directly to the course leader. These are acted on immediately and included in the report to the project steering group.

Formative tasks

Throughout the modules students are asked to complete tasks. Students are expected to complete these to reinforce their learning, but there is an acknowledgement that some topic content is well known and in these instances students will not necessarily complete all formative questions. Each task has a specified time and structure and some of the formative tasks require students to discuss issues and ideas in a blog.

Retention

Student retention for this course was expected to be a challenge and there have been 17 withdrawals. However, many of these are due to organisational restructuring with the employer. Other issues mentioned in student feedback include a lack of time, lack of access to the internet in overseas locations and insufficient time to achieve individuals' high personal standards. None of the remaining students who provided feedback cited the content or delivery method as a direct factor, but concurrent modules put students under pressure. The effectiveness of student contact is monitored and it is generally the students who fail to reply to tutors who subsequently withdraw from the course. It seems evident that students who have engaged effectively and developed strong relationships with their tutors perform better. There is always a risk of students feeling isolated. The module is very much about independent skills. McConnell advises:

> learning in groups and communities suggests forms of learning that are collaborative in nature, where students share their understanding of what is to be learned, cooperate with each other, provide support, and engage in relevant and meaningful processes that help motivate them and that require higher-level cognitive and emotional skills. (2006: 1)

This needs to be considered in future delivery of the module.

Assessment and achievement

There are two components in the assessment; the first is a reflective webfolio focusing on skills development through the module, the second is an action plan linked to personal development. Achievement for the module is very high, with 37% (15) students attaining a grade A. This is in comparison to an average grade point of B13 in leisure industries subjects. This partly reflects the students' previous experience, their employer's organisational culture and the fact that they are already familiar with the notion of personal development planning.

Student experience

Overall, the students have been very positive about the experience, although they have highlighted a number of minor issues, mainly technical or relating to supporting electronic resources, which could improve it. Where these issues relate to content, they reflect on what could be added and improved to enhance interactivity. Student comments on support from the module team and general subject guidance have all been positive, and many issues and questions can be anticipated in future module provision. For example, students have commented on the time taken to complete some tasks, and one module is already being modified in minor ways to ensure that the pedagogic approach to testing learning outcomes is both work-related and achievable in an appropriate timescale. While the lack of control over engagement with the learning materials is one aspect of further study by the pilot team the opportunities for collaboration between the study group and peer support seem to indicate that most students engage with the materials.

Face-to-face input and interactivity

When the course was written it was always envisaged that its content could be delivered in a variety of ways: as an online course and with various levels of blended learning. A number of students requested and received personal tutorials and a request from other students led to an assessment-surgery study day, which was also used to explain some of the underpinning concepts. This may be in part a reflection on the content of the module, but also the need for students unfamiliar with e-learning and unsure of the level they should aim for in their work to receive initial support and guidance. Interactivity could be developed further, for example through:

> interactions with either the content which might be text, audio visual resources, graphics, podcasts, scenarios, simulations, quizzes; or via asynchronous or synchronous online communication (O'Donoghue, 2006: 72).

The content also requires links to the teaching materials used for the taught versions of the modules, possibly through WOLF. These were avoided initially to simplify the system for the students. This would link both iterations of the module more cohesively and offer a wider range of resources to all students. As Taylor & Maor and O'Connor suggest:

> Interactivity is thought to enhance learning because feedback and reflections effectively help the construction of meaning and give structure to knowledge and information. (cited in O'Donoghue, 2006: 72)

Development of interactive FAQs and generic learning support webfolios and assessment guidance, with clearer links to the skills pages of the UoW website will help in this respect.

Evaluation

Teaching employability skills to first-year students in the classroom as opposed to via the on-line version provides an enjoyable, supported student-centred learning environment. The difference is that the taught version has the added benefit of tutor delivery allowing material to be explained and experienced through group seminar activities with tutor-facilitated feedback.

The online version of the module offers opportunities to inform ideas and best practice for the delivery of the taught module, for example the development of a fully eportfolio hosted assessment, which is more straightforward than the current approach, and will ensure students become familiar with the idea of building reflective portfolios and action plans for PDP.

A significant difference between the programmes is that the distance-learning model requires much more formal input, including regular communication, tutor led support, and intensive training in the use of eportfolio at the start of the course. Access to library facilities, opportunities to see lecturers and access training is much more limited and therefore requires a clear formal structure which is to some extent mitigated by the provision of ebooks.

In summary, the use of eportfolio in both these cases aids the student to achieve deeper learning through reflection on practice and the application of theory in the workplace. This helps to consolidate the learning that takes place and has proved a most useful tool in the delivery of modules both in the classroom and online.

References

Biggs, J. (2003) *Teaching for Quality Learning at University*. (2nd ed) Maidenhead, McGraw Hill/The Open University

Brown, S. & Race, P. (2002) *Lecturing a Practical Guide*. London, Kogan Page

Gomez, S. (2002) Electronic Portfolios in Higher Education. *Chronicle of Higher Education* 21/02/2002 Washington DC

Honey, P. & Mumford (1992) *The Manual of Learning Styles*. Maidenhead, McGraw Hill.

Knowles, M. S., Holton, E. F. & Swanson, R. A. (2005) *The Adult Learner*. (6th ed) San Diego, Elsevier

Lewis, R. & Whitlock, Q. (2003) *How to plan and manage an e-learning programme*. Aldershot, Gower

McConnell, D. (2006) *E-Learning Groups and Communities*. Maidenhead, Open University Press.

Moron-Garcia, S. (2006) What Lecturers Say Helps and Hinders Their Use of a Virtual Learning Environment to Support Face-to-Face Teaching. In O'Donoghue, J. (ed) (2006) *Technology Supported Learning and Teaching: A Staff Perspective*. Hershey PA: Information Science Publishing

Moon, J. (2004) *A Handbook of Reflective and Experiential Learning. Theory and Practice*. London, RoutledgeFalmer

O'Donoghue, J. (Ed). (2006). *Technology Supported Learning and Teaching: A Staff Perspective*. Hershey PA, Information Science Publishing

Robinson, P., Wale, D. and Wiscombe, C. (2007) An innovative delivery of Foundation Degrees: but not without its problems! In Shaping the Future of Tourism Education, 5–7th December 2007, The Subject Association for Tourism in the UK, St Anne's College Oxford

PETER ROBINSON is a senior lecturer at the University of Wolverhampton and course leader for the Foundation Degree in Travel Operations Management, Work-based Learning, CPD and Entertainment Industries Management. He has previous experience in the public, private and voluntary sectors which includes working in senior management teams in a range of roles that have included tourism development officer, visitor services manager and tourism projects manager and independent tourism consultant. Peter's research interest lies in the field of community led tourism development and sociology of tourism marketing.

CRISPIN DALE is the course leader for the BA (Hons) Tourism Management at the University of Wolverhampton, a principal lecturer who has taught strategic management for tourism at undergraduate and postgraduate level for a number of years. His research has focused on the competitive environment of travel businesses in the tour operating industry and the strategic networks of travel eMediaries. He has also researched the impact of contemporary strategic management issues on small tourism enterprises in the expanding EU.

DEBRA WALE's research area is pedagogy and her interest is in student-centred course design and teaching and learning. She moved into academia five years ago and has complemented her industry experience by developing and writing Foundation Degree courses and associated materials. She is a senior lecturer who specialises in marketing in the department of Leisure Industries Management at the University of Wolverhampton and also an experienced marketing professional who has been involved in local and national marketing projects in the public, private and voluntary sectors in the leisure and lifestyles industry. She was a brand manager in the Whitbread Group. She is also a Fellow of the Higher Education Academy.

10

From paper to eportfolio
Evolution of PDP support in a Psychology Department

Mark Moss
Northumbria University

This chapter reflects on the experiences of a small team of academics who became interested in PDP in the early 1990s. How they approached the area and introduced it formally into academic programmes is described and considered.

The Division of Psychology at Northumbria University has seen an increase in student numbers from 150 to 600 undergraduates, and zero to 60 postgraduates, in under ten years. A key challenge facing a department experiencing such growth is the successful facilitation of Personal Development Planning (PDP). Where once extensive tutorials might have been used to examine the issues and develop strategies for future development, the workloads associated with such large cohorts now prohibit this. Consequently, we have investigated new ways of delivering reflective skills development to both engage the students and be of transparent value. One avenue has been through the incorporation of appropriate activities in teaching sessions. Of equal, or possibly greater, importance has been the development and delivery of support materials that provide an active record of individuals' reflection on their learning, performance and achievement. Such a record is not only evidence of engagement in PDP activity, but also a source of reference after graduation and in at least some instances a guide to continuing professional development activities in the world of work. The division has actively developed PDP support documentation, from tutorial attendance records to on-line portfolios. This chapter considers the successes and failures that have been experienced through this developmental process.

In 1997 the Dearing Report placed PDP firmly on the agenda for all HE establishments. The QAA defines PDP as

> a structured and supported process undertaken by an individual to reflect upon their own learning, performance and/or achievement and to plan for their personal, educational and career development (QAA, 2001: 9).

This chapter highlights how, even in a department with previous experience and staff interest in the area of PDP, good practice and profitable outcome are not achieved simply as a result of government's direction to 'make it so'.

The majority of practising academics involved with PDP implementation in higher education would, I suspect, be of the opinion that it is like educating children through video games – a laudable but nearly impossible goal to achieve. From the naïve position of the principled observer, PDP is without question an essential aspect of higher education. Indeed there are those who might consider it more important than academic achievement per se. That the processes underpinning the above definition occur implicitly in nearly all students is, I believe, without question. Students enter university resembling 'rabbits caught in headlights' and leave as confident, thoughtful and evaluative individuals – clearly the result of personal development and maturation as much as of academic accomplishment. It is therefore difficult to understand why demonstrating that engagement with PDP exists, for example through files, records and minuted student contributions, is hard to do – at least initially.

Once you scratch the surface and become involved in the development and delivery of PDP recording tools it soon becomes apparent that student and staff attitudes are often in greater need of modification than the tools. The attainment of this attitudinal change and concomitant embracing of PDP practices is a challenge to everyone involved in the assessment driven environment that is higher education in the UK today. 'Evolution' is seen here as an appropriate term in development of PDP processes as there has been a delicate balance between 'extinction' and the 'survival of the fittest' with regard to documentation, practices and engagement.

Over a period of years staff in the School of Psychology and Sport Sciences at Northumbria University have developed a range of practices and materials designed to engage students in PDP throughout their academic career. In my role as Director of Student Affairs for the school I was charged with managing this development, and the application of practice to undergraduate programmes in both the Divisions of Psychology and Sport Sciences, including a Psychology with Sport Science major-minor that spans the two divisions. The journey took us from personal tutorials through paper trails to remote electronic repositories, and is still ongoing. Interestingly, the changes in attitude and expectation among the student body have meant that we are always in an active phase of development, rather than arriving at some ill-defined goal. This ever-changing system seems appropriate as well, as it is arguable that to settle on a means of achieving reflective self evaluation denies the simple truth that underpins the ability of the individual and population to change, and develop new needs and means of appreciating achievements.

Objectives

Our primary aim is to share the experiences of a small School at Northumbria University committed to the development of PDP which is at the same time experiencing a phase of rapid growth in terms of student numbers.

Context

Higher education has always placed considerable value on the opportunity for students to reflect on their learning, achievement, needs and plans for the future. However, these activities often played key roles in academic tutorial sessions rather than being explicitly part of the academic programme. I found the following in a rather aged document from another institution that shall remain nameless:

> The tutorial system underpins both pastoral and academic support ensuring that each student is treated as an individual, encouraged and supported as appropriate. Every member of staff has around ten tutees spread over undergraduate and postgraduate courses. Tutorials are held once a fortnight to discuss progress.

Higher education has seen considerable change since then. Increases in student numbers, the widening participation agenda and the modularisation of degree programmes led to a situation where students and tutors alike became unsure of the role of the personal tutor and the value of the tutorial. Such uncertainty and its impact on practice did not go unnoticed. By the early 1990s the Higher Education Quality Committee (HEQC) were regularly making audit recommendations that a university should consider reviewing the arrangements for the monitoring of the progress of undergraduates. The real motivation for a full scale development of PDP grew out of recommendation 20 of the Dearing Report (NCIHE, 1997) which specifically directed higher education institutions to develop the 'means by which students can monitor, build and reflect upon their personal development'.

Description and evaluation

In the mid 1990s the School of Psychology and Sport Sciences was still employing a personal tutoring system to monitor students' progress and provide pastoral and academic support. All students were assigned a guidance tutor with whom they had regular timetabled discussions covering their progress, concerns and aspirations. Exam results were distributed through these tutorials and this was designed to ensure student attendance – a strategy that was largely successful. The divisional student files provided the reference material and a record of tutorial activity. Over the three years of the undergraduate degree strong or at least functional relationships were built between tutors and tutees. These relationships also produced by default a level of PDP activity, as students reflected on their progress in tutorial discussions. However, the system was stretched to its reasonable limits as student numbers started to increase. Staff reported finding it difficult to remember the names of their tutees, and a number expressed the opinion that with increasing numbers the tutorial system was becoming too time-consuming. Perhaps more worryingly, students were failing to attend early tutorial sessions and many were beginning to question the value of discussions that were not directly linked to assessment.

We soon realised that this was not just something that we had 'let slip' so to speak. The change in engagement was as a consequence of the combination of a number of different influences, and we needed to develop our practices or lose something (i.e. PDP) that we felt was of fundamental importance. Our first attempt was perhaps rather predictable and consisted simply of a paper-based personal history and future aspirations record form. Students were asked to complete this form and bring it to their first tutorial to guide discussions and to encourage appropriate engagement from both staff and students. It was subsequently to be placed in the student's file for future reference during tutorial meetings. It soon became apparent that this would not 'kick start' the process. Students mislaid the documents or did not fill them in. Staff reported that they found that when used these 'crib sheets' truncated the discussion rather than stimulating it.

The first serious attempt at addressing what was becoming a well recognised problem was the production of student 'progress files'. These were produced and distributed to all new first year psychology students during Freshers' week. Our first iteration consisted of a series of 'inserts' or loose-leaf pages. As well as the (largely unchanged) personal history and aspirations sheet, students were encouraged to employ a range of forms as records of work and reflections on progress for each of the modules they studied. The consideration that students should have different folders for each module was not unreasonable, although the idea that a neatly appended file would offer them the opportunity to maintain their awareness of 'the state of the world' with regard to their learning and development was at best optimistic. After the first year of use, it was obvious that we had not hit on the simple solution we were hoping for. The personal history sheets were largely used in tutorials and interestingly received fewer negative comments than in the previous year. The module record forms were almost entirely ignored or lost. Even in instances where they had been completed by students they were not brought to any tutorials, but formed more of a personal log – which although not in itself undesirable, did not achieve what was intended.

The construction and content of these progress files soon became the subject of considerable debate. Staff–student liaison meetings discussed their worth and purpose. The subject of PDP became a standing agenda item, and therefore it is arguable that this rather ill-conceived effort made a significant contribution in its own right. Staff and students became aware of PDP and were willing to contribute ideas (and more frequently criticisms) regarding our approach and changes over time. An important consequence of this was that the subject never stagnated and we consistently attempted to move forward.

One strongly mooted suggestion was that we should make the progress file more obviously a 'file' as opposed to a collection of paper. To some extent this went somewhat against the grain of those interested in PDP. We had argued that PDP was a 'process' and not a 'thing' – and that the deliberate creation of an isolated file would lead students to approach it in either an instrumental way, i.e. 'done that' or not at all. The promotion of reflection and the importance of discussion were always going to be difficult to communicate through such a means. However, students had used progress of achievement records at school and were familiar with them, and staff felt that a well-produced file would facilitate student engagement. I got the impression that the less student-focused academics thought that it would remove the necessity for staff input, although this had never been the intention. In any event the ring-bound A4 folder complete with coloured sections and corporate logos was delivered, distributed and largely ignored.

Around this time it was felt that the practice of distributing exam marks via tutorials should be abandoned. A small number of staff were finding themselves called on to distribute marks to an ever-increasing number of students as more of our colleagues found themselves to be unavailable at these key times. Rather than abandon the process entirely, we decided on a mixed economy with students able to access their results either through their tutor or from the divisional office. The result was disappointing if not altogether surprising. With very few exceptions (a minority of third year students in the main) students used the divisional office. A number of my colleagues and I found this a disturbing development. Even those of us who wished to spend time discussing performance, successes and problems with students were unable to do so. PDP entered a rather protracted and silent era in the division – a situation that required an external driver to interrupt it.

The employability agenda reinforced the importance of PDP in Higher Education. For too long employment prospects of graduates had been based on the free education basis that graduates should satisfy 'the need for graduates to make an effective contribution to the labour market' (Committee on Higher Education, 1963). In today's climate, potential students look on employability as the opportunity to get a return on their investment. Although closely linked in the 1997 *Dearing Report*, the relationship between PDP and employability took longer to crystallise at the chalk face. This has been perhaps in no small part a result of the difficulty in succinctly defining them to the satisfaction of all. In addition to the definition of PDP given above, employability has been defined by the Enhancing Student Employability Co-ordination Team (ESECT) as

> a set of achievements – skills, understandings and personal attributes – that make graduates more likely to gain employment and be successful in their chosen occupations, which benefits themselves, the workforce, the community and the economy' (Yorke and Knight, 2006: 3).

The commonalities of these definitions are clear, and the successful delivery of PDP can without question feed employability. It was the appreciation of this link that allowed for a new impetus in the support of PDP in our programmes to be achieved.

In an attempt to move away from the folder-based PDP file, my colleagues embarked on the development of virtual forms and internet communication to reinvigorate our practices. Students were introduced to the online forms in IT workshops in freshers' week. During these sessions students were asked to complete a brief history and aspirations form. These were made available for academic tutors to consult during the initial tutorials at the end of the week. This system was certainly beneficial for those who took it on. Tutors were able to familiarise themselves with aspects of their tutees' lives prior to the meetings, facilitating discussion and increasing the sense of welcome. In addition, these records were permanently on a password-protected site, and so could be used for re-acquaintance if required. In addition to these introductory forms, the progress file forms were re-worked and added to the site for students to complete online, and this provided access for their tutors. This development in the opportunities for students to reflect on their learning and experiences was still closely linked to tutorial-based discussions and the opportunity for academic input. Although we experienced a significant increase in student engagement with the process as a result of these changes, we were made aware of the limitations in terms of student-owned records, with final-year students reporting that collation of the forms had proved difficult – requiring printing and hard copy storage.

At the time of our flirtations with web-based PDP materials, the university was embarking on its love affair with Blackboard. Such e-learning platforms are now the norm in HE and provide secure intranet environments for the storage and distribution of teaching and assessment materials. In addition, students have access to secure content areas that they can use for a range of purposes, although they are not designed as general file space for work in progress. These areas are ideal for the development of eportfolios, and it was to this we turned our attention next. A small amount of work revealed that such portfolios were easy for students to create, flexible, serially editable, and could be made available for a guidance tutor to view and comment on electronically. A final bonus was the observation that these eportfolios provided the opportunity for a permanent record of experiences, learning, achievement and reflections on university life, as students could 'zip' them and take them away to open later (as read-only) on any web browser.

Since being introduced to eportfolios in Blackboard and having decided, for the time being at least, that they provide an excellent support platform for PDP, we have attempted to address the perennial problem of engagement that dogs PDP. It has always fascinated me that the formalisation of structures and processes to support PDP has in general been met by resistance from both students and staff alike. Even when discussion with either group reveals that they see the value, indeed the necessity, of robust opportunities for personal development alongside the academic programme, they are still surprisingly recalcitrant when it comes to engaging in recorded activities. One suggestion that I have consistently resisted is that PDP engagement can be assured if it is formally assessed. I have always believed that students will be restricted in their honesty, and in their appreciation of the value of a process, if their preconceptions lead them to believe that it has a 'right' answer hidden somewhere in it. Having said that, the programme teaching timetable and activities do provide a tremendous framework for the inclusion of PDP by stealth.

Our current practice has been developed over the last four years and has been instrumental in the redevelopment of the first year of our undergraduate provision. We deliver planned initiation of PDP activities and support through module activities. Freshers' week has been slimmed down in terms of timetabled sessions, and induction has been stretched into the teaching semester. So, we are now quickly able to introduce freshers to PDP as a process 'that you will hear more of', and portfolios as an aspect of Blackboard 'that you will become more familiar with'. Meetings with guidance tutors are based around a quiz and social event. This is in contrast to our initial practice of delivering fairly intensive sessions during induction that required document completion and eportfolio production followed by discussion of these with guidance tutors, – a process that we found led staff and students to turn off when PDP was raised later in the year.

During the first teaching week, a one hour workshop session in an IT lab has been developed to allow all students to create their first outline eportfolio and place therein a template CV. This is made available to guidance tutors through Blackboard, and students request confirmation that their guidance tutors have access to it. In subsequent weeks the programme enables staff to suggest, request or require students to add examples of academic work, and more importantly reflections on their experiences and development in the first semester. It has to be acknowledged that academic staff were resistant to these activities before changes were made to the module delivery pattern to facilitate them. By the end of the first teaching semester, students have been provided with the opportunity in formal teaching sessions to add eight examples of academic work and/or reflective commentaries. This has been designed to normalise use of the eportfolio platform and to encourage spontaneous use in later stages of the programme.

Semester 2 begins with a guidance tutorial – or not, as has been our experience. Despite our best efforts to ensure that students attend tutorials at this time we have not had a marked degree of success. However, the portfolio system has allowed for the remote tutorial to be trialled. Although still in need of development, such remote tutorials consist of academics adding comments to the portfolio regarding the student's overall Semester 1 performance and highlighting any areas of concern. The students then respond to this in an overall reflection on the semester. This reflection is again ensured in a timetabled laboratory session. A new development in Semester 2 attempts to strengthen the link between PDP and employability. A module relating to careers in the psychology professions with guest lectures from experienced professionals and associated workshop activities for students to engage with has been constructed. The importance of reflection and self-appraisal in securing appointments and career development are key areas for investigation, and students are encouraged to add work that they have prepared for these sessions to their portfolio. A thread of generic, academic and specialist skills training runs through the entire first year of our programmes. This has now been incorporated into other academic modules for the first time. This change has been made in order to enhance students' appreciation of the relevance of the area in terms of their wider academic achievement and future prospects. It also allows for greater opportunities to return to the portfolio and maintain its currency.

The key aim of the activities in the first year of the undergraduate programmes is to initiate engagement with PDP that will then be continued through the later years by default. To support this we have developed a second year core strand of practical classes from all core areas of the discipline. This provides students with the directed opportunity to further develop their portfolios and maintain their involvement in remote tutorials. The final year currently sees a distinct change in student attitudes to, and participation in, PDP activities. This is not, we have observed, an intentional reappraisal of PDP by the students and staff. It is more a consequence of students developing close working relationships with their honours project supervisors. Students are entitled to half-hourly tutorials each week to support their project work and these often develop as the year progresses into evaluative discussions about the programme, student experiences and career choices. As project tutors are frequently not the same as guidance tutors, students often feel that by the time they complete their studies their project tutor knows more about the graduating student than does their guidance tutor. This is something that we have acknowledged and used to strengthen the PDP process by encouraging debate beyond the project itself in the timetabled tutorials. One caveat however, is that students report overall that some project tutors are more supportive than others and this mirrors strongly the engagement of staff with PDP and the tutorial system generally.

Conclusions

A number of years of experience have informed us that successful support and encouragement for PDP is at best difficult, and at worst apparently contrary to the wishes of both students and staff alike. Although it seems unlikely that a good alternative to in-depth appraisal discussions between academics and students will ever be realised, the endeavour to develop best practice in the prevailing climate is important. We are still learning and developing and doubtless some of our current practices will become extinct like others before them, but if we are able to continue to learn from our mistakes and our successes then we should continue to serve our customers to their best advantage.

Discussion

The major problems that we have identified with regard to PDP activity in the School of Psychology and Sport Sciences at Northumbria are essentially two-fold:
1   Positive engagement from staff
2   Positive engagement from students.

Both of these ultimately depend on two underlying factors:

1   Clearly identified value of the activity
2   Staff workload.

It is a challenge to demonstrate to students the value of an activity which does not seem to impact directly on grades or degree classification. This challenge can be most successfully addressed through the maintenance of strong links with graduates, which we consider most important. If former students are willing and able to return to university to address the current student body the impact can be considerable. Wherever possible we draw on past graduates of our programmes to deliver sessions on careers. These talks provide easily defined links between where students 'are now' and where they may 'go'. We encourage speakers to discuss the concept of graduation as a step rather than an end point, and to relate the importance of reflection and other metacognitive skills in career development. Such direct external input is highly valued by students and may leave us better able to promote PDP activities in our programmes.

Low motivation for staff involvement with PDP is often associated with workload concerns. It has long been my opinion that the issue is being looked at from the wrong perspective. PDP is seen as an 'add on' to the current workload and as such unsustainable. I would argue that PDP should be seen as the primary activity that should occupy us as academic tutors. The motivated reflective learner is far more likely to be drawn into the self-directed study that we all agree is the key to academic success. Through positive engagement with PDP activities, especially early in the student's academic life, we can reduce the burden of later requirements for increased support in terms of handouts, and requests for such unlikely aids as 'model answers'. Ultimately we will be providing a reduction in lower-level academic staff activity and administration while at the same time affording students the framework to deliver greater success for themselves as our graduates.

Finally, one aspect that informs PDP and the academic-student interaction that I have not covered here is feedback on assessment, both formative and summative. This is another hot topic: departments are faced with increasing numbers of students who ask for increasing degrees of feedback. Recent developments in software systems for online marking and feedback do not improve my opinion of the usefulness and purpose of feedback. In the years ahead I feel that academics, higher education institutions and industry need to consider further the 'product' that universities should deliver. Once this has been agreed, the metrics that gauge the product might be validated. To date, my discussions with employers have indicated that the characteristics they value most are those that reflect successful PDP. It might be the case that programmes of the future will need to re-establish the individual as the main focus for academic attention, rather than keeping to the consistently assessment driven agenda of today.

References and URLs

Committee on Higher Education (1963) *Higher Education: Report of the Committee of Lord Robbins*, 1961–63. London, HMSO

NCIHE (1997) *National Committee of Inquiry into Higher Education – Report of the National Committee.* (Dearing) Viewed at: http://www.leeds.ac.uk/educol/ncihe/

The Higher Education Academy. http://www.heacademy.ac.uk/home.html

QAA (2001) *Guidelines for HE Progress Files.* Gloucester, QAA

Yorke, M and Knight, P (2006) Embedding Employability into the Curriculum. *Learning and Employability Series One.* York: Higher Education Academy

MARK MOSS was born in Grimsby and following an education in Applied Chemistry spent ten years in manufacturing industry management before returning to university to study psychology. He gained a first class honours degree in 1995 and a PhD in 1999. He subsequently joined the full time academic staff at Northumbria where he later became Director of Student Affairs in the School of Psychology and Sport Sciences with direct responsibility for PDP activity. More recently he has taken on the role of head of the division of psychology.

11

PDP – inspiring capability

Sarah Nixon & Caitlin Walker
Liverpool John Moores University & Training Attention Ltd

We believe that the process through which we engage students
in PDP should itself be an example of the attitude and behaviours
we want them to develop! This case study demonstrates the
approaches that have been taken to enable this to happen.

Our starting point for the process of engaging students in PDP is noticing where you are and how you come to be here. We believe staff should lead the way, engaging in self-reflection, honing observation and feedback skills and deliberately creating the conditions they need to work and learn at their best. We aim to embed this philosophy in the whole curriculum until it becomes 'the way we do things round here'.

We begin with the context for our project and what we wanted to happen. Then we outline some of the philosophy underpinning our approach and introduce key features including the notion of autogenic metaphors for learning, clean (metaphor-free) questions, clean set-up and clean feedback. We continue with how we went about engaging staff and students, some challenges, learning and the impact so far, and then end with a summary of how we will do things differently this year, knowing what we know now.

Background and context for PDP development

Professional Development Planning (PDP) has been an area of interest in the Sport Development (SD) programme at Liverpool John Moores University since the course started in 1999. There is an annual Level 4 intake of 90 students and average student retention of 96%. The university requirements are for just two PDP tutorials per year, but SD views PDP as central to student development and far exceeds this recommendation.

At Level 4, Sport Development PDP is part of a year-long module. The teaching is structured around whole group lectures one week, and then small group sessions with personal tutors in the alternate weeks. Each member of staff has around nine tutees and by sharing their goals, setbacks and successes we believe that students learn more and can become more supportive of each other. They complete an assessed reflective essay on their personal goals, their learning styles and their aspirations, plus four 5-minute verbal presentations during the year on different areas of their development.

Through working with external facilitators we have formed, challenged and re-formed our thinking and our process, borrowing tools and techniques from neuro-linguistic programming, symbolic and systemic modelling. The wider university is presently taking an employability approach to its curriculum design encouraging students to develop themselves as employable graduates. The PDP process we have developed strongly supports these aims.

What did we want to happen?

Aim 1   Inspire capability in our students by building from 'where they are' and incorporating 'who they have been' into their learning

We know that our students come from a broad variety of backgrounds and many are the first in their families to attend university. We want our PDP to help them to notice the skills, decision-making strategies, learning styles and motivation they already possess. Once they know more about what they can already do, and how they do it, we want them to use these skills to adapt and grow in their life long education.

Aim 2   Students can make cross-module connections

We want our students to be able to make cross-module connections and to integrate these into their learning. To support this, we want lecturers to make cross-module connections and to have a clear model for how the whole course fits together. Lecturers often have limited understanding of one another's modules and the students are asked to make links that aren't modelled by those teaching them.

Aim 3   Build links to the world of work

As well as connecting with their past experiences and making connections across modules, we want our students to be linking what they are learning with the careers they want to develop for themselves. By enabling them to articulate their skills and experience, students improve their employability skills.

Aim 4   Develop a balance between agency and structure

Our aim is to enable staff and students to be able to maintain a sense of self and to relate effectively to external structures. We want our students to respond to their time at university as though they are the agent of their lives and not simply at the mercy of the structure in which they find themselves. At the same time we want them to develop an accurate awareness of others around them and to work collaboratively with staff and the wider university.

This balance between agency and structure, or agency and communion as Wilbur (2000) calls it, exists whether we like it or not. When students come up against difficulties – in lectures, with tutors, with peers, at work or at home – we want them to be able to affect this positively. This could be done either because they have the capacity to alter their own behaviour or learning styles in order to get more from the situation, or by receiving high quality feedback can affect the way they are being taught, managed or interacted with.

We want to create a whole-system change in the department, so that this balance, and the attitudes that come with it, are welcomed and demonstrated by staff in lectures, in meetings, staff appraisals, student assessment and feedback. We want the processes of becoming more self-aware, articulate, observant and flexible to become 'the way we do things around here.'

Key features of the approaches
Eliciting auto-genic metaphors
Following the work of Grove and Panzer (1989), Lakoff and Johnson (1980) and more recently, Lawley and Tompkins (2000) on auto-genic metaphors, we are interested in the idiosyncratic unconscious models that govern how we go about learning. Our PDP aims to bring these to conscious awareness so that students can employ the useful ones, update outdated ones and increase their capacity to learn things outside their current perception.

If a student, when learning at their best, resembles a 'magpie, liking to gather everything and take it back to my nest, sift through it and throw out the tat', this can inform both the student and their tutor how they may go about learning. If they are like a 'snail, slow and steady, but leave a glistening trail that shows exactly where I've come from', they will be a very different student from the first one, with different needs and who will have different results. However with self-awareness and a flexible tutor both students can excel on the same course.

Clean questions
The art of asking non-leading questions in order to facilitate students and staff to reflect on their own idiosyncratic thinking and internal metaphors is called 'clean questioning'. It was vital to our project that students and staff became aware of their own metaphors rather than fitting themselves into those of the facilitators. To do this we employed the clean questions, developed by Grove and published in *Metaphors in Mind* by Lawley and Tompkins (2000).

For example, students could explore the snail metaphor. When that snail leaves a glistening trail, what happens next? Or the magpie: when do you throw out the tat, what happens just before you throw out the tat? What kind of tat is it? After you throw out the tat, what happens next?

Agency and structure – the clean set-up
As people articulate their outcomes, identify individual responsibility for their state and ask for the support they need, there is an opportunity for the group to collaborate to ensure that the event is as useful for each individual as possible. These three questions, designed by Training Attention Ltd, can be asked at the start of any interaction, meeting, lecture, or project. The exact words can be changed to suit the context.

1　For this lecture to be really useful for you it will be like what?
2　For it to be like that, and you to be learning well, you'll need to be like what?

3   What support do you need to be like 2 and achieve 1?

The questions are designed to be answered and shared in small groups of up to 15.

Clean feedback

Following the notion that everyone learns and thinks differently, it is important that students and staff remember that the feedback people give is often in relation to their own needs rather than the needs of the recipient. To capture this we use a 'clean' feedback model (Table 1) to separate out what has been observed and the effect it has had (Walker & Doyle, 2005).

Table 1   Giving and receiving clean feedback – an example from a lecturer to a
          student following a presentation

Something you did which worked well for me was…(something you saw or heard)
Setting the activities clearly out on the board
I interpret this as meaning …
That you're well organised and committed to your work
Something you did which didn't work so well for me was…(something you saw or heard)
You were writing on the flip chart and talking with your back to the group
I interpret this as meaning …
You weren't aware of the group's need to hear you
Something that would have worked better for me is… (what you would have preferred to
have seen or heard)
Asking someone else to write for you or writing and then turning around to make a point
I'd interpret this as meaning …
The stuff you were saying was relevant to us and you were making sure we could hear you.

How did we go about bringing the PDP to the whole system?

Aim 1   Inspire capability in our students by building from 'where they are' and
          incorporating 'who they've been' into their learning

In order to build a congruent PDP process that works from where students are, we needed to develop the themes for the PDP from in the current student body and their learning needs. Rather than us deciding on what was important to students, we interviewed four groups of Level 3, 4 and 5 students to find out what had enabled them to get the most out of their time at university so far, what they had been attending to and what they wished they'd attended to. We used non-leading 'clean' questions in order to minimally influence their answers.

We were surprised by the topics raised by the first group of students and even more surprised when these were confirmed with later groups. The interviews were analysed and eight key themes were identified as shown in Table 2. From these themes we designed a series of self-reflexive exercises with no wrong or right answers; students investigate their metaphors for learning, their sources of inspiration etc; they compare and contrast them with peers and with interviewees shown on a DVD and then they decide how to use this information to increase the effectiveness of their learning during their forthcoming degree.

Table 2   PDP themes and resulting exercises

Theme	Focus group interest	Exercises
When you're learning at your best, what are you like?	They wished they'd known more about their learning styles earlier and how to help themselves learn better	Eliciting and developing a metaphor model for learning at your best, exploring the environment/behaviours/beliefs/values you have around learning and your identity as a student
Time	They wanted to learn about organising and managing time better	Exploring individual maps of time, how you place the past and future in space and how you plan
Inspiration and motivation	They felt that knowing what inspired and motivated them and their lecturers was important	What and who inspires or motivates you to do your best? How can you deliberately motivate yourself?
Setting and achieving goals	They wanted or had benefited from setting realistic goals and being supported to achieve them	Using the information so far, setting a goal you're motivated to achieve in a timeframe that makes sense to you
Overcoming set-backs and challenges	Identifying set-backs and how to overcome them so that unexpected problems didn't disrupt their time at university	Reflecting on times you've over-come set-backs, listening to one another's stories and devising plans to over-come any unforeseen obstacles that may arise
Making key decisions	They wished they'd thought more before making key decisions. They wanted to think about past decisions and to make better ones in the future	Thinking about how you've made key decisions so far, modelling when you've made them well. Adjusting your own strategies, borrowing other peoples or deliberately creating the conditions to make good decisions
Paying attention to the right things	Many 2nd and 3rd years wished they'd attended to different aspects of University life. They'd have liked some guidance with this; noticing where their attention was and where it needed to be to get them their goals	Exploring what you pay attention to and how to attend to the things that will get you what you want
What can they do now that they didn't think they could do	Third years thought it would have been useful to reflect on things they'd learnt in the past so they didn't become overwhelmed by the learning they were about to do	Reflecting on things you used to think you wouldn't be able to do but now do easily, exploring the conditions that allowed this change to take place and then thinking about what you may be able to achieve in the future

Students reported that after the information was delivered to them, they were thinking about:

- ❑ goal setting and aiming high
- ❑ self-belief
- ❑ realisations of how they learn in different ways
- ❑ how to learn in lectures
- ❑ ways to learn in small groups.

However, getting the students to see the relevance of the PDP in a system that predominantly values assessments and gaining marks was still a challenge; to some it seemed a waste of time and effort. We needed to increase staff understanding of the PDP themes and their links to the subject and the field so that they could respond positively to students' concerns and questions as they arise.

Aim 2   Students can make cross-module connections

As part of staff development, the staff team were asked about their mental model for the degree programme as a whole and how their modules related to it. By getting individual staff members to ask one another questions about how they view their subject and how it interrelates to other subjects they created a network of intellectual connections which in turn we wanted the students to emulate.

We changed the way students start university by having a five-week induction during which they were introduced to the degree as a whole, had mini-lectures by all staff members and were introduced to the PDP themes. They then came into contact with each of their subject modules in a relatively short space of time and were encouraged to observe how the modules fitted together and supported one another.

One member of staff stated that

> they have an understanding of the topic themes and how they relate to one another and they're trying to link things together better than they have done in the past.

Another commented that

> it was fascinating to see how we all viewed the programme and how different we all are. It really made me think about the messages we must be giving out to the students.

One of the challenges faced by the team was accepting how differently others viewed the subject or the modules and this caused some disharmony for a time. For the future it is thought that the core PDP themes can be more strongly embedded into other modules across the level, for example 'goal setting' and 'inspiration' could be incorporated into coaching and leadership modules, 'modelling time' and 'overcoming set-backs' could be included in business modules. This helps to make connections between the PDP and subject modules as well as using PDP themes to link subject modules.

Aim 3   Build links to the world of work

Who or what they already know often limits students when it comes to planning their careers. We wanted the students to hear the stories of people who they and we considered to be successful in their field of interest, people they might not get to talk to ordinarily. We asked students during the initial interviews that led to the PDP theme development, to identify those they would consider to be role models or who they'd be interested in hearing about. We interviewed a number of these individuals, asked them to reflect on the themes identified in Table 2 and incorporated this information into a DVD called *Success Journeys*. The DVD contains a set of exercises that allows viewers to self-reflect on the same themes. Students can compare their answers to those of their peers in the seminar sessions or the 'successes'. This DVD has become an integral part of the PDP process.

The DVD stimulated a great deal of discussion in the seminars and offered opportunities for the students to develop different patterns of thinking. One second year student commented:

> I hated the PDP stuff, but after being on work-based learning, I now realise it was one of the most valuable things we have done.

The DVD served to reduce dependence on the tutors running the small group PDP sessions. Some students didn't engage with the DVD as a resource; they wanted different exemplars or could see little point in the use of this type of information and linked it only to the one module. This resource will be linked to the other modules and the wider world of work next year.

Aim 4   Develop a balance between agency and structure

To encourage students to create the conditions they need to learn well, we asked them to think about learning at their best, how they differed from other students and what they needed in order to learn well. Because they did this in a small group we encouraged them to notice that staff can't satisfy all students at all times and to decide what they can do personally to stay in a good state for learning.

We ran a similar process with a small number of the staff team via a peer-coaching project. They explored what they needed in order to learn and teach well. We legitimised the idea that there is great diversity in learning and teaching and that for optimal learning to take place both students and lecturers can do some adjusting of their behaviours. We introduced the 'clean set-up' to staff meetings in order to encourage staff to articulate their own needs and to be more adept at accommodating those of others. We aimed overall to tie the DVD material, staff and student PDP experiences together.

Some staff reported that students are using them more effectively this year by asking them for the help they need.

> Last year, I didn't get my personal tutor group and others booking tutorials, this time there's been more students planning tutorial support (staff feedback).

In relation to the team

> We've got to know much more about one another, that's been really interesting. (staff feedback)

However some staff seemed to be unhappy about the increase in demands made on them by students. On reflection we have tried to introduce a number of complex changes at the same time as asking staff to deliver the PDP to students. Instead we would like to introduce the simple processes and embed them first in the staff team, allowing the staff to develop their observation skills and self-awareness before they take the process to the students.

What we will do differently as a result of what we have learned

❑ A number of staff development sessions are now organised to allow the staff time to digest and work with the processes themselves and with each other before the next run through with the students.

❑ We will arrange for staff to get observation and feedback as they deliver the PDP modules so that they can share good ideas and ask for any support they need. We can then compare approaches with feedback we collect from students.

❑ For the students, we will design a developmental activity such as a presentation or mini-essay in relation to the themes to be fed back to the tutor. This way their skills and understanding can be assessed.

❑ We will work with tutors to embed the themes in their modules so that they are also embedded in the curriculum.

❑ We will design posters displaying relevant processes for the walls of meeting rooms and lecture halls, so bringing them to everyone's attention.

❑ We are still in the process of testing, forming and reforming our PDP. At the moment we have qualitative, anecdotal evidence only. We are embarking on a formal longitudinal study tracking the progress of students through their 3 year journey beginning in July 2008.

References

Grove, D. J. and Panzer, B. I. (1989) *Resolving Traumatic Memories*. Irvington Press

Lakoff, G. and Johnson, M. (1980) *Metaphors we live by*. (2003 ed) London, University of Chicago Press

Lawley, J. and Tompkins, P. (2000) *Metaphors in Mind*. The Developing Company Press

Walker, C. and Doyle, N. (2005). Clean Feedback Model. www.trainingattention.co.uk

Wilbur K (2000) *Integral Psychology Consciousness, Spirit, Psychology, Therapy*. Shambhala Publications

SARAH NIXON is a principal lecturer at Liverpool John Moores University and the leader of the Centre for Excellence in Teaching and Learning (CETL) for the Faculty of Education, Community and Leisure. Her main teaching areas are sports management, the business of sport and PDP. Her research interests are in the area of teaching and learning, with a particular focus on PDP and the student experience.

CAITLIN WALKER is a business and educational consultant and a certified neuro-linguistic programming (NLP) trainer with 20 years experience in designing learning to learn pro- grammes in the public and private sector. Using ideas from systems thinking and clean questions from the work of David Grove, she has developed practical processes for creating learning organisations.

12

Adherence and participation factors in personal development planning

Dominic Micklewright
University of Essex

This project was designed to gain further insight about factors likely to improve learners' rates of participation in PDP and to develop a method of identifying the PDP needs of individual learners.

One of the key challenges associated with any PDP programme is engaging students and getting them to participate without using excessive levels of assessment or external rewards as motivation. In order to overcome this challenge a deeper understanding of students' perspectives on PDP is needed so that the PDP environment and PDP support can be tailored appropriately. This project was designed to gain further insight into factors likely to improve rates of PDP participation among students and to develop a method of identifying the PDP needs of individual students. A conceptual framework of salient learner beliefs about PDP was developed around the theory of planned behaviour (Azjen & Fishbein, 1980; Azjen, 1985) by conducting a thorough literature review and interviews with a range of undergraduate students.

Objectives
The two objectives of this study were to:
- ❑ Identify the antecedent motivational factors among learners that relate to their intention to engage with PDP and their actual engagement with PDP
- ❑ Develop a questionnaire that can be used to identify learners' PDP needs and support them based on their motivational profile.

Rationale
Most of the empirical studies relating to PDP have been conducted outside the UK (Gough et al, 2003: 60) and the need to build a database of UK HE empirical PDP studies has been identified (Jackson et al, 2004: 12). Therefore the broad purpose of this study was to generate some empirical understanding of PDP within a UK higher education institution.

The rationale for the specific objectives of this study are derived from Rivers & Seden (2005) whose findings suggest that PDP participation rates among learners are somehow related to their underlying beliefs and attitudes about the management, organisation, and benefits of a PDP programme. In this respect it is helpful to adopt a social-cognitive perspective of PDP in which learners can be thought of as rational decision-makers who carefully consider the PDP environment and their own past experience before engaging in any PDP activities. Social cognition refers to the way people think about their social environment and a number of social cognitive theories have emerged that have attempted to explain and predict human behaviour based on preceding social cognitions. The most widely tested and cited of these theories is the theory of planned behaviour (Azjen & Fishbein, 1980; Azjen, 1985) which, when applied to PDP, provides a useful insight about some of the social psychological factors that are likely to influence students' PDP behaviour.

Figure 1 **The theory of planned behaviour**

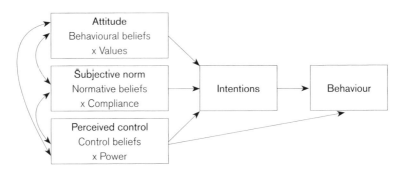

Note Straight lines with an arrow at one end indicate a cause and effect relationship. Curved lines with arrows at both ends indicate an association without any cause and effect specified.

Source: (Azjen & Fishbein 1980, Azjen 1985).

The theory of planned behaviour (TPB) illustrated in Figure 1 proposes that certain types of behaviour, such as PDP, can be predicted based on a person's intentions. According to the TPB there are three antecedents to behavioural intentions – attitudes, subjective norms and perceived behavioural control. An attitude is a positive, neutral or negative belief about a particular behaviour. For example, 'PDP improves employability' is a positive attitude about PDP. A subjective norm is an individual's perceived belief about whether significant others would want them to engage in the behaviour. For example, 'Potential employers will expect me to have engaged in PDP' is a subjective norm. Perceived behavioural control represents an individual's feelings about the degree of control they have over the target behaviour. For example, 'I do not have sufficient computer access to regularly update my eportfolio'. In the TPB, perceived behavioural control is also thought to directly influence behaviour.

The theory of planned behaviour was used as a theoretical framework to pursue the objectives of this study. Thus it was possible to collate information from learners about their attitudes, subjective norms and perceived control to PDP and correlate this information against their PDP intentions and behaviour.

Context

Institutional context

The University of Essex has approximately 8,000 students and is a campus university situated in Colchester (main campus), Southend and Loughton. The university has 18 academic departments which span the humanities, social sciences, science and engineering, and law and management. In the most recent national assessment, Essex was ranked tenth out of 136 institutions for the quality of its research, while the quality of teaching was ranked eighth in the UK in the 2007 *Sunday Times* University Guide. Essex is the UK's most internationally diverse campus university, with students drawn from 130 countries.

At the time of this study the University of Essex was in the process of developing a PDP strategy that involved a staged approach to embedding PDP in the curriculum across the various academic departments. The university provides all staff and students with the opportunity to keep an eportfolio.

Departmental context

This study was conducted with learners from the Centre for Sports and Exercise Science which is part of the Department of Biological Sciences. The Department of Biological Sciences is one of the largest departments in the university with some 45 teaching and academic staff, 40 administrative and technical staff, 35 research staff, over 600 undergraduates and about 200 postgraduates, half of whom are from outside the UK. The department offers a range of degrees such as biology, biochemistry, biotechnology, marine biology and sports science. At the time this study was conducted PDP and eportfolio opportunities were only officially available to first-year undergraduate students as part of the staged implementation plan.

A conceptual framework of learners' beliefs and attitudes about PDP

Modal salient attitudes, subjective norms and perceptions of control were identified from a review of the PDP literature and the content analysis of unstructured interviews that were conducted with nine male and nine female sports science undergraduate students randomly selected from each of the three years. This sample constituted approximately 10% of the total sports science undergraduate student population at the university. All students provided written voluntary consent to be interviewed but were paid £20 for their participation. Students were informed that they could withdraw from the study at any time without explanation. All interview procedures were approved by the University of Essex ethics committee.

Each interview was tape recorded and lasted approximately 30–50 minutes. A semi-structured interview format was used in which students were asked open questions about their beliefs and attitudes to PDP. Subjects were told the interview was about their university experiences and PDP was not specifically mentioned until the interview was underway in order to elicit spontaneous responses and minimise pre-prepared answers. At the end of each session students were told the true purpose of the interview.

All interviews were transcribed and a total of 611 statements were extracted. Each of the statements was categorised according to their relevance to each of the theory of planned behaviour stages; attitudes, subjective norms and perceived behavioural control. All the categorised statements were further inspected and organised to identify the modal salient beliefs for each TPB stage. This conceptual framework of beliefs about PDP was used for the development of the personal development planning questionnaire.

Personal development planning questionnaire (PDP-Q)

The PDP-Q was constructed around the conceptual framework about students' attitudes, subjective norms and perceived behavioural control to PDP. The initial questionnaire consisted of 51 items and was carefully worded and structured to avoid statement ambiguity, education bias, prestige bias, acquiescence effects and item order effects. A 5-point Likert scale ranging from strongly agree to strongly disagree was used to record and score the responses to each PDP-Q item. A cover sheet was also produced for the PDP-Q which included completion instructions, demographic questions and questions about students' PDP intentions.

PDP-Q trials and PDP monitoring

The 51-item PDP-Q was administered to 220 undergraduates at the university drawn from the Centre for Sports and Exercise Science, the Department of Psychology and the Department of Health and Human Sciences (PDP-Q trial 1). An abbreviated version of the PDP-Q, developed through factor analysis, was then re-administered to 169 of the original 220 undergraduate student respondents (PDP-Q trial 2). There was a three- to six-week interval between the two PDP-Q trials. PDP engagement was then measured among 37 sports-science undergraduate students (who were all PDP-Q respondents) over six months using a local eportfolio system.

Data analysis

Student scores for PDP attitudes, subjective norms and perceived control were calculated from the responses of the first PDP-Q trial. The relationships between attitude, subjective norms, perceived control, PDP intentions and PDP behaviour were evaluated using sequential equation modelling. Total PDP=Q score was also correlated against PDP adherence. Factor analysis was used to produce a shorter version of the PDP-Q.

The influence of attitudes, subjective norms and perceived control on PDP intentions and behaviour

Sequential equation modelling, which involves applying regression techniques to estimate associations and causes between variables, was conducted using PDP-Q responses to test the theory of planned behaviour. Significant associations were detected between attitudes and subjective norms ($r = .50$, $p < .05$), attitudes and perceived behavioural control ($r = .60$, $p < .05$) and subjective norms and perceived behavioural control ($r = .45$, $p < .05$). 24% of the variation in PDP intentions was found to be due to PDP attitudes ($r = .24$, $p < .05$), 1% of the variation in PDP intentions was found to be due to PDP subjective norms ($r = .01$, $p > .05$), 30% of the variation PDP intentions was found to be due to perceived behavioural control ($r = .30$, $p < .05$), and 24% of the variation in PDP intentions was found to be due to unknown factors not specified in the model ($r = .24$, $p < .05$). Results of the sequential equation model are presented in Figure 2.

Figure 2 Sequential equation model of the theory of planned behaviour and PDP

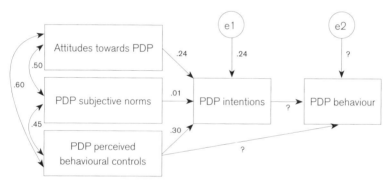

Note: Standardised residual values are shown. e1 is an estimate of variation in PDP intentions due to unknown factors which were not specified in the model (error). There was insufficient data to estimate the amount of variance in PDP Behaviour (?) due to perceived behavioural control, PDP intentions or other unknown factors (e2).

PDP-Q total score validity

Construct validity of the PDP-Q was measured using a Pearson's product moment correlation between PDP-Q total score and the number of PDP eportfolio actions performed over a six-month period. A positive correlation was detected ($r = .333$, $df = 39$, $p < 0.05$) indicating a moderate level of PDP-Q validity. A scattergram is presented in Figure 3.

A reduced version of the PDP-Q

PDP-Q Trial 1 scores were analysed using exploratory factor analysis in order to identify factors and retain selected questionnaire items that are the best predictors of each subscale (see Appendix B).

Figure 3   Scattergram of the relationship between PDP-Q score and PDP engagement.

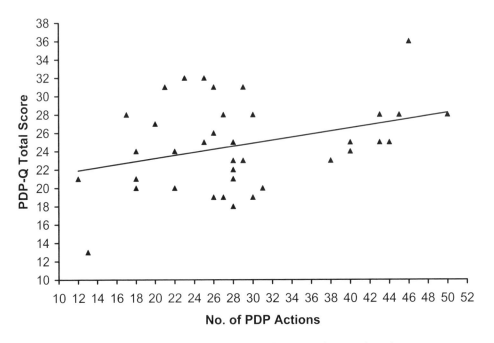

The final PDP-Q structure consisted of the following three subscales:

1   Perceived benefits of PDP
2   External influence and individual control
3   PDP motivation.

Discussion

A key finding of this study is that, in the context of University of Essex sports science, learners' attitudes to PDP and their sense of control over the PDP process are more influential on their PDP intentions and behaviour than their subjective norms are. This information is useful because it allows a more focused approach in attempting to engage learners in the PDP process. For example, from these results, it would seem sensible to arrange PDP resources so that students feel a greater sense of control over the process and to provide information and experiences that promote favourable attitudes to PDP among learners.

In this instance it seems that projecting the PDP expectations of the university and potential employers (subjective norms) is less likely to engage this particular cohort of learners. However, that does not necessarily mean that such a strategy will work with all learners. Indeed one of the purposes of developing the PDP-Q was so that the individual PDP needs of learners could be identified and then supported in the most appropriate way. The PDP-Q can be used to support students throughout the PDP process in a number of important ways such as identifying individual students' PDP needs, providing tailored individual PDP support, monitoring change and re-evaluating individual needs.

Using the PDP-Q to identify individual PDP needs

In most further or higher educational institutions PDP is usually a voluntary activity that is not summatively assessed and, despite the fairly convincing learning and employment benefits of PDP, learners often fail to engage in the process. One challenge is to recognise at the earliest opportunity the variety of PDP needs within a student intake and to identify those individuals who are least likely to engage in PDP and will therefore need the most support. Administering the PDP-Q to an intake of students at an early stage in a PDP programme will to some extent allow the diverse range of PDP needs to be explored. These initial PDP-Q results can be used to profile individuals according to their beliefs, attitudes and intentions to PDP. The results could then be used to develop tailored PDP support either at an individual or group level based on shared PDP needs.

Using PDP-Q outcomes to tailor PDP support

Once the PDP-Q profiles of individuals or groups of individuals have been identified, the logical step is to align PDP support according to their particular needs. For example, learners who score low on the PDP-Q subscale of 'Beliefs about perceived PDP benefits' could be given extra support in terms of explaining and demonstrating how engaging in PDP can help to improve their learning ability and prepare them for employment. It might be useful to give learners who score low on the PDP-Q subscale of 'External influence and individual control' extra help with managing their time, organising their resources, using the eportfolio and explaining how others, such as employers, value PDP activities.

Learners who score low on the PDP-Q subscale of 'Motivation' are most likely to be highly strategic in their approach to learning and therefore might need extra reassurance that, although PDP is not assessed, it is still nevertheless a worthwhile use of their time. PDP-Q outcomes are therefore a useful source of information that can be used to tailor PDP support. The purpose of using the PDP-Q in this way is adopt a targeted approach to promoting a favourable shift among learners in their beliefs, attitudes and intentions to PDP which will hopefully result in increased levels of PDP participation.

Using the PDP-Q to monitor attitudinal change and re-evaluate learner needs

PDP is a dynamic process through which learners' beliefs, attitudes and corresponding PDP needs are likely to change over time. Therefore, in addition to guiding initial PDP support, the PDP-Q ought to be re-administered to learners at various points throughout their PDP programme as a means of monitoring their attitudinal change to the process. This could be coordinated either through PDP support staff or even as a self-evaluation tool by the learners themselves. The important point to recognise is that the PDP-Q can be used to monitor change and to adjust and refine the level of PDP support given to learners.

Reflection

The project was successful in the sense that evidence about the antecedent factors leading to PDP intentions and behaviour was gathered and an effective questionnaire was developed to help support learners in the PDP process. It is hoped that in the future the PDP-Q will be used as a tool by practitioners in a variety of different PDP contexts and therefore it has a great deal of heuristic potential.

The PDP-Q also represents an opportunity to gather quantitative PDP data, facilitate a better understanding of students' PDP behaviour and make a useful contribution to the PDP evidence base. For example, although not included in the original project proposal, it became apparent that sequential-equation modelling could be used to further analyse the PDP-Q data and gain further theoretical insight about the relationships between students' beliefs, attitudes, intentions and PDP behaviour. As more and more data is collected this behavioural model of PDP will become much more robust which should help to inform good and effective PDP practice.

The project outcomes have so far been disseminated through several conference presentations and publications through both the Higher Education Academy and the Centre for Recording Achievement. Informal feedback from other PDP practitioners has been positive and it is encouraging that other people have expressed an interest in using the PDP-Q at their institution. One of the possibilities for the future might be to set up a PDP-Q database where FE and HE institutions across the UK can incorporate the PDP-Q into their programme and contribute their results to the study. This could lead to a huge database of PDP-Q and PDP behavioural data from a variety of contexts which would make a significant contribution to the pool of PDP evidence. The PDP-Q is currently used within the Centre for Sports and Exercise Science to evaluate, monitor and support students in their PDP.

Acknowledgements

This study was funded by the University of Essex Teaching and Learning Innovation Fund and the Hospitality, Leisure, Sport and Tourism Network 6th Round of the Pedagogic Research and Development Fund.

References and URLs

Ajzen, I. (1985) From intentions to actions: a theory of planned behaviour. In J. Kuhl & J. Beckmann (eds) *Action – Control: From cognition to behaviour*. Heidelberg, Springer

Ajzen, I. & Fishbein, M. (1980) *Understanding Attitudes and Predicting Social Behaviour* Englewood Cliffs NJ, Prentice Hall

Gough, D.A., Kiwan, D., Sutcliffe, S., Simpson, D. and Houghton, N. (2003) *A systematic map and synthesis review of the effectiveness of personal development planning for improving student learning*. London, EPPI-Centre, Social Science Research Unit

Jackson, N., Gough, D., Dunne, E. and Shaw, M. (2004) Developing the Infrastructure to Support an Evidence Informed Approach to Personal Development Planning. Paper for the Higher Education Academy Symposium: An evidence based approach in higher education – how far can we take it?' Manchester 7 July 2004

Kline, P. (1994) *An easy guide to factor analysis*. London, Routledge

Rivers, P. & Seden, R. (2005). Personal Development Planning: How can we encourage students to participate? *Centre for Recording Achievement PDP-UK Newsletter* 5 (7-8)

DOMINIC MICKLEWRIGHT is a chartered sport and exercise psychologist and a fellow of the Higher Education Academy working as a lecturer at the University of Essex in the Department of Biological Sciences. His work has focused on understanding what motivates learners to engage in the learning process particularly in the areas of personal development planning and e-learning. His research interests are on the psychological antecedents of fatigue during maximal effort exercise.

Appendix A

PDP-Q Trial 1 scores were analysed using exploratory factor analysis in order to identify BAM-Q subscales (factors) and retain selected questionnaire items that are the best predictors of each subscale. A Kaiser-Meyer-Olkin (KMO) statistic of 0.845 was detected indicating sampling adequacy among the 51 PDP-Q item responses. A screen analysis, performed in accordance with Kline (1994), revealed three factors (PDP-Q subscales) which were extracted and then rotated using the Varimax method with Kaiser normalisation since this produced the simplest structure. Six questionnaire items with the highest predictive weighting were retained in each factor to produce a revised 18-item PDP-Q A label was created for each PDP-Q subscale (factor) that broadly reflected the combined content of the component items.

Further instructions for PDP-Q use and scoring can be found at the website of the Hospitality, Leisure, Sport & Tourism Network of the Higher Education Academy: http://www.heacademy.ac.uk/hlst/projects/detail/ourwork/intentions_and_behaviour_in_personal_development_planning

Appendix B

PDP-Q

		STRONGLY DISAGREE	DISAGREE	UNDECIDED	AGREE	STRONGLY AGREE
1	On the whole, I think personal development planning at university is a good idea.	SD	D	U	A	SA
2	I would probably only participate in personal development planning if it was compulsory.	SD	D	U	A	SA
3	I think personal development planning will help me to transfer skills I have developed at university into the workplace.	SD	D	U	A	SA
4	I am NOT really interested in personal development planning since I have mainly come to university to learn about my chosen subject.	SD	D	U	A	SA
5	My chances of getting a job will probably NOT improve if I keep a portfolio of personal development evidence.	SD	D	U	A	SA
6	If I work really hard while I am at university other people may think I am a bit boring.	SD	D	U	A	SA
7	It is worthwhile participating in personal development as well as academic activities at university.	SD	D	U	A	SA
8	I would probably still participate in personal development planning at university even if the resources needed to do so were limited.	SD	D	U	A	SA
9	I think employers will be more interested in my academic qualifications rather than my personal characteristics when it comes to getting a job.	SD	D	U	A	SA
10	I would find personal development planning useful if it helped me to reflect on my performance at university.	SD	D	U	A	SA
11	I do NOT think there are many opportunities at university to develop transferable skills.	SD	D	U	A	SA
12	I am NOT usually very good at organizing my studying time.	SD	D	U	A	SA
13	I would always try to find time for personal development planning, even if I was very busy with other academic activities.	SD	D	U	A	SA
14	Other people might think I was wasting my time if I participated in extra activities designed to improve my personal development.	SD	D	U	A	SA
15	I am NOT confident that I will be in full control of my personal development while I am at university.	SD	D	U	A	SA
16	It is important for students to spend some of their time at university on personal development planning.	SD	D	U	A	SA
17	There may be better ways than personal development planning for me to record my progress at university.	SD	D	U	A	SA
18	There is NO value in trying to develop transferable skills at university since they do not count towards your degree.	SD	D	U	A	SA

13

Stepping Stones 2HE
Fresh thinking for introducing PDP to freshers

Christine Keenan
Bournemouth University

Effectively engaging students is often cited as a 'problem' for personal development planning. This chapter shows how to stimulate their interest from pre-induction into the first term, by relating it to student experience and aspirations, and involvement in curriculum design and assessment.

This chapter describes an approach to introducing new first-year students to personal development planning from the pre-induction phase. *Stepping Stones 2HE* (Keenan, 2006; 2008) is an initiative that engages new students with an on-line resource which aims to ease the transition to HE by providing students with information, resources, learning activities and a reflective questionnaire prior to their induction week. The broad aim is to provide students with the information they need to make the transition into HE a less daunting process, and reduce the problem of information overload during induction week. Students are also provided with learning activities to work on before induction and then, during induction, they collaborate with their peers to share what they have already been doing and work towards an output, for example, a presentation or poster. The resource also provides a section on personal development planning (PDP) as a means of introducing students to PDP. We do this by explaining why we think PDP is a useful process for students and we point them to pertinent aspects of our PDP website, for example preparing for your first tutorial and study skills, among others.

The *Stepping Stones 2HE* materials are linked with induction week activities and provide students with the opportunity to contribute to the design of part of their curriculum. The activity described here took place with students studying *Multimedia Network Systems* within the School of Design, Engineering & Computing (DEC) at Bournemouth University in the autumn of 2007. Four seminar groups of ten students each were involved. The students were predominantly 18-year-old males with just two females in the cohort.

This approach allowed students to contribute to the design of their curriculum content for the first term of a 20 credit professional studies module and allowed them to personalise their assignment for the module. Although for this example there is a focus on *Multimedia Network Systems* students, the concept is transferable across other disciplines. It aims to contextualise PDP and demonstrate relevance and applicability to the students to encourage their engagement.

While it is acknowledged that some students needed more encouragement than others to buy in to the idea, the overall results (2007–08) showed a significant improvement on previous years and there was greater satisfaction within the cohort. It will be interesting to work with them again as they enter the second year of their course to ascertain if they feel, on reflection, that their self awareness and better understanding of their learning made a difference that will sustain them through placement and on to graduation.

What we were trying to achieve

There is plenty of anecdotal evidence to support the notion that engaging with PDP enhances the student experience. At Bournemouth University we believe that employability and personal development planning is about developing the whole person, and we encourage students to think about themselves not just in terms of understanding their learning, but also in how they engage with the wider university community through clubs and societies and volunteering. We also actively work with our student union which offers a leadership award and runs PDP sessions every Wednesday afternoon, known as *Your Best You*. It is believed that developing meta-cognitive skills in reflection and self-awareness provides a strong basis for successful student progress. However, it is sometimes difficult to persuade students of this and engage them in the process. This case study describes a process by which we set out to achieve the engagement of students.

The key features

❑ Development of pre-induction resources to promote PDP within the *Stepping Stones 2HE* approach

❑ Allowing students to be involved in design of the curriculum in a way that con-textualises PDP and makes it relevant to them

❑ Allowing students to express their feelings about PDP within the first assignment which had to be a 1,000 word essay (with this constraint, students had autonomy in terms of the assignment title)

❑ As this was the first academic essay for these students at university, the students had a lecture on academic writing/critical thinking and a seminar session during which we explored examples of writing.

The activity

New first-year students receive a link to the on-line *Stepping Stones 2HE* resource once they receive confirmation of their place at the university. The resource provides information for students about university life, study skills, news about the broader university, an opportunity to provide us with their reflections on their previous learning experiences, and to think about their expectations of themselves coming to university and of the institution. There is also a section on PDP.

The resources introduce the idea of PDP to students in a way that makes sense to them. It explains why we think PDP is useful and important, and, it walks them through our PDP website, directing them to useful resources that will be of immediate help to them. In this way, we hope that students will arrive at university with a sense that this is 'what we do' at Bournemouth University and that we value not just the learning that takes place, but also that we actively support and promote the development of well-rounded students who graduate with a strong sense of self and a strong understanding of themselves as global citizens.

Late in summer 2007, I was tasked with 'teaching the PDP unit' to the incoming cohort of the Multimedia Network Systems course. I wanted to find a way to make this an active and relevant experience for the students, contextualised in a lively way, and give them some control over the content.

I wrote to the students during September 2007 and reminded them to visit the Stepping Stones 2HE website and in particular to visit the PDP section, to ensure they had carried out the learning activities provided by the staff and to complete the on-line reflective questionnaire. I also asked them to bring a number of job advertisements to the induction week. I asked them for examples of jobs that they might aspire to on graduation and to include a range of other job advertisements not necessarily related to their own discipline.

During the first introductory session with the cohort at induction, I brought along members of the student union who worked with the students on an informal activity to help them identify what sort of learners they are as individuals and how they relate to others in groups. This led to a lively and stimulating session which was particularly useful because it was led by union staff who related very well to the group. The students enjoyed the session and often referred back to it during the first few weeks.

During the first seminars, the students and I analysed the job advertisements that had been collected. The students were encouraged to identify the skills, competencies, attributes and qualities that the job adverts called for. We had a scribe in each seminar group who noted everything down on a large sheet of paper. We then clustered what had been jotted down and the students identified a range of elements including:

❑ being self-motivated
❑ team working
❑ creativity
❑ communication skills (and listening)
❑ organisation skills

- ❑ enthusiasm
- ❑ taking responsibility
- ❑ multi-tasking
- ❑ interpersonal communication skills
- ❑ attention to detail
- ❑ being able to analyse situations
- ❑ commitment
- ❑ good health
- ❑ language skills
- ❑ time management
- ❑ personality
- ❑ professionalism
- ❑ using own initiative – working on own interests outside the workplace
- ❑ hardworking
- ❑ flexibility and adaptability
- ❑ tenacity
- ❑ being trustworthy
- ❑ subject knowledge.

This led to discussion about many 'factual' requirements or 'skills', 'competencies' and 'qualities', coming under the umbrella of what are termed transferable skills. Once again I demonstrated how these transferable skills were articulated and described on the university PDP website. The next part of the activity was for me to cluster these together and negotiate the module programme for the rest of the term with the students.

Module design: intended learning outcomes

The students were involved in developing the intended learning outcomes for the first term module. The outcomes state that, on completion of the first term, they will have:

- o started to develop their own ideas of what PDP is about
- o understood how engaging with PDP can give a clear idea about the kind of life and work that you want for themselves
- o linked the idea of PDP with developing confidence in their skills, qualities and attributes
- o thought about how to articulate their skills, personal qualities and competencies to potential employers
- o developed a positive attitude and approach associated with success
- o understood many of the terms associated with PDP.

They receive a paragraph from me on each of the following:

PDP is about enhancing your learning

PDP is about enhancing your experience as a student

PDP is about enjoying the present and planning for the future

Module design: schedule for Term One

The Term One content negotiated with the students from the list identified through the job advertisements was:

- ❏ approaches to learning
- ❏ group working
- ❏ communication skills
- ❏ presentation skills
- ❏ critical thinking
- ❏ extra-curricular activities
- ❏ self-management
- ❏ career management
- ❏ leadership.

I then prepared the unit guide, which provided students with the weekly schedule, plus a range of resources, reading and preparatory work, of which this is an example:

19.10.07	Seminar

Learning
Approaches to learning, action plans, portfolio and evidence building
Using the PDP Website exercises:
- ○ Set up a file/portfolio in which to keep PDP activities and evidence
- ○ Approaches to learning and studying questionnaire
Academic work and life in general survey
- ○ Goal setting and action planning for learning
- ○ Read and critique Christine Keenan's PDP chapter [see unit materials in *MyBU*]
- ○ Read Chapter 1 *Essential Study Skills* (Burns and Sinfield)
- ○ Read Chapter 3 *The Study Skills Handbook* (Cottrell)
- ○ Try *Your Best You* – LearnHigher Room (Library Courtyard), Wednesday pms

Where possible, speakers from the wider university were invited to work through the sessions with students. The student union were much involved in a number of the sessions. This was particularly helpful as it ensured that there was a variety of people for students to interact with.

The premise for this approach was that if students had ownership of the module and saw for themselves that it was relevant and contextualised, they would invest in engaging with it.

Assessment

Assessment for this module is prescribed as a 1,000-word academic essay. This was the first academic essay of the course, so I delivered a lecture and seminar on essay writing and critical thinking. We looked at Harvard referencing and I explained about marking criteria. We also talked about both formal and reflective writing styles and we looked at previous examples of student work.

The students were given the freedom to choose their own essay title, the criterion being that the title needed to encapsulate their thinking about this module. Students were provided with guidance in terms of developing the content of the essay, for example, reflecting on why they chose Bournemouth University and this course in particular, their personal strengths and weaknesses, and what they were looking forward to studying in Year Two. The main point was to explore these issues within the context of the work we had been doing in the first term.

It was felt really important that the marking criteria should not penalise these novice writers, so they were weighted primarily in favour of the content and how students argued their case, and with lower weighting for accurate referencing and structure. I felt this was important in order not to penalise students for their lack of experience.

❑ structure of essay: 20%
❑ quality of argument and reference to sources: 50%
❑ conclusions: 20%
❑ Harvard referencing: 10%.

Some examples of titles students gave to their work were to the point:

'An explorative essay documenting my self development and understanding in order to choose my university and course of study'

'Career ambitions and gaining success at university'

'Why I am studying digital media development at Bournemouth University and how I intend to gain the most from this opportunity'

Others were quite imaginative:

'Back to the future!'

'University life, the unit and me'

'My development, my future'

'Reflections of a DEC Freshman'

'PDP and personal exploration: A useful or useless process?'

Students were encouraged to reflect on strengths and weaknesses and marks were gained for self-awareness and insights into personal characteristics developed through engaging in PDP:

I need to let other people take charge sometimes and have control and lastly have more self control so I am not impatient all the time.

I am now heavily involved with the wider university and feel that I am getting the best possible experience from the opportunities presented to me. I am to increase my involvement in the second year by joining the PAL scheme [i e becoming a peer-assisted learning leader].

Before I can continue to develop further into the person I want to be, I need to look at past work, to reflect back on who I was back then and how I've developed into the person I am today.

It is my intention to begin attending yoga at the university to allow some time-out in this age where time is a precious commodity.

In my opinion, for many this self-objectivity or introspection [of PDP] is a difficult struggle, or fear of change too strong for the process to be of benefit, but for the others personal development planning offers focus for targeted personal evolution and growth, perhaps even the beginning of a lifetime's obsession.

One critical student who was very resistant to PDP suggested:

The course is not what I expected; there were a few contents on the course that I did not know about. These are Personal Development Planning and Marketing. However I will look to give time for these to adjust and for me to do research to enable me to not fall behind. I will have to motivate myself as the course itself is not doing this.

Others commented:

Within the first few weeks of starting the course I recognised certain strengths and weaknesses that stood out, which I realised I could improve or capitalise on.

Choosing my course of study at university was not easy. The complex decision-making process, my entire life in a single set of applications and projecting my future career was a daunting thought.

I have been challenged by the idea of personal development planning, and now admit that I already find it extremely useful. I am looking at the subject of learning in a completely different light than six weeks ago, and I fully see the benefit to myself of self-analysis and recognising skills that I would normally just take for granted, with no real idea how to improve or change them in the past. I realise that I must regularly update these skills and ask myself 'how am I doing'.

Effectiveness and appropriateness of this approach

Further research with this cohort when they begin their second year of study will help provide evidence for what they consider to be the effectiveness of this approach in the first term.

Attendance did drop off once the assignment was submitted. The students who committed to attending throughout the term suggested that other students were using the PDP seminar hour (timetabled on a Friday) to prepare other assignments.

At the end of the first year, after exams, the first-year students brought all the technical and 'soft' skills developed during the year together into a simulated business week which also formed part of the assessment for the module. During the week they had to work in small teams and build a web and network system to promote the services of a garden centre. This integrated the subject knowledge they had gained during the first year across all the units and it drew on their increased understanding of team working, communication skills and dealing with conflict.

It is interesting that this cohort had one of the best sets of final results seen at a first-year exam board in the school and the external examiner commented on the very high overall marks achieved by the cohort. I plan to work with the group next year to see if it is possible to attribute this phenomenon to the approach taken of allowing the students to take ownership and some control over the content and direction of the PDP element of the course.

It would be interesting to carry out further analysis of:

❑ The students' perceptions of personal development planning as they enter their second year of study.
❑ Which elements of PDP students explicitly thought about in terms of their approach to study.
❑ Whether students realised their stated aims of joining volunteering groups, clubs and societies, and other wider university activities.
❑ Whether students have maintained their use of action plans, and evidence building in personal portfolios.

What enabled the practice to work

The first-year student experience is a cornerstone of the university education enhancement strategy and *Stepping Stones 2HE* is integral to this. As an institution we are developing expertise in understanding how to support students during the difficult and formative transition stage. The institution has also stated that 'PDP is literally and metaphorically at the centre of what we do here' (Curran, 2006). The university also has responsibility for the learning topic area of PDP within the LearnHigher CETL, and, we are partners in a national teaching fellowship scheme led by the University of Bolton investigating developing research practice in PDP.

Within the university we have a range of provision and approaches for PDP and we introduce new students to PDP at the very start of their university experience, through the pre-induction resource. We believe that it is important to overcome any perception that PDP is an inconvenience. From the outcomes of this case study, contextualising PDP in a subject and demonstrating for students its relevance to the outside world – and its benefit to their personal effectiveness – does make a difference.

Barriers and challenges faced

Although universities are required to provide opportunities for students to engage with PDP, there is a lack of published research in the sector to provide evidence to demonstrate that 'it really works'. Academic staff often cite this lack of reliable quantifiable evidence as a reason for their lack of confidence in PDP. Although there are a number of case studies providing examples of practice available through organisations such as the Higher Education Academy, the Centre for Recording

Achievement, and the LearnHigher CETL, it is recognised that more research and evaluation in the subject would improve confidence. Funding through the National Teaching Fellowship Scheme is currently providing an opportunity for a number of HEIs to conduct research projects over a three-year period. It is anticipated that the research outcomes will provide the evidence that the sector is seeking to give confidence in PDP as an approach to providing students with the scaffolding to develop their meta-cognitive skills, self-awareness as individuals, their understanding of how they learn and their relationship with their peers, communities and environments.

At Bournemouth, there was a pocket of resistance within one seminar group, led by a very vocal student who felt that PDP was a waste of his time. He wanted to get down to the technical aspects of the unit and felt that PDP was an imposition that he did not want to subscribe to and claimed furthermore that the course had been misrepresented to him because of it. I did extend this conversation to the rest of his seminar group, which he claimed to be representing in his views as I felt it was important to give voice to the other students. Although he was having an influence on the group, the rest of the seminar group did indicate that the others did not share his strength of opinion against the principles of the unit.

Key lessons learnt

- Engaging students with PDP resources in the pre-induction transition phase sets an expectation – students arrive with the expectation that this is what happens at university.
- Working with the students to contextualise PDP within their university, social and personal lives helped to provide relevance and a base to work from.
- Allowing students to develop the learning outcomes of the PDP element of the module gave them some control over their learning.
- Working with the students to develop the curriculum content was useful to empower them and provide relevance in terms of what they believe was important to them professionally, academically and personally.
- Time put aside within the teaching schedule for giving insight into the requirements of academic writing and allowing discussion time to explore examples of academic writing was felt to be very helpful.
- Giving students the opportunity to provide the title for their assignment allowed them to shape their assignment but still work within the criteria.
- Providing marking criteria that rewarded reflection, insight and exploration of self in relation to university and the course, and that did not penalise them for what they did not already know (for example, accurate Harvard referencing) boosted confidence early on in the course.

Conclusions

Although this case study describes the experience of *Multimedia Network Systems* students, the concept is transferable across disciplines. The central concept is seeking to find a way to gain student engagement with PDP. This is clearly one of the key 'problems' of PDP and yet it seems that, when students do engage, it enriches the whole of their experience and provides them with the self-awareness and self-reliance that will underpin their personal, professional and academic futures.

This case study describes one example of engaging students with the concept of PDP. Students are introduced to PDP prior to enrolment within a suite of other transition support materials and resources. This introduction to PDP is developed further through supported activities during induction week. Students are then involved in the design of the curriculum by being allowed to include content based on their own aspirations and what they perceive to be important to them, personally and academically, in the first few weeks of term. The overall impression at the end of the unit is that the students in this particular cohort have done exceptionally well in terms of their progress and final marks.

It is hoped that further study with this cohort will help to identify what made the difference. Given the reflective nature of PDP, I hope to work with these students as they enter the second year of study, and again when they enter the final year of study, to see whether it is possible to identify the impact that the PDP section of the professional studies module made. Given the insights provided by the students in their assignment, it is anticipated that this style of working with them in helping them to determine the shape of the curriculum and assessment may well have made the difference in terms of fresh thinking for introducing PDP to freshers!

References
Burns, T. & Sinfield S. (2008) *Essential Study Skills*. 2nd ed. London, Sage

Cottrell, S. (2003) *The Study Skills Handbook*. Basingstoke, Palgrave

Curran, P. (2006) Vice chancellor's speech opening the LearnHigher CETL social learning space at Bournemouth University.

Keenan, C. (2006) *Stepping Stones 2HE*: Bridging the Transition Gap. In *Exchange Magazine HEA* 3 p 31. Available at: http://www.heacademy.ac.uk/resources/publications/exchange

Keenan, C. (2008) Students getting down to work before they start at university: a model for improving retention. In Crosling, G., Thomas, L. and Heagney, M. (eds) *Improving Student Retention in Higher Education: The Role of Learning and Teaching*. (Routledge Abingdon)

CHRISTINE KEENAN has a learning and teaching role at Bournemouth University working with both staff and students in a range of learning development activities. Her teaching responsibilities include a social psychology unit on a communication and media undergraduate degree, professional studies and postgraduate research methods. Christine gained a Learning and Teaching Fellow award at the university to develop her work supporting students in transition to HE (*Stepping Stones 2HE*), and, is involved in a number of externally funded projects investigating aspects of first year experience and personal development planning.

14

Enhancing student learning
Managing tensions in a large undergraduate module

Graham Baker and Robert French
Bristol Business School, University of the West of England

Implementing a graduate development programme has raised major
questions about the nature of teaching and learning in a business school

This chapter describes the agonies and ecstasies of implementing a university-wide innovation in the context of a large Level 4 undergraduate module (c. 1,000 students). This innovation has involved the introduction of a Graduate Development Programme (GDP) into an existing, compulsory module, *Management and Organisational Behaviour* (MOB). The experience has challenged many of our preconceptions and assumptions about the nature of teaching and learning in the business school and has made us question the aims of the course, its content and structure, and the nature of the student–tutor relationship. At the end of the first year of implementation, we are in a position to report on what we have done, but also on the challenges which it presents. We believe that the potential interest for others may lie as much in the *questions* the experience has raised as in any local solutions we may have found.

Summary
This case study investigates the attempt in 2007–08 to transform the experience of teaching and learning on a well-established Level 4 undergraduate module at a large business school. It looks at the experience of developing a new-style module within the confines of the existing university structures and reflects on the learning from the first run-through, the challenges that arose, and the issues which remain.

At the heart of the transformation was an attempt to develop our relatively traditional *Management and Organisational Behaviour* module into a new student-focused module. In particular, the case study will focus on the manner in which this university-wide GDP initiative was incorporated into the MOB syllabus, and the impact of this innovation on the experience of teaching and learning for students and staff.

Objectives

Following a wide-ranging review by our incoming vice-chancellor, new energy was brought to bear on the student experience at the University of the West of England (UWE). The central concern, shared in the business school and among staff on MOB, was simply that we were not getting the best out of our students. Among the many factors influencing this situation, we believed it resulted in part from the nature of what we were offering. In particular, the impact of increased student numbers and widening participation initiatives meant that the assumptions underpinning much of what we were doing no longer held true or, at the very least, were in need of some reassessment.

This was the context which led to the idea of introducing a Graduate Development Programme (GDP), intended to run alongside and to support students, from the start of their courses through to graduation and employment. As information to students puts it:

> The GDP is an essential and integral part of your academic programme. It will enable you to:
> o manage the transition into your first year at UWE and as you progress from one stage/level to the next
> o develop your university-level learning skills and styles
> o develop the capacity for effective group work and learning with and from your peers
> o see the importance of your role in UWE life and as a member of your subject degree group
> o develop a rounded appreciation of your academic programme and the connections between your modules and the wider world
> o plan your own 'preferred future' and develop the graduate skills, attributes and abilities that will help you achieve your goals
> o recognise, describe and demonstrate your academic achievements and graduate skills.

The GDP offers a common approach to student learning that aims to contribute to the development of a distinctive 'UWE Graduate'. It focuses on learning skills such as academic writing, development of the skills and attitudes needed to be a successful student, personal development, working in groups, employability and academic achievement, and, underpinning all of these, the student role itself. The programme is supported through the pedagogy of 'facilitated learning' and takes place in peer groups of 15–18 students.

Rationale for the course

In the academic year 2006–07, the University ran some pilot courses based on a free-standing model of delivery within faculties. These included one small programme cohort in the business school, consisting of two groups of around 25 students. The pilots were evaluated and the decision to expand the programme across the whole university was ratified.

In October 2007, GDP was, therefore, introduced as a compulsory element for all first-year students. In the business school, the decision was taken to implement GDP through the MOB module. The aim was to locate the innovation in an existing module, although we already recognised that with experience, we would almost certainly want to expand the approach into other modules. MOB was seen to be the most appropriate vehicle for GDP for a variety of reasons:

1   The 'vehicle' of an existing course would ensure that the new approach was fully 'owned' by someone from the start.
2   MOB is a compulsory module for nearly all Level 4 students (between 900 and 1,000 in total). Any attempt to introduce GDP as a stand-alone element within the student experience would have been problematic as the timetable is too tight to allow for what would amount to a new module.
3   We doubted our ability to persuade students to take the idea seriously if it was not attached to an assessed course.
4   Several of the elements of GDP were closely related to MOB content – such as the idea of the 'student role' – and the use of experiential learning approaches in MOB closely paralleled the facilitated learning approach to be adopted for the delivery of GDP.

Elements of GDP which did not fit with MOB, such as numeracy, were to be delivered through other modules.

Context: the MOB course

The MOB module is delivered by staff in the Department of Organisation Studies. It is an introductory course to the issues of people in organisations and is a core module in all the programmes offered by the Business School, with the exception of a small number of joint-honours students taking Economics. It also forms a core module in the management courses run at Hartpury College, an affiliated, land-based college in Gloucestershire, and an introductory module at Taylor's College, a higher education institution in Malaysia. As a result, it is the largest taught module in the university, with over 1,000 students and 16 staff, running on three separate campuses and over two continents.

The MOB course has evolved over many years, changing its name, focus and content at each stage of its evolution. In recent years, we have grown sceptical over the impact of textbooks in our field. We have grown to think of them as a form of unintended 'tyranny'; we choose the textbook we think most closely 'fits' with our own course – but the impact of the choice is to remove choice, as the textbook itself begins both to dictate to us what it is that we teach and to become, in the eyes of many students, the repository of 'answers', in a subject in which the very notion of answers is misleading. As a result, we have continually found ourselves adapting what we would *like* to teach to the requirements of the book; students, for their part, often end up giving the textbook the status of an original, research-based text and, despite all encouragement and inducements, seldom if ever read an original journal article or research monograph.

The pedagogical requirements of GDP acted, therefore, as a catalyst for a fuller review of the MOB course, in terms of content, delivery and assessment. This review became crucial from the moment the business school decided to embed GDP into the MOB module, rather than producing a free-standing GDP course, as was the case in other faculties.

As a subject, MOB encourages the application of learning to the students' own experience. However, the tendency is to work either from theory, more or less for its own sake, or from case-study material. The changes we had introduced over the previous few years reflected a desire to move from a content-driven learning experience to one which was more relevant to the needs of our students. We wished to recognise two things:

1   That our own passion for our subject, as staff, is based on an engagement with theory which has helped us, through the encounter between theory and practice, to make sense of and draw meaning from our own experience in and of groups and organisations.

2   That this could also be the key to bringing the subject alive for students, but only if we were prepared to acknowledge that they too have a wide-ranging experience of groups and organisations, one which neither they nor we have tended to value.

We had already been developing the course in a way which was more activity-based and less didactic, encouraging a focus on the student experience, which anticipated the approach embodied in GDP. Our inability to find an appropriate textbook for the course was a further contributory factor to the need to change. Finally, we had, for some time, been working to address our concerns over the nature and quantity of assessment on the existing module. While these concerns – such as fairness, standardisation and moderation – may be common to all assessment, they are exacerbated by the scale of this module both in terms of the student group and the staff team, which, at the time, included a significant number of visiting (now 'hourly-paid') lecturers.

Description

The resulting course was ambitious in intent. We continued to address selected themes from the MOB syllabus, such as management, leadership, change and motivation. In addition, we introduced or developed for GDP several themes and approaches:

❑ the use of learning journals
❑ tutoring
❑ feedback

❑ reflection – in class, in seminars and through writing
❑ library awareness
❑ the use of academic language
❑ the evaluation of theory
❑ learning as a topic
❑ the use of experience to critique theory and *vice versa*
❑ experiential workshop activities.

The changes were intended to develop the skills and abilities of students, to help them develop as independent learners. Specific academic skills such as referencing, using the library, academic writing, and receiving and working with feedback were mixed in with MOB areas of interest, such as working and understanding group dynamics, approaches to learning, and managing individual and institutional change and transition. Some lectures focused specifically on GDP issues, while most of the seminars were student-focused with a range of whole seminar group, small-group and individual student activities. Many of the activities were backed up by a learning journal, which required students to reflect on their experiences as a way of developing themselves as students. The traditional assignment of the past was replaced by a short, non-assessed writing activity which was marked solely for feedback purposes and followed up by a personal interview and an entry in the learning journal, where students indicated how they would improve the piece of work as a result of the feedback.

Evaluation

At the time of writing, it is hard to draw any conclusions that are other than provisional, as the dust from the first storm of activity has not yet settled. However, it is possible to make a preliminary evaluation of the relative successes and failures in this first stage.

Relief rather than triumph!

In terms of our regular measures of success – pass rates, average marks, and student feedback – there appears to have been a clear, but by no means dramatic, improvement. Problems regularly encountered here, and across the HE sector more generally, in relation to attendance and engagement, were no worse than in recent years. There was some evidence of several encouraging trends:

❑ An increased understanding of the overall 'thrust' of the subject – i.e. its relevance as a perspective which allows for reflection on, and learning from, organisational experience
❑ An increased awareness of some academic skills, such as referencing (though attributing this to changes in just one module out of six is not possible)
❑ More evidence of the ability to differentiate and use key skills in relation to theory: description, application/ analysis, and evaluation

❑ Students also reported more frequently than in the past that they had benefited from tutor support. This may have reflected something of the intended shift of staff-student relationship, as giving students a sense of belonging was one of the aims of GDP.

Perhaps the most important positive outcome, especially for the longer term, was one we had not predicted, that of a significant increase in *staff* engagement with the course beyond the immediate task of 'delivering' workshops/seminars. Some of the reasons for this are discussed below.

'Could do better…'

The most obvious *dis*-satisfaction reported from the first year of the new MOB–GDP module, derives precisely from the ambiguity of the hyphen: MOB-or-GDP? Some students and some staff clearly found that the new course opened up their understanding and application of the subject and enhanced their sense of its *relevance* for the student role and beyond. However, others experienced a 'watering down' of the subject content, with fewer subjects being covered, in order to make space for GDP-related activities. There certainly was a reduction of the quantity of MOB material, but elements of *quality* were also felt to have been compromised: for some students, we felt that the level of academic challenge was reduced; some staff felt that the opportunity for input, in terms of individual academic interests and beliefs was absent; and, due to the need to standardise workshop activities, the opportunity for teaching and debate was also reduced. Some staff felt that this affected the development of their own identity as lecturers.

Ironically, the attempt by the module leaders to escape from the 'tyranny of the textbook' led to a different form of tyranny, this time based on the module leaders' own interests and preoccupations! What was experienced as liberating, innovative and exciting by the module leaders, was experienced by some staff as imposing a one-size-fits-all approach, which left them with less autonomy as teachers. This is an aspect of large-module teaching which is well known, but it was influenced by a significant influx of staff relatively new to teaching, as well as by the changes to the course. Attendance issues also have an impact; at a visceral level, the experience for staff of low student attendance and engagement can be extremely undermining. Changes made to the course do not seem significantly to have improved this situation over other years (although, again, there are many variables affecting attendance). Whether or not one believes in the process of projective identification, it is not too far-fetched to assume that this experience on the part of staff is likely, in some way, also to be a reflection of the emotional experience of students.

Discussion

This innovation has highlighted some key issues for us – obvious, perhaps, in retrospect, but difficult to see at the time. They revolve around tensions that exist in relation to teaching in this context:

1 'structural' tensions between the course and the institution
2 tensions within the course itself – some in relation to the staff team, some in relation to students, some in the relationship between the two.

1 Tensions between the course and the institution

The GDP project was introduced and implemented according to timescales set by the University which were very short, and this large, 'flagship' initiative was introduced within an existing, very complex system. The issues of implementation were further complicated by the decision in the business school to embed GDP in an existing module rather than it being free-standing. This meant that every workshop, lecture and assessment had to be planned anew, in order to ensure that the demands of the GDP were being met throughout the whole module. As a result, many of the well-known problems of large student numbers had an impact on the implementation of this specific change; for example

❑ timetabling issues
❑ resource requirements and provision
❑ pressure on administrative procedures
❑ assessment regulations.

Backing from the Bristol Business School executive was essential to the success of the innovation, in terms of delivery and content, making it possible to address structural issues in the areas of timetabling and resourcing which underpin the whole programme.

2 Tensions within the course

Within the course team

The normal anxieties resulting from the teaching role were exacerbated by three factors:

 i this was a new course for *all* staff, even though some had been teaching on MOB for many years
 ii seven staff were entirely new to the course
iii five were newly appointed to the university, of whom three were new to teaching and three to the UK.

The sector-wide tension between centralised control and academic subject freedom for teaching staff was brought into focus by the innovation. For example, the new approach, together with the size of the staff team, made it necessary for module leaders to provide workshop guidelines each week. While this was welcomed by some, it was experienced by others as an unnecessary and irritating constraint.

Both of these issues had been predicted. More interesting, perhaps, and unpredicted, was the fact that the change made three quite different 'groupings' visible within the staff team. These represent or reflect key aspects of our subject in its context: academic research, practice in organisations, and teaching and learning, which match the three elements underpinning the work of a business school: as a centre of research, a centre for training managers and for knowledge exchange, and a centre for teaching and learning. This, in turn, maps onto three primary identities or roles taken up by business school staff: the more or less 'pure' academic, the consultant or manager, and the teacher.

Within the student body

These tensions within the staff group were paralleled by differences within the student body. Some students are indeed aspiring academics but a much larger majority is focused on future employment, while a significant number have decided to take a degree, but without either a particular commitment to, or even understanding of, the subject area or a clear career focus. Consequently, the tension, for both staff and students, is between education as training and education as developing thoughtful citizens, able to question and challenge organisational and social structures and values. In both groups, students and staff, such tensions can clearly be linked intimately to an individual's values and sense of personal and professional identity.

3 Implications

This innovation has highlighted issues of leadership and staff development in ways we did not predict at the outset. In terms of leadership, a key question has involved a sense of ownership of the innovation. Of necessity, the planning was led by only two staff, but the programme was eventually delivered by 16 individuals with a wide range of experiences and interests. The issue of ownership was highlighted by the fact that some members of the teaching team simply could not identify with the course content and/or the teaching approach. As a result, they found it hard genuinely to engage the students.

The tensions described above have made it clear that to succeed with this innovation we have to work in a focused way on both areas of tension. First, we have to develop the *staff team*, working with the tensions and differences between ourselves, in the hope of providing a playful and challenging experience for staff and students. Secondly, we have to start where the *students* are, *not* from where we think they should be, or we would like them to be, or where we think we were when we were students, or indeed, where the textbook says we should *all* be.

4 Conclusions

On reflection, we feel the above account does not put effectively into words either the agonies or the ecstasies of the past 12 months of change and innovation. We would, therefore, like to conclude by stating what is to us obvious, but may not be to the reader.

At this point last year, we had only just started work on the implementation of GDP into our module – and with only the vaguest understanding of the whole project, very little awareness of how much we might gain, but quite a strong sense that this might suck the soul out of us and the course. Looking back, however, we now realise that the renewed energy we have had for this work, and the remarkable levels of engagement from many of the staff team, have been a direct result of the change. Our sense is that there have been two key elements to this. The first is team working. While as module leaders we may, initially, have chosen to work together for survival, we have increasingly realised that this initiative has enabled us to bring together in a new way our many years of experience of teaching in different contexts. The experience has been both creative and even, at times, exhilarating, both in relation to working in the module leadership pair and with the wider teaching team. In our experience, this is not a common reaction among those involved in the teaching of large undergraduate modules, who often describe this work as a painful chore, rather than a stimulating challenge.

The second element is that we have been forced to do things which we probably should have done long ago! One side of this relates to the internal management of the course; this was a large module which needed a fundamental review, in terms of content, assessment and teaching approaches, including the way we used lectures and seminars. The other side is that we have been unable to avoid engaging in 'political' activity on behalf of the course, in terms of how the module is prioritised in the timetable, teaching loads and 'credits' for module management and for teaching and student support. We have been able to put back into the course some of the valued aspects of teaching, in particular, closer working relationships with colleagues and with students that the recent increase in numbers had driven out. In that sense, we have been forced to change – more or less against our will at the start – but we have, to our surprise, been able to use GDP as a lever to introduce wider innovations of our own.

GRAHAM BAKER is senior lecturer in organisation studies at the Bristol Business School, University of the West of England where he is the deputy module leader for *MOB* and module leader for *Organisational Leadership* at Level 6. His research interests are based around discourse and power relations in the public sector. Before joining the university he spent 18 years teaching in a variety of secondary schools.

ROBERT FRENCH is reader in organisation studies at Bristol Business School, UWE, and also works as an independent organisational consultant. He has particular interests in issues of teaching and learning, in friendship in organisational settings, in leadership, and in the application of psychoanalysis in group and organisational contexts. He has written widely in these areas and recently edited the papers of David Armstrong *Organization in the Mind* (Karnac, 2005). He has also co-edited two books, *Rethinking Management Education* (Sage, 1996) with Chris Grey, and *Group Relations, Management and Organization* (Oxford University Press, 1999) with Russ Vince.

15

Against the grain?
Introducing experiential and enquiry-based learning to final-year students

Louise Grisoni, Carol Jarvis, Margaret Page
Bristol Business School, University of the West of England

This chapter describes the introduction of enquiry-based approaches
(EBL) to learning and teaching on two final-year undergraduate modules
in organisation studies as part of a general business studies award.

This chapter developed out of a co-enquiry undertaken by the authors with the Business Management Accountancy and Finance Subject Centre (BMAF) small-grant funding. It looks at the introduction of enquiry-based approaches to learning and teaching (EBL) in two final-year undergraduate modules within the field of organisation studies: *Managing Change* (an elective attracting some 85 students in 2007–08) and *Organisational Analysis* (a core module taken by more than 400 students). Most of the students on *Managing Change* (80%) also study *Organisational Analysis*.

The modules are at different stages of development with regard to EBL and we have found similarities and differences in the opportunities and challenges they face. Our case study shows that experiential and enquiry-based learning approaches can encourage students to develop their self-awareness, to explore wider aspects of their own experience, and to link theory and practice.

Objectives and rationale

The *Organisational Analysis* and *Managing Change* modules form part of a general Business Studies award. The development of these modules during the course of 2007–08 has built on previous work, with a particular focus on:

❑ How to work with the subject content and assessment processes creating resources that will develop critical thinking and writing skills and be consistent with values held by staff and students in relation to enquiry-based approaches.

❑ Exploring the emotional dimensions of student and staff experiences in relation to this approach – in particular the role of anxiety in relation to learning.

Kolb and Kolb (2005) note that most management education adopts a text-driven approach to teaching and learning. The text-driven approach sits comfortably with the preferred learning style of almost half (46%) of the management students they surveyed while only a fifth (21%) preferred experiential approaches. Much text-driven management education tends to put the focus on providing answers, whereas experiential approaches and EBL place the emphasis on questioning and asking good questions. Daudelin (2001) notes that while in the complex world of organisations that students will face when they graduate, reflection and enquiry are core skills for managers, it is not always easy to convince students of their value. Often there can be a big 'so what?' question in students' minds when they are first introduced to these approaches.

The context

EBL can often provoke strong responses – both positive and negative – in students, generating comments like:

'The reflection on the learning helps ideas and theories to stick in the memory for the long term.'

'[I like] the encouragement to build my own opinion on things.'

'Good way of making me think about practical work experiences – useful for theory and practice.'

'I didn't like any of the OA module.'

'You can't be taught experiential learning it happens naturally. Everybody uses their experience differently.'

[*Liked most*] 'Freedom to ask questions.' [*Liked least*] 'There are no definitive answers.'[1]

Our experience suggests that some students struggle to accept that we really mean it when we say 'there is no one right answer' (even when as tutors we role model this approach), fearing that they will be somehow penalised if they fail to agree with the tutor's viewpoint. For many students in their final year their focus is, quite naturally, on assessment and successful completion of the modules. It is perhaps no surprise then that discovering how to engage with a new approach to learning can be anxiety provoking for students. Staff also experience considerable anxiety in relation to holding on to the principles of student-led enquiry as an approach to learning under considerable pressure from students to revert to more familiar approaches and a wider system that is designed to support more didactic approaches.

Description

It is in this context that we developed and adopted the hybrid enquiry-based learning (HEBL) approaches (CILASS, 2008) described below.

---

1 These comments have been taken from responses to a student designed and administered questionnaire on the *Organisational Analysis* module. Research was conducted during lectures in March 2008, towards the end of the module.

Managing Change

The *Managing Change* module was taken by 85 students in 2007–08 and was re-designed over the three preceding years specifically to adopt a strong emphasis on enquiry-based learning (EBL). The design was modified in response to student feedback in each successive term and changes are summarised in Table 1. This is an iterative process, in which tutors responded to requests from students by offering clearer links between teaching, learning and assessment, and more teaching input on enquiry skills to support and encourage a student-led, research-based approach to learning and teaching. Most students on *Managing Change* were also enrolled on the *Organisational Analysis* module and therefore experienced the EBL approach in two contexts. This made a considerable difference to staff and students in both modules.

Teaching input in 2007–08 offered a lecture and tutorial session on reflective writing, in which students explored their experiences of a visit to the Port City exhibition on migration and change at a local art gallery; more on 'story' and narrative methods for research and analysis; and more explicit modelling in lectures by tutors of critical dialogue with core texts on 'managing change'.

Assessed work consisted of 60% coursework assignments and 40% exam. There were three coursework assignments: the first was an individual reflection on three enquiry questions brought by the student to the module; the second, a group research project presented in the form of a 'storyboard'; and the third was an individually written essay. Each of these assignments was designed to build on the previous one, encouraging students to identify what it was that they wanted to learn, and to learn through a group and then an individual research process. Topic areas relate to big picture change issues: climate change, the energy crisis and globalisation, equality and diversity. Students were thus encouraged to locate the business perspectives of the 'managing change' literature within a social context, and with their own experiences of change in personal and employment contexts. Results suggest an improvement in average coursework marks with each successive year (see Table 1).

Students this year (2007–08) have made more explicit links between experiences of change in personal and organisational domains, and seem more able to make links between business and social contexts, and to identify related moral and ethical concerns. The depth and breadth of their enquiry is demonstrated in visual images and narratives in their storyboards and in their reflective writing about their experiences of change in a variety of business and personal contexts. Many students have expressed enthusiasm for the approach, and appreciation for tutors' availability in tutorials to support their engagement with this approach to learning. Levels of anxiety about assessment have to date been considerably lower than in previous years as tutors have become more confident and explicit about their expectations. The module leader has a sense that reduced anxiety and increased confidence on the part of both students and staff have been enabled by iterative feedback and response, and that this process has been essential for tutors to find forms of teaching and learn-

...g approach to EBL on managing change

Changes to design	2005–06	2006–07	2007–08
Overall approach	EBL introduced first lecture in handbook and in marking criteria. Core text is Senior, B. (2002) *Organization Change*. Harlow, Pearson education	As 2005–06 and modelled by tutors individually, with a few co-taught sessions. Core text is Senior, B. & Fleming, J. (2006) *Organizational Change*. 3rd ed Harlow, Pearson Education	As 2005–06 and modelled by tutor interaction in lectures and tutorials. All lectures and some tutorials co-taught. Core text is Senior, B. and Fleming, J. (2006).
Students' enquiry questions	Students asked to write about their enquiry questions. Feedback indicates students found writing in first person for first time challenging and queried 'How can we ask questions before you have told us what the module is about?'	Three enquiry questions modelled by tutors in first lecture. Tutorial to help students develop enquiry questions from their individual experiences of change. More explicit introduction of learning from critical reflection.	Visit to Port City as stimulus to reflect on dimensions of change. Lecture and tutorial to introduce and practise reflective writing to explore experiences of and responses to Port City visit.
Coursework and assessment	Coursework remains unchanged (review of academic article; essay). However first coursework (article review) shows students unaccustomed to developing critical review of texts based on a view of their own. Newly introduced unassessed Powerpoint presentations linking social change to business responses popular with students but under-developed responses; feedback suggests: if you want us to prioritise, you must assess!	First assignment changed to writing up enquiry questions. Storyboards introduced as assessed group assignment, with posters replacing Powerpoint. Final coursework is extended essay exploring enquiry questions in context of social change. Libraries brought in to tutorials to introduce critical research skills. 'Narrative' introduced as a concept. Peer feedback on presentations.	Storyboards introduced with tutor-identified organisations to research. Stronger tutor input on narrative and on data-collection methods. Peer-feedback discussion focused more on narrative, construction of analysis, and presentation skills alongside issues/content.
Lectures: introducing theory	Lectures based on core text with some introduction of tutor case study experience, research interests (action enquiry, psychoanalysis, narrative) and use of video case study.	Lectures continue to use core text and introduce new material on complexity, psychological contract and extended material on narrative. Video/ film clips/ case study from experience.	Lecturers model critical engagement with core text from research perspectives – illustration using video/film clips and refs to current news. Dialogue between tutors in lectures (all jointly attended) models asking questions (in contrast to finding answers) as a method for learning
Exam: same structure, new content	Analysis of live news report replaces case study. Open question option invites application of selected theory to selected change situation. Final section – critical reflection on learning – remains.	Analysis of live news report continues. Open question option invites application of selected theory to selected change situation. Detailed application of theory in tutorials (Term 2) and practice for each section of exam includes reflective writing. Final section – critical reflection on learning – remains.	Analysis of live news report continues. Open question becomes single compulsory questions replacing choice between questions relating to specific theory. Final section – critical reflection on learning – remains.
Student responses	Very high anxiety and some hostility before end of Term 1: how to revise for the exam. Tutors not accessible enough! 4% achieved a first class mark in 2004/05	Less anxiety and more enjoyment. More use of tutors but still sense that some don't get it. 17% of students achieved a first class mark. Average mark increased from 56.7% to 59%.	Less anxiety, more students initiated contact with tutors. Higher marks for coursework assignments.

ing that best evoke qualities of enquiry, and demonstrate how these are rewarded through assessment. While the principles of EBL remain constant, they need to be 'translated' into a form that can best be worked with by specific tutors and students, and in this sense need to be 'reinvented' from year to year. However, EBL is not the preferred learning approach for all students, and tutors continue to work with the challenges of finding a level that is generative and fair to the cohort as a whole.

Organisational Analysis

The *Organisational Analysis* (OA) module faces different challenges and opportunities. *Organisational Analysis* is a core module across a range of programmes within the business school at undergraduate Level 6. It is taken by more than 400 students each year. Assessment currently includes both coursework (learning diary and extended essay) and examination (short-answer case-study exam, and extended-essay exam). The module places an emphasis on the use of Multiple Perspective Analysis in exploring organisations and encourages students to take a critical approach. The teaching philosophy is based on Kolb's (1984) learning cycle and the current core text is Morgan's (2006) *Images of Organisation*. Students are encouraged to attend their timetabled workshop (20–25 students) and lecture (c 200 students) each week, but this is not compulsory.

Assessed learning diaries were introduced onto the module in 2006–07. Students are asked to write a couple of pages for each topic covered in lectures and workshops. The template provided is structured to encourage students to make links between theory and their own experience and each topic has four sub-headings: thoughts; personal experiences; reflections; and applications. Our first year of using the assessed learning diary suggested that students found keeping the learning diary beneficial. Although some found the volume of work involved high in relation to the proportion of assessment marks attached to it (5% of the total module mark), others claimed it was an important aid to their learning and revision for exams.

With more than 400 students and a staff team of seven, module handbooks, other materials and activities are planned well in advance of the new academic year, leaving less flexibility to make significant changes mid-module. This year, external research funding and internal funding of research and development through work and development credits, has allowed an increased flexibility through the introduction of optional workshops. These workshops have been designed and delivered in response to student and staff feedback on areas where students desire additional support. Workshops have covered:

❑ reflective writing
❑ writing and analysing a case study of personal experience
❑ interpreting and applying the marking criteria (including practising peer assessment).

A strong emphasis has been placed on learning from peers in tutorials (something many students have been reluctant to take seriously in the past). This is beginning to have an impact so that, for example, students have initiated a series of group-revision sessions, for sharing readings and practice answers, co-ordinated via a Facebook group. Staff involvement has been limited to booking rooms and publishing the Facebook link on Blackboard.

On a module of this size, the competence and confidence of staff in working with these approaches is also important. Staff support and development activities in the last two years have included the preparation of detailed briefing and debriefing papers on experiential workshops and a session to explore what we mean by 'effective scholarship' in the context of the module (the output has been built into the assessment criteria and marking grid and is given to students in advance of their coursework hand-in date). A reflective-writing workshop and experiential-learning session are planned for May 2008.

Table 2 summarises developments in the module over the last two years and proposed changes for next year. Average marks have shown no real shift over the last two years, with mark averages for coursework steady at around 60%. However, student feedback suggests that anxiety levels have been reduced – a significant benefit in its own right.

Evaluation

Student responses: opportunities and challenges

Feedback from students suggests that our approach to teaching is perceived as different and difficult. Many experience high levels of anxiety around the approach and particularly around assessment; in a final-year core module which has to be passed if the student is to graduate, submitting a piece of assessment that is 'different' is seen as 'risky'. Yet the message is that to achieve a high mark, students need to take the risk. Anecdotal evidence suggests that some students who find the approach too different and difficult make a strategic decision relatively early to disengage and do just enough to pass. In an attempt to address this issue, this year we introduced lectures on reflective writing (*OA* and *Managing Change*); a timetabled workshop on the learning diary (*OA*); and optional workshops on reflective-learning logs in the first half of the first term (*OA*). The aim here was to encourage students not only to begin to reflect more deeply on their experience, but also to recognise and value their experience as an important and valid source of learning and enquiry.

In an *OA* seminar last term, students discussed their approaches to completing their assessed learning journals and the challenges they faced in getting started. As we explored why this might be, they suggested it was a need to feel that they were progressing and that always required starting at the beginning with the first entry. If you start anywhere else at some point you find yourself 'going backwards' which they saw as stressful – more stressful even than a blank page – and deeply unsatisfying. No wonder then, that for some students, experiential and enquiry-based learn-

Table 2 The evolving approach to HEBL on *Organisational Analysis*

Changes to design	2006–07	2007–08	Proposed for 2008–09
Overall approach	Emphasis on use of Multiple Perspective Analysis in exploring organisations and encouraging a critical approach. Teaching philosophy based on Kolb's (1984) experiential learning cycle. Core text is Morgan (2006) *Images of Organisation*.	As 2006–07. Introduction of lecture and tutorial dedicated to reflective writing, as well as more material on Blackboard and optional additional sessions.	As 2007–08. Core texts Morgan (2006) and Cunliffe *Organisation Theory* (Sage Publications, London 2008).
Lectures	Introductory and revision lectures and two lectures on each of eight perspectives discussed in Morgan – first lecture introduces key theory; second looks at theory in practice using lecturers' own experience, case studies, and video clips. Each lecture delivered twice.	Drop one perspective (complexity) to allow introduction of guest lecturers to talk about their experience of important organisational issues – very well received, although some students feel they are 'pointless.' Introduce lecture dedicated to reflective writing. Greater use of video clips.	Trial use of 'PointCast' (online PowerPoint slides with voiceover attached) to create space for some Q&A sessions in lecture slots.
Tutorials	Topics follow lecture content in the same week. 20–25 students per tutorial, working in learning groups of four or five. Term 1 makes use of a lot of case studies; Term 2 more challenging, experiential exercises. Each learning group encouraged to run one seminar (unassessed).	Dedicated sessions on reflective writing and critical reflection or learning from experience. Optional seminars on reflective writing; coursework; and revision prove popular and are well-attended. Greater emphasis on peer learning and assessment, although encouraging students to value this can be difficult.	Larger tutorial groups to be taught two-up to provide opportunities for role modelling of critical engagement and allow assessment of student presentations and participation under controlled conditions.
Assessed coursework	Term 1 – introduction of learning diary, where students are asked to complete a couple of pages on each of the topics covered. Some students find it a really helpful way of engaging with the material and a useful revision tool; others feel it is difficult and time-consuming in relation to marks available. Term 2 – extended essay using multiple perspectives to analyse experience in learning group/on the module. High levels of anxiety exacerbated by dissertation hand-in.	All coursework moved to Term 1 to reduce student stress around pre-Easter period, when dissertations and a number of other significant coursework assignments due in. Second assignment based on narrative case study of student's own experience. Anxiety levels are much reduced but there is a negative impact on attendance in Term 2.	Learning diary to be redesigned and extend into Term 2, with formative feedback in Term 1, and to include a critical reflection on learning on the module. Introduction of assessed presentations (peer and tutor) and marks for participation.
Exams	Short answer case study exam split from May exam and held in January. Average marks increase by nearly 10%. Two-hour exam in May contains two extended essays.	No significant change.	Drop January exam in favour of increased emphasis on assessed coursework, made possible by changes in PSRB requirements for exemptions from professional exams.
Student responses	High levels of anxiety around the introduction of new ways of learning at Level 6, when the stakes are highest and students feel their workload increases significantly.	Anxiety around introduction of new ways of learning at Level 6 remains – do not want to take risks in final year, but feel they have to. Anxiety around coursework reduced.	Developments on core OS module at Level 4 expected to help contain anxiety over coming years as approaches will be more familiar.

ing approaches, which, like experience itself, are messy and confusing, are seen as difficult and even threatening.

At the outset of both modules, students tend to polarise in their attitudes to the modules and their learning approaches. Our experience suggests that few students feel indifferent about the approaches. Vince (1998) suggests that one of two cycles is generated in response to the anxiety provoked by learning. In one of these the individual or group moves through the anxiety, taking risks and arriving at new insight (promoting learning). In the other she or he succumbs to defences against anxiety that block learning. Where there has been an opportunity for dialogue with tutors, many students who are initially hostile in their response become strong advocates.

We have found that student anxiety has tended to rise again as they approach revision for the exam, and the final coursework assignment. At this point tutors have introduced Vince's (1998) model and invited students to use it to map their own responses to anxiety provoked by assignments. In subsequent assessed work, students reflecting on their learning have described how they have been able to use this model as an enabler for moving through anxiety triggered by the EBL approach, towards more risk-taking which has enabled learning. This was a surprise to tutors, who were also contending with high levels of anxiety and concerned that they had underestimated the stresses and risks for students induced by introducing EBL in their final year of assessment. Thus the model offered a shared sense-making frame that enabled staff and students to 'contain' and work with anxiety in ways consistent with the principles of EBL – student self-managed and self-directed learning.

When students do embrace these more enquiring approaches, the effects on their levels of self-awareness can be profound and can generate real excitement and enthusiasm, as well as anxiety. Students begin to make new connections between different areas and aspects of their life and in a 'safe' tutorial environment will often share deeply personal insights with their peers and tutor, insights that suggest they have developed real confidence in the value of their own experience.

Staff responses: opportunities and challenges

Ogbonna and Harris (2004) suggest that work intensification arising from cost pressures and increasing student numbers requires more emotional labour and emotion work (Hochschild, 1983) on the part of staff in terms of class management as well as meeting the demands and expectations of larger groups of diverse students. Our research suggests that the resistance from some students that can accompany experiential and enquiry-based approaches can serve to intensify this emotion work.

Our research among colleagues teaching on these modules suggests that EBL requires us as teachers to engage emotionally with our teaching. Similarly when, as teachers, we engage emotionally with our teaching our hope and expectation is that students will do likewise. As one colleague expressed it:

> [I feel] satisfaction if they [the students] seem engaged, even if they don't do it the way I would or I asked them to.

By contrast when we perceive that students are not engaging, we may look for someone to blame. Sometimes this leads to a questioning of our competence:

> I worry that I am not giving them enough theory and that this reflects what I do in my own research, I don't use enough theory.

and sometimes to attaching blame to the students

> What do they see as learning? Being spoon-fed?

If anxiety is ever-present, we need to consider what provokes anxiety that discourages us as teachers from learning and what enables us to contain or hold anxiety sufficiently to promote learning? Our research suggests that one important factor is autonomy in the form of our perceived ability to respond in a way we feel is appropriate to meet the group's needs:

> If you respond to the group's emotion, you know what will work and what won't.

By contrast these tutors felt that, on modules where the content and delivery of seminars is more closely prescribed, they have less flexibility and are less effective as teachers: students may see them as competent in neither their subject nor their teaching. Some tutors spoke of 'content' as a container for anxiety for both student and tutor. A paradox here is that while students may question the tutor's subject expertise when they are not given answers, to teach effectively using experiential and enquiry based learning approaches requires tutors to engage philosophically, as well as intellectually, with the material they are teaching and to be able to respond, in the moment, as discussion unfolds. In other words, they should be expert (Dreyfus, 2002; Dreyfus & Dreyfus, 2004) in both subject and teaching approach.

Tutors in our research study noted that there are times of year, particularly when teaching Level 6 undergraduates, when:

> Students and tutors are totally wiped out.

At these times the tutor is seen to have responsibility for the emotion work necessary to generate energy in the room. The emotional dissonance involved in displaying an emotion the tutor does not feel means the emotional cost of doing so can be significant (Zapf & Holz, 2006). Constantly testing boundaries by adopting more questioning approaches to learning and teaching involves emotional labour and emotion work – for students as well as tutors. No matter how experienced the tutor, this emotion work is not without its cost as well as reward.

Tutors all recognised the rewards in terms of their own learning when adopting EBL approaches and had stories relating to the 'buzz' they experience when students really engage with the subject and the approach – for example:

❑ emulating the tutor's style and approach when making a presentation
❑ emailing articles and web links that have excited them to the tutor
❑ describing in seminars how they have applied their learning on other modules or in other areas of their life.

These responses are by no means predictable, even for the same tutor working with the same group. Thus the anxiety is ever-present.

Discussion and conclusions

Our case study of two modules has shown that experiential and enquiry-based learning approaches can encourage students to develop their self-awareness and to explore and exploit wider aspects of their own experience, to link theory and practice. Hybrid approaches to EBL have been adopted to meet the needs of student groups that differ in size and level of initial engagement with the module, and both modules have adopted iterative processes that have allowed them to develop in response to student and tutor feedback. *Managing Change* has a stronger EBL focus, while *Organisational Analysis* takes a more hybrid approach, and is developing in a different but complementary direction. This raises an issue around the broader institutional context and the introduction of new approaches to learning and teaching in the final year of undergraduate studies.

Staff commitment to the learning and teaching approaches is seen as vital to their successful implementation. We suggest that tutors need both stronger content knowledge and developed skills in coaching and facilitation to support guided enquiry. To encourage students to be enquiring, teachers not only need to 'live life as enquiry' themselves (Marshall, 1999), but they need confidence in their own grasp of the material to allow students to question it. In this way, the teacher can promote a learning space that models 'safe uncertainty' (Mason, 1993) and that is conducive to developing genuine enquiry skills. Tutors describe being 'drawn back' towards chalk and talk methods when they are feeling tired and/or students are resisting and these can be characterised as defence mechanisms against anxiety. When they succumb to this pull, tutors feel they have let both themselves and the students down and the emotion work involved in dealing with this can add further to the time and tiredness involved.

Student feedback suggests that co-teaching can also bring significant benefits to students and staff. Students suggest that seeing tutors voicing their differences gives credence to the idea that there is no single right answer and helps students to give voice to their own ideas and insights. Reflective writing has proved beneficial in its different forms on both modules. Our research among *Organisational Analysis* students suggests many students value lively classroom discussion more highly. *Managing Change* already includes some classroom-based assessment, and this will be introduced to *Organisational Analysis* next year.

This case study has developed out of a co-enquiry undertaken by the authors with BMAF small grant funding. As a project team, we have experienced many of the frustrations that students complain of when adopting EBL in relation to the need for:

- ❑ clarity in relation to the project (students wanting to be given 'the right answer')
- ❑ time available to work on it (more work in relation to other modules)
- ❑ the need for a sense of plan and achievement of successful outputs for our work (what response will we get to the risks we have taken)?

This has led to some interesting insights into the concept of 'mirroring', the reality of collaborative working, creating 'boundaries' in relation to what's in the project and what's outside it, when we work on the project in work time or personal time, and whether having fun and being creative is an acceptable way to conduct research.

References

CILASS (2008) 'Enquiry-Based Learning (IBL)' Centre for Enquiry-Based Learning in the Arts and Social Sciences. University of Sheffield http://www.shef.ac.uk/cilass/ibl.html Accessed 20/02/08

Daudelin, M. (2001) Learning form Experience through Reflection. *Organizational Dynamics* **24** Winter pp 36–48

Dreyfus, H. L. (2002) Intelligence without Representation – Merleau-Ponty's Critique of Mental Representation. *Phenomenology and the Cognitive Sciences* **1** pp 367–83

Dreyfus, H. L. & Dreyfus, S. E. (2004) The Ethical Implications of the Five-Stage Skill-Acquisition Model. *Bulletin of Science, Technology & Society* **24** June pp 251–64

Hochschild, A. (1983) *The Managed Heart.* Berkeley and Los Angeles, University of California Press

Kolb, A. Y. & Kolb, D. A. (2005) Learning Styles and Learning Spaces: Enhancing Experiential Learning in Higher Education. *Academy of Management Learning & Education* **4** (2) pp 193–212

Kolb, D. (1984) *Experiential Learning.* Englewood Cliffs NJ, Prentice Hall

Marshall, J. (1999) Living Life as Enquiry. *Systemic Practice and Action Research* **12** (2) pp 155–71

Mason, B. (1993) Towards Positions of Safe Uncertainty. *The Journal of Systemic Consultation & Management* **4** pp 189–200

Morgan, G. (2006) *Images of Organisation.* London, Sage

Ogbonna, E. & Harris, L. C. (2004) Work Intensification and Emotional Labour among UK University Lecturers: An Exploratory Study. *Organization Studies* **25** (7) pp 1185–203

Vince, R. (1998) Behind and Beyond Kolb's Learning Cycle. *Journal of Management Education* **22** (3) pp 304–19

Zapf, D. & Holz, M. (2006) On the Positive and Negative Effects of Emotion Work in Organizations. *European Journal of Work and Organizational Psychology* **15** (1) pp 1–28

LOUISE GRISONI is head of School of Organisation Studies and was Director of Learning and Teaching 2006–07 at Bristol Business School, University of the West of England. Her teaching interests include organisational analysis and behaviour and organisational learning and leadership. Her interest in experiential and enquiry-based pedagogy has been developed over many years.

CAROL JARVIS is a lecturer in organisation studies at Bristol Business School, University of the West of England, Bristol. Her research interests include: unwritten contracts; emotional labour and emotion in organisations; complexity and emergent approaches to change; coaching and mentoring; and the use and development of enquiry-based learning approaches. Before joining the University full-time in 2006, Carol spent 20 years as an independent management consultant, specialising in organisational and marketing research; organisational effectiveness and change; and internal communications.

MARGARET PAGE is a senior lecturer in organisation studies at the University of the West of England where she co-directs the Leadership and Organisation in Public Services MSc and is module leader for the Level 6 undergraduate elective Managing Change. Her publications are concerned with action-enquiry-based methodologies for teaching and learning, and engaging with the dynamics of gender, power and change in organisations. She is currently interested in metaphor as a means of inquiring into modalities of knowing, learning and organising.

16

Embedding PDP in an academic subject

Jacqui Gush
Bournemouth University

By embedding PDP in the curriculum, using reflective writing and
the encouraging self-awareness in students, this chapter shows how
PDP can be meaningfully integrated into a subject. Thus learning
outcomes associated with PDP complement subject-based learning.

Context

In the School of Services Management at Bournemouth University most undergraduate programmes have a common unit of study at the second level called *Managing People & Personal and Professional Development* (MP&PPD). This draws on the body of theory from organisational behaviour as well as covering some key principles and practice of human resource management. The purpose of the unit is not to develop participants as specialist HR managers but as managers of people in their chosen sector of the service industries. Students learn about key theoretical areas such as personality, motivation, leadership, group work and conflict.

However, an integral part of learning in this academic unit is the development of skills that underpin management competences. This provides an ideal opportunity to marry theory to practice to develop students' understanding of the challenges in the management of people. At the same time it allows them to assess and reflect on the development of their own attributes and behavioural practices as a person, an employee or a manager. Thus this aspect of learning represents the personal and professional development of the student as they are encouraged to follow a PDP process.

As these programmes are all sandwich courses with a 40-week paid work placement, normally in the third year of the four year programme, the MP&PPD unit of study enables students to understand and develop themselves in preparation for role responsibility within the workplace the following year.

Intended learning outcomes of the unit include the ability to:

❑ Apply concepts, theories and knowledge from social psychology and management theory to the management of people at work.

❑ Set personal objectives and take a pro-active approach with regard to planning for their placement year.

❑ Secure a suitable placement using skills for completing job applications, managing interviews and assessment centres.

❑ Complete a personal development portfolio and demonstrate the benefits to be gained from this.

❑ Through reflection, demonstrate improvement in transferable skills for the workplace and identify areas for ongoing development.

Main features of the approach

To illustrate the main features of the approach, the teaching, learning and assessment methods used in the module are examined. Students have three elements of assessment in this unit:

❑ student-led workshop presentations

❑ a time-constrained essay

❑ a personal and professional development portfolio.

This diet of assessment approaches is designed to strike a balance between the theoretical and practical components of the unit, where the essay tests their knowledge of theory and the workshop allows them to develop and demonstrate skills. The capstone assessment is the portfolio which will be discussed further.

Teaching and learning methods used have traditionally been a mix of lectures and seminars. Lectures have been used to deliver an introduction to the topic and outline the main theoretical approaches. Increasingly as teaching materials are available through the university VLE, large group sessions are used more for discussion and questions and answers based on prior reading of these materials.

Small group seminars are used for the practical aspects of the topics. These may include discussions and assessments to build self-awareness and knowledge, or practical exercises based on case studies or role plays.

Some sessions are designed to support the placement search effort which takes place during this year of study. For example, building knowledge of personality is linked to developing a personal SWOT analysis and from here a CV; communication theory is linked to building skills and knowledge of recruitment and selection; and interview role-playing is undertaken. As well as looking at the theory of learning we take the opportunity to help students understand their own learning styles and to develop their skills of reflection.

In addition, students are encouraged to integrate learning from other concurrent units. For example, students usually undertake a large group-work project during their second year. Their learning within MP&PPD enables them to understand the theory and principles of group work, which they are then able to relate directly to their practical experience and gain a critical awareness of skills and behaviours being demonstrated by themselves and others.

The student-led workshops, when students working in small groups are assessed, also take place during seminars with the rest of the student cohort peer-assessing their presenting colleagues. The presenting groups are given a topic and expected to design, organise and lead a 50-minute practical, participant workshop for students, so their peers learn from participating in the workshop. Students are introduced to the university PDP website as a key resource. Examples of workshop topics include:

❑ Stress and emotional intelligence
❑ Motivation
❑ Group work
❑ Perception and attitudes
❑ Leadership.

Designing appropriate delivery patterns was crucial in order to facilitate this close relationship between understanding the theory and using this knowledge to develop self-awareness and a personal skills set. In 2006, the traditional lecture-and-seminar timetabled sessions were abandoned and instead a whole day within a rota of block teaching replaced the weekly sessions. This was designed to imitate a professional training day. It also offered more flexibility and allowed for movement between theory and practical exercises throughout the day. We believed that it would produce more opportunity for discussion and the development of areas of interest. However, the day was very tiring for the tutor as well as the students. Organisation had to be meticulous or time could be wasted; the day's programme could become unbalanced and thus even more tiring. In the following year, the principle of a block of dedicated time was retained, but the duration reduced to a regular weekly half-day session within the first semester. This proved quite popular, was less tiring and allowed similar benefits to be gained.

The development of the portfolio assessment

The purpose of the portfolio assessment is to encourage students to complete a reflective account of personal and professional development over time supported by evidence. Students are encouraged to be selective in their development of themes, (which do not have to be directly drawn from within MP&PPD) and to relate reflection and analysis of development to their forthcoming work placement, and to discuss how they intend to use this year to further develop themselves personally and professionally. This results in clearly expressed pre-placement objectives.

Once out on placement, students are expected to complement their work-based learning (WBL) with a reflective work diary. This diary records their work experience and until this year was not directly associated with the MP&PPD unit. However, as students are expected to reflect critically on their learning and development in the context of their organisational work, this is in effect continuing their PDP work.

Figure 1 could be useful in illustrating the challenge presented to students of under-

Figure 1 Mapping the different approaches taken to a reflective task

taking reflective work in a workplace setting. It shows the four quadrants into which students' accounts can fall. Because it is not really possible to be reflective in a purely technical account of one's work experience, the best and most successful option is a critical reflection on behaviour in a work (or technical) context, as indicated by the position of the star in the diagram. In contrast, the lowest marks come from students who stick exclusively to a factual account of what they did or what happened, and do not explore how they or others did what they did, and do not reflect and analyse the challenges, skills, the theory and learning that underpinned the experience. These are represented by the top right quadrant.

In the last year, the school has undertaken a radical change to the portfolio whereby the second year MP&PPD portfolio and the WBL diary are combined. This establishes a formal link between the learning within MP&PPD and the workplace, and students' workplace learning is assessed within the unit.

This change to the assessment has the advantage of emphasising the seamless developmental journey over time, and reinforces the theme of personal and professional development and the need for a behavioural dimension. It allows the student to develop an analysis of selected themes over time and to establish the link between their development as a student and as an employee. Because practical work-based learning is now a meaningful part of the academic curriculum, there is congruence with the three main tenets of the PDP process, academic, personal and career or employability.

Evidence of effectiveness

The first measure of effectiveness and the easiest source of evidence is at the level of student reaction. This emerges through the various mechanisms, both formal and informal, used to obtain student feedback. In class, students enjoy the practical side of the subject, but not always the theoretical side, and frequently they cannot make the connection between the two. This is evident in the assessment where marks are consistently higher for the student led workshop presentations than for the essay.

Peer feedback on the student-led workshops is usually very positive, stating that it has helped their learning. Although a natural inclination may be to claim 'they would say that wouldn't they', I have found students to be constructively critical of their colleagues when given the responsibility to peer assess and I find that their comments and evaluation usually reflect my own.

The portfolio is challenging for students. They find it difficult during the second year to understand what is required of them and with little or no work on reflective skills undertaken during Level 4, they are challenged by the concept of reflection. However, it is evident that for most students the experience of submitting a reflective portfolio before they go on placement helps with their second piece of reflective work during the placement. Students frequently comment, following the second year portfolio and more so following their placement work, that it has helped them to learn and understand themselves and to see the relevance of the learning in their subject.

'Doing this work has helped me to understand myself better'.

'I feel much better prepared for placement now.'

'I enjoyed learning about personality and felt I did a better CV after this.'

Although there is no evidence of a direct correlation, students frequently exceed the expectations of employers, certainly with reference to the transferable skills now so widely recognised as key workplace skills, but also with attributes such as self-awareness, willingness to learn, self-motivation, resilience and reliability.

A good percentage of students receive offers to return to their placement organisation and about 20% of students do so.

'The feedback from stores and regional managers has been that Nigel is very eager to learn... He takes things more seriously than most members of staff.' (placement development advisor report)

'He clearly sees the relevance to his degree and looks for the links.' (employer)

'The student has impressed me immensely.' (employer)

This reflects the skills and attributes identified as part of the USEM model in the work of Yorke and Knight (2004) as part of their Skills Plus project. Their research findings culminated in a model which highlighted four important dimensions to student employability, namely; understanding, skills, self-efficacy and metacognition. It would seem that the type of work done in this unit and the close link to the work placement has a positive impact on students' employability.

This may also be at least partly responsible for the maturity with which students return to their final year and their different attitude to their studies and the skills that they bring to this pressurised and important year, such as self-organisation, time management, resilience, emotional intelligence and generally a higher level of self-efficacy. Would this have happened anyway without the requirement to consciously capture, reflect, analyse, monitor and review their journey of learning? Kolb (1984) did not think so and his learning cycle demonstrates the important role for reflection in facilitating learning.

The external examiners have been particularly supportive of the design of this unit.

In particular, one examiner who is a manager in a local council's tourism department expresses enthusiasm for the employability benefits the work brings to students.

Enablers, barriers or challenges

The two most important enablers of success for the practice have been:

1 Achieving an effective delivery approach given the usual constraints and logistical challenges of a university timetabling system and estate.
2 More negatively, the ability to impose assessment on the students, without which the benefits of a structured and systematic reflective appraisal of themselves and their developing competences would most likely not have taken place.

The importance of class contact for this type of work with students is beyond doubt, particularly where the challenge is relating theory to practice. I consider tutor facilitation in PDP work with students to be crucial in encouraging student engagement. Therefore, a significant barrier is the declining class-contact time with students. Growing pressures on staff time and the need to reduce assessment workloads also threaten the continuation of the traditional portfolio as a method of assessment.

A further issue in this unit is the extent to which this type of work should be student-initiated and directed, as opposed to tutor-facilitated. As far as the portfolio is concerned, there was never any question of whether it should be assessed. However, as the tutor, I was loathe to prescribe to students what it should contain and how they should set about it, apart from establishing guidelines of broad principles and themes. However, students become frustrated without very clear directions and structure, and over subsequent years of setting this work, I found I was adding more and more detail in the brief to students, and hence increasingly setting the agenda. I try to keep the 'helpful hints' to generic points of principle, but they want to know what is good practice and ask to 'see examples from last year'.

Students' frustration with not understanding the principles behind the portfolio has been reflected in the end of year student feedback. On more than one occasion, the score for the question 'What is expected has been made clear to me?' is lower than for other criteria, despite a genuine willingness on my behalf, through dedicated time slots, to helping them to engage with this type of work.

There are also concerns with the student-led workshops. I worry that the group as a whole will have missed vital learning if the presenting group does not do what I consider a good job, and key aspects of learning are missing, such as important self-assessment material which facilitates important learning about oneself. Thus I always brief the presenting group, agreeing learning outcomes and suggesting approaches and/or content. However, am I placing conflicting demands on the students by tending to impose my agenda and my expectations as tutor, while at the same time telling them that they need to take ownership of their presentation? The difficulty of making assumptions about what and how others are learning is illustrated in the way that I am sometimes surprised to find that a presentation that I was not satisfied with is viewed as a positive learning experience by the class. This supports the need for the tutor role to be one of facilitating and supporting others' learning through process, rather than dictating content and following our own agenda. This is a difficult balance to strike with this type of work when serious marks are at stake and there is a set of assessment criteria which is broadly tutor-set.

Conclusion

Lessons learnt from running this approach to PDP for several years now have been outlined in the sections above. In summary, important lessons include:

❑ The importance of assessment, but at the same time, recognition of the challenges that assessing this type of work brings.

❑ The importance of achieving the right teaching and learning approach along with the right delivery pattern.

❑ The need for students to be introduced to reflection in the first year of their university programme.

❑ The value of real work experience as a focus for personal and professional learning and development.

This case study of practice has illustrated how PDP can be meaningfully integrated into the curriculum. Although the nature of the subject provides a natural substratum for embedding this type of work, the marrying of the technical and behavioural dimensions and the ability to reflect on action is central to learning for success in all endeavours and subjects, whether that be as a student, an employee or a human being.

This approach to working with students is relatively time-intensive and as pressures on staff time in higher education continue to reduce class-contact time, the challenge for the future is to find an effective way to engage students in this type of work without the degree of tutor support that has been illustrated here.

References

Kolb, D. (1984) *Experiential learning: experience as the source of learning and development*. London, Prentice Hall

Yorke, M. & Knight, P (2004) *Learning, Curriculum and Employability in Higher Education*. London, Routledge

http://pdp.bournemouth.ac.uk/

JACQUI GUSH was Head of Learning & Teaching in the School of Services Management at Bournemouth University 2002–07. During that time she led the introduction of PDP for the university and designed and developed a comprehensive PDP website. She subsequently led a strategic employability initiative through an Employability Steering Group, working closely with the Careers Service. As well as continuing to teach, she also developed successive formats for work-based learning for the School. She now heads the Graduate Employment Service for the university which incorporates the Placement Development Unit.

17

To embed or not to embed?
The embedding of PDP in the curriculum

Dorota Ujma, Mark Atlay, Petia Petrova
University of Bedfordshire

This chapter outlines some of the key aspects of a project to explore students' perceptions of PDP and to evaluate their learning needs and shows how our approach to PDP in tourism has changed.

This chapter is based on the Tourism Personal Development Planning (PDP) Module Evaluation and Redesign Project in the Division of Tourism, Leisure and Sport Management. This intervention was funded by the University's Centre for Excellence in Teaching and Learning (Bridges CETL) with the intention to explore students' perceptions of PDP and to evaluate their learning needs. It considers how issues arising out of the work of the Bridges CETL could be incorporated into the redesign of modules to support the overall objectives of PDP. The changes are discussed in the light of various PDP models that are employed in UK universities, and concludes with a set of suggestions for curriculum designers.

Objectives for change in the tourism curriculum

There are various models that enable curriculum designers to build PDP into study programmes. These models are still developing; as Atlay (2006b) points out, they are built on the premise that academic staff should work towards adding value to the learning-teaching experience, helping students take greater responsibility for their own learning and providing more focused and effective support and guidance. Considering these factors, the tourism course team wanted to provide students with an educational structure and process that enables them to develop towards their future successes in personal and professional areas by:

❑ relating their learning to a wider professional context
❑ improving their general skills for study and career management
❑ articulating their personal goals, enhancing opportunities and evaluating progress towards their achievement.

Rationale behind the changes

PDP is intended to improve the capacity of individuals to communicate their learning to others who are interested, such as academic staff and employers, to self-reflect, to plan and monitor the achievement of personal objectives (QAA Website 2004). In the tourism courses there are modules that deal with improving students' skills and reflection on their development. The module *Personal Development Planning (PDP) in Tourism* was introduced in 2003 to enhance students' awareness and understanding of careers within tourism, and to develop knowledge and skills to enable students to make and implement their career decisions, both now and in the future.

The PDP module is of great potential benefit to tourism graduates who, when considering career options, face an uncertain economic environment, the burden of tuition fees, increased competition for traditional graduate positions, and the fact that tourism degrees often have low value within the tourism industry (Petrova and Mason, 2004b). The industry perceives tourism degrees as broad-based, providing generic knowledge, intertwined with business studies and economics, while the tourism industry values highly personal skills such as communication and numeracy (Amoha and Baum, 1997). PDP is a process embedded in the curriculum which should support students in facing these challenges and improving their skills.

Context

For the last eight years the University of Bedfordshire has been developing a distinctive undergraduate curriculum model which supports the personal and professional development of students through integrating PDP, transferable and career management skills into the academic curriculum. In 2005 the Bridges CETL was established to build on the experience of embedding PDP processes, incorporating skills in the curriculum, fostering employability and sustaining excellence (Petrova and Ujma, 2006b). Bridges is involved in supporting PDP implementation across the University. It is intended that regardless of discipline, PDP should enable students to make links and gain a (holistic) overview of their studies, reflect critically, become more independent, adopt a more pro-active stance in their academic study, extra-curricular pursuits and career planning, and capitalise on their learning in a variety of contexts (Atlay, 2006b).

The tourism department has long been committed to students' personal development and employability prospects. It has been involved in researching its tourism students' career expectations and aspirations (Petrova, 2001; Petrova and Mason, 2004b; Petrova and Ujma, 2006a); the impact of work experience on student development and the relevance of tourism degrees to the tourism industry across the UK (Petrova and Mason, 2004a; 2005). The department has also worked towards improving students' career prospects and taken steps to embed PDP and employability in the tourism curriculum in a strand of inter-related modules.

The changes in the Tourism PDP

The tourism PDP strand consists of three modules across the programme. The *Personal, Professional and Academic Development Planning* (PPAD) module in Level 4 of tourism degree courses was introduced in 2003. PPAD concentrates on the development of academic skills in our new students. Students then progress onto the *Personal Development Planning (PDP) in tourism* module in Level 5 and are encouraged to take their development a step further, to enhance their career-related and employability skills, through interactive exercises, group activities and individual reflection. The strand is completed at Level 6 in the final-year project.

Low grades and poor attendance on the Level 5 PDP module suggested that prior to academic year 2005–06, *PDP in Tourism* was not maximising the potential benefits for students – or staff. It was also observed that neither staff nor students were particularly happy with the module and did not entirely understand its aims and objectives. To investigate the reasons behind this, an evaluation of our PDP provision was conducted. Funding from the CETL Bridges and the Fund for the Development of Teaching and Learning Phase 5 (FDTL5) project into feedback supported the evaluation. Independent researchers conducted surveys of students' views, observation of teaching practice, focus groups with students and meetings with members of staff involved in teaching and supporting the PDP provision. Following this evaluation, changes in the PDP provision have been gradually introduced to the tourism curricula.

Module changes at Level 4

At the same time as the changes in the Level 5 PDP module were undertaken, parallel research was carried out on the Level 4 PPAD. It focused on the use of feedback by tourism students (Lawrence and Ujma, 2007). This research is not discussed here in detail, as its impact on the PDP module re-design was somewhat serendipitous, rather than carefully planned and designed.

The students' limited awareness that feedback is part of the learning process at Level 4 was somewhat surprising. As a result of the research, workshops are now embedded in the Level 4 Tourism PDP curriculum aiming to raise awareness and empower students to ask appropriate questions, and to encourage reflection, critical in creating lifelong learning (Hinett, 2002). The course team are now considering ways of optimising feedback throughout the PDP undergraduate curriculum, so that tourism students leave university as self-regulated learners who can genuinely use feedback and understand its value. This is congruent with the development of life-long learning skills, part of the PDP objectives.

Module changes at Level 5

The re-design of the PDP in tourism module consisted of four stages which included module evaluation, development, testing and dissemination of results. The module evaluation stage began by assessing the provision of the module, establishing areas of strength and weakness, including assessment and student experiences. The outcomes of the evaluation were reported in previous selections of case studies (Becket and Kemp, 2006, Petrova and Ujma, 2006a) and in a conference presentation (Petrova and Ujma, 2006b). The new module was introduced and subsequently evaluated with the tourism and leisure students (81) and three members of staff in academic year 2006–07. The new module has been assessed by students, staff and external observers, using a combination of evaluation tools, and additional changes have been incorporated in the current academic year 2007–08 as now detailed.

First, a questionnaire survey of tourism, leisure and sports students was conducted to investigate their career aspirations and steps taken to date in their personal development planning. Further to this, lectures and seminars were observed, and student feedback was sought. Two focus groups were conducted with sport and leisure and then tourism students. The results suggested that students did not see the module as practical or challenging. They felt they knew the basics and the module went over familiar ground. Students also indicated that they liked the opportunity to talk and did not like being 'talked at', suggesting that more interactive workshops, rather than the traditional lecture and seminar delivery, might be more productive. Some even questioned whether lectures were needed. Students did like the first assignment – a job study and comparison between skills required for a job and the personal specification of the student applying for it. Although they may have not found the module 'interesting', they admitted that the module made them think about their career objectives. The module achieved its aim of enhancing students' awareness of careers via the assessments administered, but not necessarily through the delivery of content.

The questionnaire survey showed that students are interested and committed to the industry and increasingly more and more of them work part-time during their study, often in a subject-related area. However, they were lacking awareness of industry skills needs and in the ability to assess their own skills against industry requirements. So in redesigning the module we considered academic and employability skills, peer- and self-assessment of skills, and industry demands in relation to skills. (Petrova and Ujma, 2006b). Changes have been introduced to the module in three areas: teaching methods, the role of technology and assessment.

Teaching sessions were changed from lectures and seminars to workshop sessions, with a smaller number of students in each workshop (up to 20). This has given the teaching team an opportunity to get to know the students better. On the other hand, it was also more resource-intensive, as more staff hours were needed.

Technology has become more important in the module delivery, both in 'spicing it up' and in engaging students with new technological solutions. A new Breo[1] design

---

1   BREO is the name of the University of Bedfordshire VLE Blackboard system and stands for the Bedfordshire Resources for Education Online

offering tools for online reflection and access to notes/handouts and teaching materials, which students needed to use independently between scheduled sessions, played an important part in the new module delivery. New teaching rooms, designed in an office-like layout, introduced an exciting change to the teaching environment. The layout proved conducive to group work (each group having access to a computer) and has had a positive impact on students' experience. Students' views about these changes have been recorded occasionally throughout the semester in their reflections, and in the last week of teaching, in a FacilitatePro[2] online meeting session designed for that purpose. FacilitatePro software was used to get a better insight into students' opinions of the module, submitted in an anonymous brainstorming session.

The assessments were also changed. The job study now has an added element of action-planning to encourage thinking about future career plans as soon as possible. The second assessment was changed from the submission of an application pack to a process of mock interviews, crucial as a training process for real job interviews. Submitting an application pack before the mock interviews has become just one of many steps students need to complete the interview process. On the day of the mock interviews students are all 'performing' on both sides of the process, role-playing employers and employees. The interview panel (a team of students performing as employers) needs to select the best candidate for the job for a given vacancy and provide feedback to the successful and unsuccessful candidates. The students are observed in the process, mainly by staff from the careers centre at the university, who also provide feedback on the performance of the panel and individual interviews. The process is not assessed, but reflections on it must be included in the final individual and graded report.

Mock interviews, although very complicated and labour-intensive, have offered students the opportunity to develop as self-directed learners. Interviewing has numerous impacts on the students' learning experience. For example, it enables them to realise the value of preparation before the session, makes them see how not co-operating in group work may affect other students, allows them to master peer assessment and self-assessment processes and helps to develop reflective practices.

All these changes were introduced in order to help students focus more on their future career choices, and to enhance their opportunities and ability to evaluate progress.

Evaluation of the PDP practice

The effectiveness of the changes introduced in the Level 5 PDP in Tourism module has been analysed through a set of specifically designed tools, presented in a separate detailed report, produced for the Bridges CETL (Petrova, 2007).

In addition, the module was also evaluated using the Student Perception of

2 FacilitatePro is an online collaborative meeting software designed to support collaborative group brainstorming and decision-making processes (http://www.facilitate.com).

Module (SPOM) Questionnaire, a standard module evaluation tool at the University of Bedfordshire. It consists of 20 questions designed to elicit views about the quality of the learning experience and is distributed during the teaching sessions around weeks 11-12 of the 15-week semester. It is a part of the standard quality assurance procedure. The results are analysed centrally and forwarded to teaching teams.

Figure 1 Mean results for the Student Perception of Module (SPOMs) for PDP in Tourism – comparison of results before and after interventions

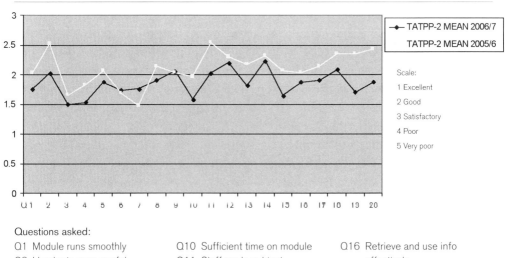

Questions asked:

Q1 Module runs smoothly	Q10 Sufficient time on module	Q16 Retrieve and use info effectively
Q2 Handouts were useful	Q11 Staff made subject stimulating	Q17 Comm/present info effectively
Q3 Opportunities to ask questions	Q12 Feedback record was informative	Q18 Apply method to problem solving
Q4 Module information available	Q13 Good explanations	Q19 Work well with others
Q5 Accurate information available	Q14 Usage of knowledge & skill	Q20 Rate module
Q6 Aims of module were clear	Q15 Staff interested in student views	
Q7 Module assessment clear		
Q8 Correct level of skill assumed		
Q9 Correct prior knowledge assumed		

SPOM results for the Level 2 PDP module (Figure 1) confirm that changes have positively impacted upon students' experience. The chart shows that the redesigned module is graded higher than previously, in all aspects, apart from three questions related to the module aims, assessment and required level of skill, indicating that the changes were beneficial to students' experience. Further to the changes to the PDP strand outlined above, there have been a number of other developments introduced to the tourism curriculum over the last five years. The following section explores how these changes fit within the various models of embedding PDP in curricula.

PDP and the curriculum

Atlay (2006c, 2008a) suggests that five main approaches to PDP in the curriculum have been adopted by various universities. These include a *discrete* model, where PDP is additional to the curriculum; *linked*, with PDP in parallel to the curriculum – but not integrated; *embedded modular*, embedding PDP in certain modules; *integrated*, with PDP embedded across the whole curriculum (in some cases as 'curriculum carrier') and finally, an *extended* model.

These approaches, as explained in the following sections, are not mutually exclusive, and mixed or intermediate models are also possible. Each has its own value and those designing curricula need to find a model which works best for their subject and, particularly, their students. The nature of the student body, the curriculum, the institutional and wider context and the aims of the course team are all factors which need to be considered when incorporating PDP into the curriculum.

Model 1 Discrete / additional: PDP as additional to the curriculum

In this model students are provided with opportunities to engage in 'PDP activities' and encouraged to undertake them, but these are additional to the curriculum. Students maintain their own PDP, often in the form of a portfolio, deciding what to include and undertaking their own analysis and reflection. This model might be seen as one which best prepares students for their continuing professional development (CPD) since the onus for its operation is in their hands.

This model existed in the tourism department in the early 1990s. Students were encouraged to keep a paper-based PDP folder and collect information about their professional and academic progress throughout the course, even though these may not have been assessed in any way. Some examples of the activities (surviving to this day) include becoming a student representative or taking part in additional activities (to the obligatory diet of modules), which may lead to obtaining some certificates and/or enriching their CVs.

Additional activities and lectures are provided, for example by the Bridges CETL 'U CRe8' Club (2008) and within the Knowledge Hub (2008). The 'U CRe8' Club invites all students to themed creative sessions organised co-operatively by students and staff. These sessions build on practical skills and develop creative thinking and employability in a friendly environment. The 'Basics of Building a Business' (B3) is a free lecture series from the Knowledge Hub, running through the autumn and spring terms. The lectures are open to all, including local people, start-up companies, staff and students of the University (Knowledge Hub, 2008).

Students often participate in these options. They search for additional knowledge and skills, but full advantage is gained when students engage and reflect, often telling staff about these experiences during the PPAD and PDP modules.

Model 2 Linked: PDP in parallel to the curriculum, but not integrated

In this model, the PDP element and the curriculum are distinct. The linkages may only occur at certain points (related, for example, to activities in certain modules / units) or throughout the course. Students are given activities as part of the course which emphasise PDP and consciously link these to their personal progress.

Before introducing the PDP strand in each level of the tourism courses, a personal tutoring system was tested with Level 4 and 5 students. When the PDP in tourism on Level 5 became a core module, the personal tutoring system was replaced by the PDP strand described earlier. Students are encouraged within the PDP modules to take an opportunity to discuss their future careers with a number of academic and support staff at the University, but it is left to them to arrange. They can do so with academic advisors within faculties and centrally in the Professional Academic Development (PAD) section, career advisors, study exchange and work placement and learning resource teams at any stage of their studies, when they feel the support of those various groups is needed. The PDP module serves to an extent as a place where these additional services are being promoted to students.

Sessions in the Bridges CETL, designed to share the teaching activities between staff from different subject areas, helped the tourism course team realise that most of the modules offer opportunities for students to reflect on their learning process and show links between theories studied and world-of-work practices. For example, in sport tourism at Level 5, students examine customer services and are encouraged to write a job advertisement, detailing selection criteria and skills required to perform a particular job in the industry. Students need to research the job requirements and the employment market and discuss the selected characteristics during seminar sessions. In this work, they follow PDP practices, even though they may not realise that this is the case. Within a number of modules (especially those involving group work), students are encouraged to keep a log of activities undertaken in specific projects with a view to strengthening their reflection on the 'learning curve' and to realise the 'distance travelled' in the learning process. These activities are most effective not as a one-off, but when they are incorporated, structured and supported within a curriculum.

Model 3 Embedded modular: PDP in certain modules

The modules designed to provide the main support for PDP may serve to link with material studied elsewhere and the student's progress file or portfolio. Such modules may have a focus on skills and/or a subject as well as emphasising PDP processes. The tutors for these modules tend to take primary responsibility for PDP development and support within their curriculum area. There may be any number of such modules within the curriculum, but they tend to be more likely at higher education Levels 4 or 5. At higher levels students normally take responsibility for their own learning and PDP. This model appears to be the dominant curriculum model emerging in many higher education institutions.

Members of staff are encouraged by various initiatives at the University of Bedfordshire to practise this approach to PDP. The Employer Liaison Scheme offers financial benefits to interested members of staff, as well as opportunities to develop their own personal development planning. This approach has worked in some instances and students have benefited from practical PDP-related options being introduced to the course diet.[3]

For example the *Airport Services Management* module is based on the Servisair training programme delivered by their staff at London Luton Airport in co-operation with our employer liaison fellow. (Servisair is a global operator in aviation ground services http://www.servisair.com). Students who achieve good results on the module are offered short-term employment with Servisair during the summer.

Practical modules that develop employability are popular with our students. *Airport Services Management* gives students the opportunity to experience the realities of working in the industry, and to compare it with their own expectations and dreams of working in the aviation sector. They comment on and discuss their development during the workshops and in the structured reflections in their PDP module, rather than in the *Airport Services Management* module itself. This practice stresses the value of a structured and supported PDP process, exploring links between modules and 'real-world' practices.

Model 4 Integrated: PDP embedded across the whole curriculum
Where the whole curriculum embraces a PDP-based approach and most modules or units involve activities which adopt PDP processes, PDP is embedded in all or most of the experiences of students. In such a model, reflective approaches underpin the delivery of the curriculum. Curricula seeking to address employability issues particularly lend themselves to this type of approach.

So far the tourism PDP strand can be placed somewhere between models 3 and 4. The PDP strand across Levels deals specifically with reflection on skills developed. These processes often pose problems to students, so to facilitate them the course team works closely with the university's Centre for Personal and Career Development.

PDP aids students' ability to look at the course, and skills development, as a whole. It teaches them how to assess and apply their skills within different contexts and to reflect on other modules on offer as part of our tourism courses. To enable this process the tourism PDP co-ordinators explore the links with other modules within the tourism curriculum, particularly where there is an emphasis on the development of practical skills and reflection on the overall development of our students. The challenge is to extend this responsibility to all members of the teaching team.

Model 5 Extended model
PDP processes are embedded in the curriculum and also serve consciously to integrate activities which occur outside the curriculum. Such a model is most often found in professional programmes where students are working in an area related to the topic they are studying. Here PDP serves to provide the link between the academic

3 'Working in Partnership' Event was a direct result of the Employers Liaison Scheme and is summarised on http://newsweaver.co.uk/corpnews/e_article000861289.cfm?x=b11,0,w

curriculum and these wider experiences.

Usually in tourism, mature students can see clear links between the practice in their jobs and some aspects of the course. Their younger colleagues, despite having worked in a number of tourism-related part-time jobs, need to be prompted to notice the links between the 'two worlds', which they often compartmentalise and treat as separate entities. Students have the opportunity to apply for accredited prior experiential learning (APEL), where the experiences from the world of work are credited at the university and count towards their degrees.

The extended model includes negotiated programmes. Independent study modules, where the learning outcomes are negotiated between the tutor and an individual student, are considered mini-examples of this practice and provide a strong personalised input in learning. Similarly, in the Level 6 Final Year Project, a relationship between the student and his / her supervisor provides some personalised structure to the research-centred PDP approach.

Advantages and disadvantages of the models

Effective curriculum design is dependent on a wide range of factors and each of these models presents distinct challenges to staff and students. The possible advantages

Table 1 Advantages and disadvantages of models of PDP integration (Atlay 2008a)

	Advantages	Disadvantages
Discrete / additional	Simple, places onus on the student, minimal disruption to the existing curriculum, less resource required	Not all students will engage, students' experience will vary; resource and opportunity may be wasted. Doesn't prepare students for the transition into employment
Linked Parallel – not integrated	Student experience is more controlled, there is some (but minimal) disruption to the curriculum and can build on existing activities such as induction and tutoring	Students may still choose not to engage and hence the impact on student learning and employability for those most likely to gain may be minimal
Embedded modular	All students will experience PDP at some stage. PDP can be controlled and built on	Experience may be fragmented, staff and students may see PDP modules as being of low value. Only those teaching the modules know what PDP is
Integrated	Becomes part of student and staff thinking in all modules and hence an approach to work and study. PDP helps provide coherence to students' studies	Difficult to get all staff to implement, maybe become so embedded as to be invisible (and non-existent)
Curriculum carrier	Provides coherence to students' learning and enables a high degree of personalisation of the curriculum. Only the staff running the core PDP spine need to fully understand PDP processes	Resource intensive, student experience can still feel fragmented. Providing time within the curriculum for the PDP spine can be difficult. Students need to engage with the PDP element and see its advantages
Extended	Becomes a holistic way of working, draws in work and life experience	Activities beyond the curriculum are varied and uncontrollable, learning will be as well. Some may see this as a problem – particularly those who like to have clear outcomes

and disadvantages of each are shown in Table 1.

The advantages of embedding the PDP in curricula

Why embed PDP in the curriculum?

Atlay (2008b) lists the main reasons supporting integration of PDP into programmes as follows:

❑ It supports learning

PDP prepares students for academic study by emphasising learning processes and skills. Students often have a poor understanding of their learning processes and how to maximise their potential. By introducing activities allowing students to recognise their learning styles and allowing them to make mistakes (for example in the mock interviewing process), they get an opportunity to make the most of their learning potential.

❑ All students can benefit from PDP

Embedding ensures equality of provision where all students get the opportunity to become more effective, independent and confident self-directed learners. True PDP processes should help and support the effective learning of a wide range of students and help them to become more confident in the 'world of work' and in life. At the end of the course all students will have experienced similar opportunities, aiding teaching and student management.

❑ More effective use of resources

When PDP processes are integrated within the curriculum, resources may be saved in the longer term in comparison with an additional optional process, which if it duplicates modules, may waste scarce resources. Changes introduced in the PDP strand in tourism were resource-hungry in the first instance, but the materials produced will be used in the future, saving time and energy, even though contact time and staff hours increased.

❑ Preparation for life beyond university

PDP processes are widely used in 'professional' life as part of continuing professional development and all students need to be prepared for this as well as for life beyond university.

The relationship between PDP and the curriculum

Regardless of the type of PDP model adopted, curriculum designers often choose to emphasise one particular aspect over another, depending on the issues they wish PDP to address in their own course or their own perspective on the role of PDP in relation to student learning. When embedding PDP they may focus on one of the three purposes for PDP: student learning, careers and employability, or students' personal development.

For example, vocational courses are more likely to emphasise educational and career dimensions while more traditional academic courses may emphasise personal and educational aspects. Tourism students tend to value the practical elements of their course, especially if they see the relationship of this to their increased employ-ability. As mentioned earlier, through various staff schemes the university encourages development of practical modules in the curriculum and employer engagement. This aspect is popular amongst staff and students. However as we see in tourism, the vocational aspects of the course can be so satisfying to some students, that they can neglect educational dimensions. To avoid this, the notion of students taking respon-sibility for their own learning and development in a structured and supported way, should be at the heart of any approach to PDP and all three purposes of PDP should be balanced in course delivery.

In a true PDP curriculum, students' self-awareness and their ability to use feedback and to take responsibility for their learning and development will all be emphasised – at all levels. PDP becomes a philosophy which underpins curriculum delivery, and fully embracing the notion of PDP is thus an issue for the whole institution. In this approach the development of PDP can't be marginalised, or left to individual ele-ments within the curriculum or particular members of staff. If this is to work across all areas, there must be a common language and understanding amongst course teams, support services and the student about what PDP is and its value in support-ing student learning. The challenge of this approach should not be underestimated.

Challenges

The main challenges, not in any particular order, arising from attempting to fully embrace PDP in the tourism and other curricula at the University of Bedfordshire are:

❑ Achieving an appropriate balance between learning, career and personal develop-ment and ensuring that one is not over emphasised to the detriment of the other two.

❑ When PDP is seen as only about skills and not about process. This happens when the careers and employability strand is interpreted exclusively in terms of stu-dents getting jobs at the expense of acquiring the ability to change roles and continuously develop their careers.

❑ PDP can be marginalised and not seen as an important part of the curriculum or the learning process, if it is given to specific members of staff and not embraced by whole course teams.

❑ A PDP curriculum should be more student-centred than tutor-centred. The needs of individual students are as important as the demands of the curriculum. The tutor becomes a facilitator of the learning process and needs to be supported in this role.

❑ Systematic and sustained staff development is required to support staff awareness and understanding of PDP and its application. It is good supporting practice for staff to 'role-model' PDP processes on the ways in which they themselves work.

❑ Difficulties in getting students to see the value in PDP immediately – the views of students are largely formed by the views and attitudes of the key staff they interact with.

PDP as a process

We have listed a number of practices within tourism courses at the University of Bedfordshire. We are in the process of reviewing our curriculum, so that the best student-centred designs are implemented.

The tourism example shows that just because we might have a range of activities that we broadly label PDP, it does not mean that we are necessarily 'doing PDP'. PDP is not an event or a series of unstructured and unrelated activities but a 'structured and supported *process*'. Events such as case studies, employer visits and group work often cited as meeting the career dimension of PDP, only become true PDP activities when students are engaged in a process which actively and consciously supports their learning and the making of connections. There are various examples of processes which can be followed – these are discussed in detail in Kumar (2007).

The questions below guide us in monitoring whether our curriculum allows PDP to be 'structured and supported' and they can be recommended for that purpose in any institution.

Some questions to make PDP events a *structured* PDP process

❑ Do students consider that what they've done prior to the activity has a bearing on it? For example, if it is a group work activity, does it start by looking at the group work activities they did the previous year or in their pre-university studies – and what they learned from these?

❑ Do students assess their own abilities in relation to the task and consider how they might improve? This can be done at the beginning, middle or end of the activity.

❑ Do students consciously reflect (in a structured way) on what they've learned during and/or after the activity?

❑ Are students helped to make connections between what they learned in the activity and future planned activities or the world beyond their current course? This might be in their personal life, in future study or in employment.

Some questions to make PDP events a *supported* PDP process

❑ Are students provided with clear guidance as to what PDP is and how it is supported?

❑ Are students supported in seeing the activity in context? Are they provided with guidance on what is different about this activity from similar activities they've done in the past, (such as the nature or the level of the intended outcomes)? Are they helped to see how it relates to their wider academic study, to the attainment of learning outcomes and to the world beyond the university?

❑ Do students know of sources of help (staff, written material, e-learning guides) with the key elements of PDP (task-specific requirements, self-awareness assessments, reflection)?

❑ Are they guided as to how to keep records of their reflections and activities (using notes, blogs, portfolios, journals)? The recording is not an essential requirement but it can help with contemporaneous and subsequent reflection and is a means of evidencing development.

When activities are set in context and explicitly linked, where addressing the above sets of questions becomes a way of working for staff and students, then we will have a real PDP curriculum – a truly structured and supported learning process. We are still in the process of finding the best match between our own and our students' needs in the tourism courses, but we hope that the changes introduced and planned for the future will help us to create an exciting curriculum, structured around PDP practices, benefiting staff and, most importantly, our students.

References and URLs

Amoha, V. A. and Baum, T. (1997) Tourism Education: Policy Versus Practice. *International Journal of Hospitality Management* **9** (1)

Atlay, M. (2006a) *CETL Report September 2005 – February 2006, Laying the Foundations*. University of Luton. http://www.beds.ac.uk/bridgescetl Accessed 03/05/2006

Atlay, M. (2006b) *A Guide to Progress Files and Personal Development Planning*. University of Luton. http://www.beds.ac.uk/bridgescetl Accessed 03/05/2006

Atlay M. (2006c) *Embedding PDP practice in the curriculum in Personal development planning and employability*. Learning and employability series 2 CRA/Higher Education Academy

Atlay M. (2007) *CETL Bridges Evaluation Report July 2007*. University of Bedfordshire. http://www.beds.ac.uk/bridgescetl/dissemination/workingpapersreports Accessed 16/04/08

Atlay, M. (2008a) *Curriculum models and PDP Practice*. BRIDGES: Working Paper on http://www.beds.ac.uk/bridgescetl/dissemination

Atlay, M. (2008b) Embedding PDP Practice in the Curriculum. BRIDGES: Working Paper, on http://www.beds.ac.uk/bridgescetl/dissemination

Atlay, M. and Kumar, A. (2004) *Bridges – Supporting Personal, Career and Professional Development through the Undergraduate Curriculum*. University of Luton. http://www.luton.ac.uk/bridgescetl Accessed 03/05/2006

Becket N. and Kemp P. (2006) (eds) *Enhancing Graduate Employability in Business and Management, Hospitality, Leisure, Sport, Tourism*, Newbury, Threshold Press pp 148–54

Bridges CETL 'U CRe8' Club http://www.beds.ac.uk/bridgescetl/events Accessed 26/04/08

Higher Education Academy Website (2008) http://www.heacademy.ac.uk/projects/detail/projectfinder/projects/pf2255 Accessed 28/05/2008

Higher Education Academy Website (2003) http://www.heacademy.ac.uk/assets/hlst/documents/projects/Employability/employability_project.pdf Accessed 28/05/2008

Hinett, K. (2002) *Improving Learning through Reflection – Part One*. http://www.heacademy.ac.uk/resources/detail/id485_improving_learning_part_one Accessed March 2008

Knowledge Hub http://www.beds.ac.uk/knowledgehub Accessed 26/04/08

Kumar A. (2007) *Personal, Academic and Career Development in Higher Education SOARing to Success*. Routledge

Lawrence L. and Ujma D. (2007) Optimising feedback throughout the Tourism PDP curriculum. Presentation to the 'Shaping the Future of Tourism Education in HE'. Association for Tourism in

Higher Education (ATHE) Conference 2007, St Anne's College, Oxford 5–7 December 2007

Petrova, P. (2001) *Tourism Students Career Expectations and Aspirations: An Examination of Attitudes, Perceptions and Expectations of Current Undergraduate Tourism Students at the University of Luton of Tourism Degrees and Tourism Careers.* University of Luton.

Petrova P. (2007) *Redevelopment of module TATPP-2 'Personal Development Planning in Tourism'.* Bridges CETL Internal Final Project Report

Petrova, P. and Mason, P. (2004a) How Valuable Are Tourism Degrees? Tourism Industry Views. Presented at the Critical Issues in Tourism Education Conference, Association for Tourism in Higher Education, Great Missenden Management Centre, Buckinghamshire Chilterns University College 3 December

Petrova, P. and Mason, P. (2004b) The Value of Tourism Degrees: A Luton Based Case Study. *Education + Training*

Petrova, P. and Mason, P. (2005) Employment Practice in Tourism – Limits and Opportunities to Potential Employees. Paper presented at the International Conference on Critical Tourism Studies, Dubrovnik, Croatia 30 June–03 July

Petrova P. and Ujma D. (2006a) Students' Awareness of the Importance of Transferable Skills for Employability. In Becket N. and Kemp P. (eds) *Enhancing Graduate Employability in Business and Management, Hospitality, Leisure, Sport, Tourism.* Newbury, Threshold Press pp 148–54

Petrova P. and Ujma D. (2006b) Drive for Excellence in Personal Development Planning (PDP): the Case of Tourism Courses at the University of Luton. Presented at the 24th EuroCHRIE Congress 'In Search of Excellence for Tomorrow's Tourism, Travel and Hospitality', Makedonia Palace Hotel, Thessaloniki, Greece hosted and co-organised by the University of the Aegean, 25–28 October 2006

QAA Website (2004) Progress files for Higher Education, http://www.qaa.ac.uk/academicinfrastructure/progressFiles/default.asp Accessed 28/05/2008

Servisair website http://www.servisair.com Accessed 26/04/08

MARK ATLAY is Director of Teaching and Learning and the University of Bedfordshire's Centre for Excellence in Teaching and Learning (CETL). Mark worked at the University of Glamorgan and at the Open University before moving to Luton where he has worked in a number of areas including quality assurance, staff development, quality enhancement and educational development. His co-ordination of the development and implementation of the university's curriculum model involving a revised approach to skills development linked to progress files and PDP led to the designation of the university as a CETL. His current role involves responsibility for the development of the university's curriculum and teaching on a postgraduate course for new academic staff.

PETIA PETROVA is lead researcher (scholarship and curriculum) in the University of Bedfordshire Teaching and Learning Directorate. Petia is responsible for introducing initiatives which ensure that staff research has an impact on the learning experience of students across the university. She is also an associate of the university Bridges CETL. Petia was previously a research fellow at the division of tourism, leisure and sport management, responsible for re-designing the content and delivery of the 'Personal Development Planning in Tourism' module. She has just completed a PhD on tourism employers' views of the value of tourism degrees.

DOROTA UJMA is a senior lecturer and a field chair in undergraduate tourism studies at the University of Bedfordshire. Previously she taught at the Krakow University of Economics in Poland. She completed a masters degree in Krakow, and a PhD on tourism distribution channel relationships at the then University of Luton. Her current research interests are focused on tourism marketing, specifically distribution in tourism and hospitality, health resorts and tourism associations and their role in the travel trade. Dorota is a member of the Tourism Society and the Higher Education Academy, as well as a Bridges CETL Fellow. As such, she focuses on employability issues and links between employers and curriculum, as well as on the processes guiding development of tourism career management skills.

18

Space to learn?
Learning environments in higher education

Colin Beard
Sheffield Hallam University

What form would your ideal teaching space take? In this chapter I encourage the consideration of issues raised by Jamieson et al. (2000) about the relationship between teaching and learning and the physical and virtual spaces and places used to facilitate and enhance the student learning experience.

The shift in language from the historical 'classroom' to contemporary 'learning environment' is symbolic of the transformation in progress. Let me offer some images, a glimpse of some *real* learning spaces I have come across around the globe. Some interesting trends might reveal themselves in your mind (see also Beard & Wilson, 2006). Consider the following:

❏ seat hammocks in lecture theatres in Turku Polytechnic in Finland
❏ large Mongolian style tents in the countryside campus of Lancaster University to teach outdoor education and outdoor adventure
❏ moveable indoor 'igloo style walls' for privacy in Glasgow Caledonian University learning centre
❏ classrooms located in department stores in Thailand
❏ education and training of Omani senior civil servants on board a tallship

and think about those well-known structures called sheds, where significant inventions often occur. Learning is migrating out into the corridors beyond the classrooms, into informal spaces, to the outdoors, locating within local communities and beyond immediate home shores. In the opposite direction, nature is moving indoors, with plants and other 'landscaped' learning spaces on the increase: wooden decking, water features, beanbags and sofas, even straw bales (with removable plastic covers for seats), and carpets with outline grids built into their design .

The traditional classroom has colonised the psyche of higher education institutions over many years and it has dictated many teaching behaviours. It is said that students in higher education will have spent over 20,000 hours in 'classrooms' by

179

the time they graduate (Fraser, 2001): classroom residence has perhaps taken centre stage for far too long. The places and spaces in which students learn are changing, dramatically affecting both learning efficacy and the experience of learning. Could this time spent learning be more productive if it was located within a more diverse range of places and spaces? Such questions now have to be addressed by lectur-

Figure 1
Hammocks in Turku
Polytechnic lecture
theatres

ers, as committed pedagogic specialists; our current understanding of the impact of physical space on the accomplishments of those who occupy them perhaps remains disappointingly low and this important question of *optimal places to learn* remain for the most part unanswered.

Let's talk about the pedagogy of space

Becher & Trowler (2001), using an 'ecological' approach to space design in the workplace, refer to the need to observe the movements of people or 'tribes' and their creation of 'territoriality'. In order to understand the way the traditional 'classroom' approach has become entrenched in the HEI psyche, there is a need not only to appreciate the sub-cultural differences between disciplines and fields of study concerning space for learning, but also to explore the overarching and broader conflicting discourses that occur between the space providers (facilities managers), space consumers (academics and students), space designers (such as architects), and institutional senior managers.

Estates staff are the people we need to talk with; however, their focus will be on efficiency of use, durability in performance, and density of occupation. They will declare their intention to provide adequate numbers and sizes of classrooms, in the appropriate locations to serve academic needs. For these staff the learning environments are operational places to manage, through measures and costs, inventories, equipment lists, offering an educational 'service' with limited pedagogical data or expertise. Durability, efficiency, use of space (occupancy x frequency), percentage of seats filled, number of rooms used, return on investment, health and safety issues and theft and security problems all become part of the statistical data that form the basis of important managerial decision-making. Individual lecturers and schools might usefully contribute a pedagogical voice to the space management debate.

So how do we collectively make learning spaces more suitable and personal for all of us? At present many lecturers and students migrate at frequent intervals to

Figure 2
Yurts at Lancaster
University

'given' timetabled spaces; this creates some ambivalence towards the given space. The campus pulsates to hourly rhythms. Powerpoint projectors start up, plasma screens light up, and aged overhead projectors add to the clutter of technological gadgetry at the front of the classroom 'occupied' by us. As lecturers we can feel coupled to the lectern, console, mouse and microphone, powerless to leave the immediate space, so reinforcing the perceived separation of lecturers from 'audience' (Beard, 2005). As lecturers we do need to understand such 'territorial' issues, and the associated politics of power and ownership in the use of learning spaces.

How else can we help students?

For many years I have observed the way students occupy, colonise and modify spaces for their own purposes, particularly in uncontested, often unclaimed informal spaces within and around universities. The evolving landscape of learning is interwoven, in a complex way, with student behaviour. Many lecturers and schools are encouraging such trends in proactive territorial behaviours by putting extra tables, chairs, sofas and technological enhancements in these areas, to support the student occupation of hitherto underused spaces. At Sheffield Hallam University there are many suites of fast-food-style stand-up computers for short-term usage in the corridors and reception areas. Form usually follows function but sometimes the reverse is true as students modify the 'given' to suit their requirements. In between classrooms some large spaces have been appropriated by students; equipped with technological mobility students surreptitiously borrow furniture from elsewhere and increasingly their learning spills out of the formality of classrooms, libraries and learning hubs, and moves into informal corridors and cafés (see case study *Using Informal Space*). We can facilitate this reconfiguration of learning spaces by providing more opportunities that allow students to collaborate in the re-shaping and re-designing of the psychological, physical and IT enabled spaces.

So why do students need to come into university in the first place? Besides seminars and lectures and other face-to-face learning, the university acts as a place to meet *people*, such as peers and tutors, to access *resources*, and for access to those special *spaces* that possess *an ambience for learning, thinking and collaboration*. Space becomes a place, as part of student identity: a place to be seen, a place just to '*be*', to '*belong*', and be met. Yi-Fu Tuan (1977: 6) notes, 'what begins as undifferentiated space becomes place as we get to know it better and endow it with value'. These social dynamics coalesce with the educational experience.

Continued transformational change in the design and use of learning environments will occur more rapidly in the near future. The shift from 'transmission' approaches to active or experiential engagement suggests one way forward: we are witnessing more co-operative multi-disciplinary projects, new forms of placement (e.g. 'service learning'), more law 'clinics', more simulated environments (e.g. hospital wards), more virtual field trips (rather than, or as well as, real ones), learning 'studios' (of the art and design style – see Jamieson et al, 2000; Carbone & Sheard, 2003), 'learning cafés' (see JISC, e-Spaces study) different kinds of 'laboratories', news production rooms for journalism (http://www.adm.heacademy.ac.uk/resources/case-studies), real restaurants and real customers in hospitality 'suites'. These signpost innovative trends. As we begin to realise the limiting effect of the page and (computer) screen on our capacity to learn, so floors, walls, glass, IT, informal and unused learning territory all become ripe for the development of innovative learning ideas. The film *Minority Report* offers a glimpse of the future of IT developments that will overcome this restriction on brain capacity using large glass IT enabled screens.

The 'coffee and papers' case study below highlights one very simple approach to the use of informal space (cafés and outdoor spaces) for the development of relaxed alertness. It can engender the pleasure of the 'reading of the text', producing more of a sense of excitement about learning.

A simple practical case study

Using informal space – 'Coffee and Papers'

Reading and the creation of the state of relaxed alertness

Underlying principles

❏ This session uses the principle of mood setting and relaxation to create a pleasurable flow experience of reading (of articles) for a limited period of time

❏ Learners are given (or can bring – or both) a large choice of 'papers' to be read

❏ The session uses informal learning spaces in a creative way and the principle mood setting metaphor is taken from the idea of relaxing on a Sunday reading the papers.

What it achieves

❏ Uses space and place (e.g. university café, atrium, outdoors) in a creative way to develop the pleasure of the (critical) reading of the text and the notion of different spaces for different learning functions

❏ Improves levels of (post-reading) collaborative discussion in a course, develops critical reading and debate, and introduces a literature base to a topic/subject

❏ Deeper thinking and reading (of the text) skills by students

❏ Higher cognitive processing skills are developed within a short space of time because of group collaborative sharing when the knowledge base is high from reading.

Description

This technique has been tried with over 6,500 people from around the world in different cultural settings. Used with FE students, FE lecturers, HE students and HE lecturers, corporate clients, public sector staff (e.g. NHS) and many others.

I use the mood setting 'frame' of **lounging about reading the Sunday newspapers** – but instead of newspapers academic journal articles are supplied and/or brought to the event by learners from a range of well-known sources.

The scene. The participants drift off with their chosen papers into a plethora of spaces both indoors and outdoors. Some go off to the café, others sit on the floor at the back of the lecture theatre. Some have their shoes off, sitting or lying on comfortable sofas in the glass conservatories. Sometimes the classroom has soft background music playing. In hotel settings with our MBA students or corporate events, coffee percolators bubble away, Earl Grey tea is on offer and lemon scents the air.

The articles might be from scholarly and professional journals: *People Management,* and *Management Learning, Management Education and Development, People and Organisations, Training and Development, Industrial and Commercial Training, Sloan Management Review, Harvard Business Review* and many others. Hardly Sunday morning reading! Subtly included in the reading material are articles that encourage students to be aware of themselves and to be critical of these articles.

We are encouraging students to become more relaxed about the 'literature' associated with their subject, to encourage them to share, become fascinated, get copies of lots of material because they want to take it home, and to learn to communicate and explore their findings with each other.

Following the reading I act merely as a scribe and facilitator – letting go of my concerns about my expertise and as a result the sessions produce much debate. The subsequent evaluation of one particular session showed that students wanted more time in future to repeat these explorations of the literature and to **play with concepts and ideas** in this **relaxed** way. One student said:

> One of the more effective learning community development exercises, in my view, followed the coffee and papers sessions each morning. During these sessions, differing

views concerning the same articles were discussed and new insights developed based on individual experience outside the articles. This led to a spin of ideas that spurred more new ideas, and re-shaped some of my initial thoughts of the articles. It appeared that many of the participants shared this experience regarding the coffee and papers sessions.

In the corporate world where this technique has been used, one chief executive sat in her stocking feet on a stool in a hotel lounge, surrounded by strawberries coated in chocolate, and coffee and croissants and said:

Colin, I am in heaven. I never have the time to read any more. I have lost the power to think or read with any depth these days... I am enjoying this experience!

For first year tourism students I have used weekend travel sections from newspapers and the students have explored the text in the broadest sense: image analysis, titles and sub-titles, anthropomorphic language, concepts. The students involved in these sessions made an important contribution to the thinking behind a chapter on wildlife adventure tourism in the first international book on adventure tourism (Swarbrooke et al, 2003).

Pedagogy and space usage: a typological checklist

Students, and lecturers, learn in an increasingly diverse range of places and spaces. Emerging definitions of 'learning environments' are conceptually expanding and I tentatively offer the following:

A sufficiently diverse and varied, physical or virtual, natural or artificial place and/or space that, wherever and whenever, can facilitate and engage people in the wide range of learning activities, through connectivity and community, cultivating and sustaining psychological, intellectual, emotional, social and political development...

Within these broad defining parameters I offer the following checklist/typology of learning environments for individuals and schools in higher education to use as a tool aid for the design and/or use of learning space diversity.

To what extent do you and your learners:

Use informal and formal spaces within and outside university (e.g. cafés for reading, corridors for provision of more computers)?

Use indoor or outdoor spaces (e.g. larger glass whiteboards, large glass roof areas[for natural lighting gives more energy], plants or flowers, amphitheatres, outdoor space use)?

Work with both physically active and/or passive techniques? (e.g. Silence, solo, regular movement of people and information).

Use both quiet and/or interactive periods?

Use public and private spaces?

Mix teacher-centred and student-centred approaches?

Consider and discuss the ownership of your learning spaces?

Manage the intellectual learning environment? (problem solving, intellectual challenge and risk, developing innovation etc).

Manage the physical learning environment? (seating, movement, use of the body in learning – see *Walk the Talk* case study in chapter one of this book, p. 8–9)

Manage the social learning environment? (interaction, collaboration, notions of constructionism, competition)

Manage the emotional learning environment? (see Mortiboys, 2002)

Manage the virtual learning environment? (IT, i-pods, mobiles, blogs, voting systems, multi-media)

Within all these categories there is a diverse ecology of sub-categories.

Virtual learning environments (VLEs) might well reconfigure learning practices. Sub-divisions might include questions about your use of:

❑ Mobile learning (laptops)
❑ Ubiquitous or 'everyware' learning (almost imperceptible but everywhere around us.... embedded in e.g. objects, surfaces, clothing or body. Examples include using smart clothing technologies or wearable computing, 'smart' furniture, 'smart' doors, floors and corridors within buildings).
❑ Social interactive learning ('social media' or web 2.0 technologies for networking learning such as MySpace, YouTube, Bebo, Second Life).
❑ Visual interactive learning (e.g. video conferencing)
❑ Audio interactive learning (e.g. Teleconferencing)
❑ Connected learning (wireless/wired)
❑ Supported learning (e.g. information points on plasma screens)
❑ Augmented reality (e.g. implanted chips that enable people to feel each others' emotions, enhanced beyond the real thing such as brain scan data that has been augmented or enhanced for medical learning, flight simulators)

Three very different learning environments are now briefly explored giving further illustrative snapshots to amplify the scope of the debate about learning spaces.

Silent spaces

Research into the pedagogy of silence (Behuniak, 2005) explores the provision of solitude for learning. Concerns are expressed about space provided within educational learning environments, as public spaces are diversifying while private spaces are declining:

> given the need for solitude, it is ironic that what most universities do is to create an environment in which students are rarely alone. Intent on forming a campus community, campus architecture creates communal spaces: classrooms, student living quarters, outdoor quads, dining halls, recreation centres, and now even libraries are places to be designed to be with others. Where, then, do they go to be alone.....Where is the private space? (Behuniak, 2005: 11)

Paradoxically, contemporary educational thinking calls for greater student reflection about personal and professional development within formal education. Reflection can be significantly enhanced by both private thinking space as well as social thinking space. Outdoor educationalists are familiar with the role of the 'solo' and silence in reflective learning.

Adventure

Underpinning learning is the notion of a lifelong journey, and it is hoped that this will be an adventurous and exciting learning journey. Adventure, of course, whether indoors or outdoors, requires an element of risk (real or perceived). This risk, in a learning activity, can be physical, emotional, intellectual or material. 'Outward Bound' is a nautical term referring to the outward journey of a ship: Outward Bound schools always had a strong focus on outdoor learning through sea 'expeditions'. The many dictionary definitions of the term 'expedition' include the idea of a journey with a definite purpose. Education might take note of one specific market trend highlighting an abundance of 'adventure learning activities' currently on offer in a range of locations around the world; adventurous travel and 'experience' based learning are being seamlessly combined. Eco-adventure travel, for example, is an area that has increased rapidly over the last decade to become one of the leading income generating themes within the tourism industry. Greenforce, Frontier and Earthwatch are three such organisations that offer a new and unusual combination of learning journeys that I have termed '*edventure*' (education plus adventure).

These organisations are constructing new learning experiences for young people, creating a subtle mix of educative features for self-development, including adventure, travel, environmental or community development work, and skills in scientific wildlife monitoring. These organisations are usually charities recruiting paying volunteers to support wildlife projects around the world. Frontier, for example, is a non-profit organisation promoted by the Society for Environmental Exploration, and has the following in its 2000 brochure:

> Many former volunteers have used their expeditions as the basis for project and dissertation work for bachelor's degrees and master's degrees. Frontier is also a 'sponsoring establishment' for research degrees through the Open University, the ONLY volunteer conservation organisation to have achieved the status of a field university. If you want a career in conservation and overseas development work, Frontier is the only option. With all volunteers eligible for a Level 3 BTEC qualification in *Tropical Habitat Conservation* just on the strength of ten weeks of training and work on a Frontier expedition, becoming a volunteer gives you a chance to kick start a career in this highly competitive field. A recent survey found that 62% of ex-Frontier volunteers have achieved such careers thanks to their experience with Frontier.

Simulation and gaming

The outdoors can also be brought indoors through simulation. Learners can create the outdoors through fantasy. Many years ago Saunders (1988) described a number of examples of indoor 'simulation gaming' under the umbrella of experiential learning. He includes an example of a game called *Island Escape*, where participants are stuck on a volcanic island that is about to explode, and comments that 'while this is a fantasy game, participants rapidly introduce themselves to other people, and reveal their backgrounds, interests and skills' (1988: 136). Saunders argued then that simulation gaming combines the features of games (rules, players, competition, co-operation) with those of simulation (incorporation of critical features of reality), and suggested that these can be used very effectively for encouraging communication, both as a diagnostic and prognostic instrument.

'Diagnostics' involves detective work to identify issues for people to work on, with case studies that replicate the essential features of real-life situations, while 'prognosis' involves predicting people's future performances. In researching epistemologies of contemporary immersive video gaming, Turner (2005) suggests that gaming design principles offer education new forms of literacy within a virtual learning environment interface. Video games, she suggests, can engross players in complex and challenging activities. E-learning is undergoing dramatic changes, with noteworthy developments in social networking. There is increased interest in the virtual-real interface becoming more experiential and leading to the emergence of new term, e^2-learning environments (electronic-experiential learning) (Beard et al, 2007).

Some concluding comments and 'overarching principles':

This chapter has explored a diverse range of environments for learning, and taken a brief snapshot view of the emerging pedagogy of space and place. The traditional classroom is evolving fast and this is being driven by a number of stakeholders. Academic staff and students might usefully contribute to these changes. Much has been learned from developments in IT and we are witnessing constant shifts in indoor and outdoor learning space boundaries. The classroom and its occupants are reaching out into other spaces, into other communities, aided by technological developments; learning is moving onto the streets, into local communities and beyond. Student learning journeys are increasingly taking many different routes.

Academics at individual and school level can work to improve and diversify the physical, intellectual, psychological, technological, and social environments that facilitate learning through connectivity and community. Shifts from directive learning to active or experiential learning mean that spaces require a multi-functionality, offering lecturers and students more flexibility, more mobility for themselves, their learning objects and furniture. The *space* configuration, the furniture, artefacts and technology all need to be rapidly moveable to suit our distinct academic needs. Information is becoming more e-accessible so that we can (re)-construct it in different ways. Wireless connectivity connects people across many places and spaces, and e-mediated learning increasingly opens up the *mobility* of learning.

While the form of the learning environment is often centred around the learning activities we conduct (*functions*), function can also follow form. Students and staff who occupy 'given' environments need to be able to shape and reshape them in different or unanticipated ways; people can adapt to space form. As academics we can encourage this behaviour and be more sensitive to the *politics of space and place* – whose territory is it, who owns it and who occupies what?

These are exciting times as environments for learning continue their journey of transformation. Fish might have finally discovered the water surrounding them.

References

Beard, C. (2005) *Student Achievement: The Role of Emotions in Motivation to Learn – Emotional Maps, Pedagogic Research*. Report, Higher Education Hospitality, Leisure, Sport and Tourism Network, January 2005

Beard, C. and Wilson, J. (2006) *Experiential Learning: A Best Practice Handbook for Educators and Trainers*. (2nd ed) London, Kogan Page

Beard, C., Wilson, J. and McCarter, R. (2007) Towards a Theory of e-Learning: Experiential e-Learning. *Journal of Hospitality, Leisure, Sport and Tourism Education* 6 (2)

Behuniak, S. (2005) Finding Solitude: The Importance of Silence and Space for Thinking. Paper presented to Design For Learning, the 12th International Conference on Learning, Granada, Spain 11–14 July

Belcher. T. & Trowler, P. (2001) *Academic Tribes and Territories: Intellectual enquiry and the culture of disciplines*. Buckingham, SRHE/Open University Press

Carbone, A. & Sheard, J. (2003) Developing a model of first year student satisfaction in a studio based teaching environment. *Journal of Information Technology Education*. Informing Science Institute, USA.

Eyler, J. & Giles, D. (1999) *Where's the learning in service learning?* San Francisco, Jossey-Bass

Fraser, B. (2001) Twenty Thousand Hours: Editor's Introduction. *Learning Environments Research* 4 pp 1–5

Greenfield, A. (2006) *Everyware: The dawning age of ubiquitous computing*. Berkeley CA, New Riders Publishing

Jamieson, P., Fisher, K., Gilding, T., Taylor, P. G. & Trevitt, A. C. F. (2000) Place and Space in the Design of New Learning Environments *Higher Education Research and Development* 19 (2)

Mortiboys, A. (2005) *Teaching With Emotional Intelligence: A step-by-step guide for higher and further education professionals*. London, Routledge

Saunders, D. (1988) Simulation Gaming: Three aspects. *Training Officer* May 1988

Society for Environmental Exploration (2000)

Swarbrooke, J., Beard, C., Leckie, S. & Pomfret, J. (2003) *Adventure Tourism – The New Frontier*. London, Butterworth-Heinemann

Turner, T. (2005) Video Games as Eduction and Literacies: What we Have to Understand about Video and Computer Games and Technological Environments to Accomlish Learning and Literacies. Workshop Presentation Abstract, Design For Learning, The 12th International Conference on Learning, Granada, Spain 1–14 July

Yi-Fu Tuan (1977) *Space and Place: the perspective of experience*. London, Arnold

See also:

Space management: www.smg.ac.uk/about.html

E-learning and pedagogy: www.jisc.ac.uk/elearning_pedagogy.html

COLIN BEARD is a faculty teaching fellow at Sheffield Hallam University. He is also a National Teaching Fellow and Fellow of the Royal Society of Arts. Colin advises many higher education institutions on innovations in teaching and learning, and he works extensively with international companies advising on the effective experiential education and training of staff.

Index